ALSO BY TERRY TEMPEST WILLIAMS

*The Hour of Land*

*When Women Were Birds*

*The Open Space of Democracy*

*Finding Beauty in a Broken World*

*The Illuminated Desert*

*Red*

*Leap*

*Desert Quartet*

*An Unspoken Hunger*

*Refuge*

*Coyote's Canyon*

*Earthly Messengers*

*Between Cattails*

*Pieces of White Shell*

*The Secret Language of Snow*

# Erosion

ESSAYS OF UNDOING

# Erosion

Terry Tempest Williams

SARAH CRICHTON BOOKS  FARRAR, STRAUS AND GIROUX  NEW YORK

Sarah Crichton Books
Farrar, Straus and Giroux
120 Broadway, New York 10271

The following essays originally appeared, in slightly different form, in
*The New York Times*: "Keeping Our Fossil Fuel in the Ground," as "Keeping My
Fossil Fuel in the Ground," March 29, 2016; and "Will Bears Ears Become the
Next Standing Rock?," as "Is Bears Ears the Next Standing Rock?," May 6, 2017.

"The True and the Real," in "Heart of the Matter: Erosion of Fear," originally
appeared as an opinion piece in *The Salt Lake Tribune*.

Library of Congress Cataloging-in-Publication Data
Names: Williams, Terry Tempest, author.
Title: Erosion : essays of undoing / Terry Tempest Williams.
Description: First edition. | New York : Sarah Crichton Books / Farrar,
    Straus and Giroux, [2019] | Includes bibliographical references and index.
Identifiers: LCCN 2019017871 | ISBN 9780374280062 (hardcover : alk. paper)
Subjects: LCSH: Erosion. | Self (Philosophy) | Ecology. | Environmentalism.
Classification: LCC PS3573.I45575 A6 2019 | DDC 814/.6—dc23
LC record available at https://lccn.loc.gov/2019017871

Designed by Abby Kagan

Our books may be purchased in bulk for promotional, educational, or business
use. Please contact your local bookseller or the Macmillan Corporate and
Premium Sales Department at 1-800-221-7945, extension 5442, or by e-mail
at MacmillanSpecialMarkets@macmillan.com.

www.fsgbooks.com
www.twitter.com/fsgbooks • www.facebook.com/fsgbooks

10  9  8  7  6  5  4  3  2  1

Frontispiece and part-opener art: Tree by Luis Leamus / Alamy Stock Photo

*Dan Dixon Tempest*
1962–2018

*There are no beautiful surfaces without
a terrible depth.*

—FRIEDRICH NIETZSCHE

*All souls come here to rub the sharp edges off each other.*
*This isn't suffering. It's erosion.*

—CHUCK PALAHNIUK

# ❖ CONTENTS

## ❖ PREFACE: THE TURQUOISE TRIANGLE

If the world is torn to pieces, I want to see what story I can find in fragmentation. I have taken to making collages. I want to see whether a different narrative might arise from poring over American magazines, tearing them up, and putting them back together in a shape that makes sense to me. When everything feels like it is coming apart, the art of assemblage feels like a worthy pastime. It is said that when John Ashbery lived in Paris, from 1958 until 1965, he took to making collages because he felt so "isolated from America and its language." He said, "You can make a collage on a postcard and write a poem about it."

Perhaps these essays are my postcards from home, a cutting and rearrangement of "the collusions and chance associations" I am witnessing in the American West. This is a moment of strange juxtapositions. On one day, I am undone by the absolute stillness of where we live in Castle Valley, Utah. On another day, we awake to what sounds like war games: helicopters buzzing Adobe Mesa, with filmmakers hanging halfway out the aircraft as they attempt to document a superathlete traversing the world's longest slackline, stretched across a sandstone formation called The Priest and Nuns to Castleton Tower. What is home to some is a playground for others. Every day brings a different surprise.

A new road is being cut into a canyon for natural gas extraction. Another town meeting takes up a proposed coal plant or the return of uranium mining on the rim of the Grand Canyon.

We can take nothing for granted.

I am aware of my restlessness. I am waiting—waiting for what? Scenes from Samuel Beckett's play *Waiting for Godot* keep returning to me: *Was I sleeping while others suffered? Am I sleeping now? Tomorrow when I wake, or think I do, what shall I say of today? That . . . at this place, until the fall of night, I waited for Godot?*

After a season at home, I left Castle Valley for work in Santa Fe. I had heard of a family of artists named Namingha, of Tewa-Hopi descent, Dan Namingha and his two sons, Arlo and Michael. I went to their gallery before I had to teach. I walked in, and before my eyes could adjust to the light pouring in from outside I saw an aerial photograph on the wall: the Colorado River meandering through the sage desert with a large turquoise triangle made out of plexiglass cutting into the landscape. It was an installation called *The Escalade Project*, by Michael Namingha. Tears started streaming down my cheeks. I couldn't say why. All I knew was that I was feeling something again. My heartbreak was being met. I sat down on the floor, took out my notebook, and started writing. Words flowed onto the pages like water.

Michael Namingha introduced himself. He saw I had been moved. We stood in front of his installation and talked about what moved him to create it: a tramway perched on the edge of the Grand Canyon, designed to take tourists down to the confluence of the Little Colorado River, a sacred site of origin for the Hopi. He spoke of how the Turquoise Triangle represented, for him, both the land itself and the spiritual essence of the land being lost as it was being cut out, removed, destroyed, disappeared. What I hadn't been able to articulate verbally for months, Michael had articulated for me visually. The emotional dam I had constructed for myself since the 2016 election, broke. I watched the words buried deep in that reservoir of grief surface.

This is a collection of essays written from 2012 to 2019, a seven-year cycle exploring the idea of erosion: the erosion of land; the erosion of home; the erosion of self; the erosion of the body and the body politic. It is a book of competing dreams and actions—the arc between protecting lands and exploiting them and, for many, not seeing them at all; between engaging politics and bypassing them; and the spectrum between succumbing to fear and choosing courage.

This is a gathering of stories, poems, and pleas in the name of Beauty in an erosional landscape sculpted by wind, water, and time. It is also a book of questions. Whom do we serve? How do we survive our grief in the midst of so many losses in the living world, from white bark pines to grizzly bears to the decline of willow flycatchers along the Colorado River? How do we hold ourselves to account over our inescapable complicity in a fossil fuel economy that is contributing to climate change, as well as ravaging tribal and public lands in the American West? What are the necessary actions we can take in order to realize justice for all? And how do we find the strength to not look away from all that is breaking our hearts?

The paradox found in the peace and restlessness of these desert lands, where rockslides, flash floods, and drought are commonplace, allows us to embrace the hardscrabble truths of change. In the process of being broken open, worn down, and reshaped, an uncommon tranquility can follow. Our undoing is also our becoming.

I have come to believe this is a good thing.

TERRY TEMPEST WILLIAMS
*Vernal equinox 2019*

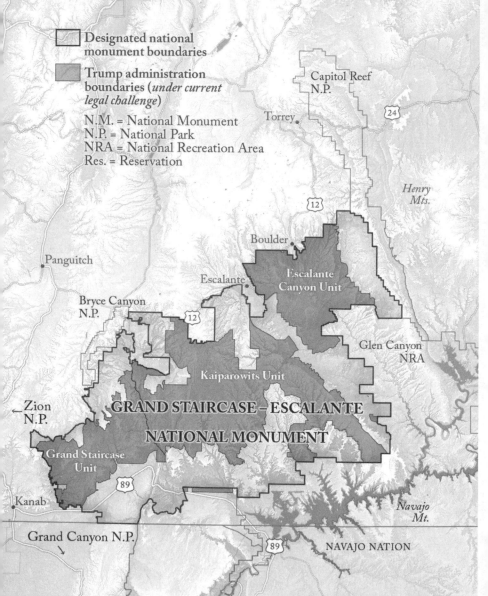

# Eroding Public Lands

Designated national monument boundaries

Trump administration boundaries (*under current legal challenge*)

N.M. = National Monument
N.P. = National Park
NRA = National Recreation Area
Res. = Reservation

70

Capitol Reef N.P.

Torrey

24

Henry Mts.

12

Boulder

Escalante Canyon Unit

Panguitch

Escalante

Bryce Canyon N.P.

12

Glen Canyon NRA

Kaiparowits Unit

Zion N.P.

GRAND STAIRCASE–ESCALANTE

NATIONAL MONUMENT

Grand Staircase Unit

89

Kanab

Navajo Mt.

Grand Canyon N.P.

89

NAVAJO NATION

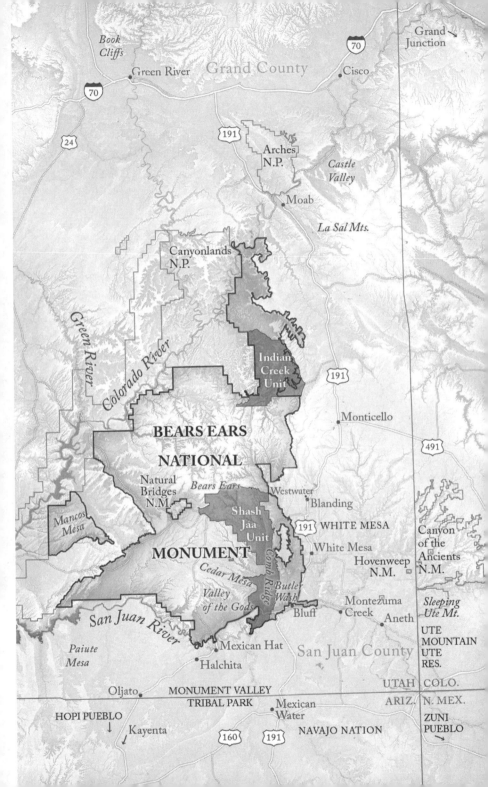

1

An equality of survival does not exist . . . We have both the responsibility *and the ability* to protect one another.

—ELAINE SCARRY, *Thinking in an Emergency*

## ❖ THE CUTTING EDGE OF TIME: EROSION OF HOME

Not long ago, a friend visited us from New York City, planning to stay several days in the desert. But after her first night, we awoke in the morning and found her with her bags packed, standing at the front door. She had changed her plane ticket for an early return to Manhattan. Her last words to us as she left were "Aren't you afraid you will be forgotten?"

What I wanted to say but didn't was "I hope so."

None of us see landscape the same.

Each of us finds our identity within the communities we call home. My delight in being forgotten is rooted in the belief that I don't matter in the larger scheme of things, only that I tried my best to be a good human, failing repeatedly, but trying again with the soul-settling knowledge that my body will return to the desert.

Robin Wall Kimmerer tells the story of a beloved professor who had the initials NYS written behind his name. It stood for "not yet soil." Amen.

For those of us who live in arid country, red dust devils as commonplace as sage sandblast any notion of self-importance right out of us.

Yet still, we forget.

I write to remember.

It is dark, the sun has yet to rise, and a candle is lit on my desk. It is the last day of the year, a difficult year, and I am up early, unable to sleep. People often ask how we can stay buoyant in the face of loss, and I don't know what to say except the world is so beautiful even as it burns, even as those we love leave us, even as we witness the ravaging of land and species, especially as we witness the brutal injustices and deep divisions in this country—as exemplified by the separation of families seeking asylum at the southern border; the blatant racism exposed in Charlottesville; or the students' encounter with a Native elder drumming at the Indigenous March in Washington, D.C. The erosion of democracy and decency feels like a widening crack on the face of Liberty.

How do we not fall into a perpetual state of despair?

My father said to me the other day, "We have to stare it down." *It* being grief. It being everything he can't control, like age, the waning strength in his legs, or the loss of another son.

I am aware that we hold a multitude of emotions at once. They are not contradictory; they are siblings. One minute I can hardly breathe—and in the next, I am in gales of laughter. Humor is the match I strike to see where I must go, especially when my vision is blurred by sorrow.

Just the other day, I had to leave a lecture I was asked to attend, "Egyptian Hieroglyphics and Practices of Tantric Sex Among Stick Figures" or something like that. It wasn't that the lecture lacked compelling material—it was that I didn't have the bandwidth to absorb the information. For me, it became esoteric chatter. I was ready to explode. I tried to discreetly exit the room and quietly close the door behind me. But the second I stepped outside I broke into wails of laughter— what I think the Brits call "corpsing," when you laugh at a nonhumorous performance. One of my fellow residents at the Center for the Study of World Religions (which we lovingly call "God's Motel") heard my hysteria and followed me upstairs to my apartment to see if I was okay. She couldn't tell if I was laughing or crying, and in truth neither could I. All I knew in that moment was the rising pressure of too many minutiae, too many bloodless words, and no air for me to breathe—a feeling brought on when a small group of people talk only to themselves.

After the event was over, I stood outside and howled like a coyote, a way to release my pent-up energy. At my core, I am feral. This is how I survive. With a family name like Tempest, I can only contain myself for so long until an eruption occurs: anger, joy, irreverence, love.

These essays are my howl.

Like the red rock desert before me, I, too, am eroding. Nothing fixed. Nothing static. Only a steady state of flux. I live by disturbances. They keep me awake, a physical stay against complacency. This is my privilege and preference living in the outback of southern Utah.

If you have been here, you understand it is a place of sand so hot in the summer, bare feet burn. If you have not yet encountered the high desert of the Colorado Plateau, it might surprise you to learn that rivers freeze in winter, looking like shattered glass. In spring, we are drawn to the river's edge before we realize we are being sucked into the depths by quicksand, stuck, immobile, the future food of vultures.

In the desert, I try to stay alert. Mistakes are costly. Home is the place of my attention.

For now, I am migratory—living in Utah half the year and working at the Harvard Divinity School the rest, an unexpected surprise that came when I was in my own depths of undoing, unknowing what was next.

I am learning to trust.

I am learning to pray again, not in the way I was taught as a child, but in all the ways the desert has taught me to listen.

I am trying to stay open to what is coming, understanding that uncertainty is the way of the world.

And I am growing more comfortable with waiting, watching, being patient and impatient until, in the middle of the night, when most people are asleep, the hours when owls fly, I make my move. What I once believed to be madness I have come to see as night vision—what every animal knows as it remains vigilant in darkness, moving freely in the shadows. I will find my way into new country that beckons me to take unexpected risks, which turn out not to be risks at all, but the next step.

There are practices I turn to: morning mind is the gift that comes after dreaming. If I have asked my psyche a question the night before, by dawn the answer is waiting for me. Rarely does this received information deceive me, and it is usually accompanied by a moment of awakening in the living world.

A chevron of geese will fly past our window. Canada geese. I hear them first and see them second. Sound shapes our perceptions in inexplicable ways. On another day, I noted the snapping of wings; it was a dragonfly whose name I learned is meadowhawk. Our windows are always open. Wildness enters our home.

This got me thinking about wings. I remembered a photograph taken by Lukas Felzmann. The image is of a human figure casting a long shadow that appears to be attached to a large wing made of mirrors lying on the sand. The figure's arms are raised, hands open, fingers splayed, creating the impression that this shadow body is about to take flight.

I don't know why this image flew into my mind on that

particular morning, followed by the word "imago," but I took it seriously and sought definitions:

noun
1. Entomology
   The final and fully developed adult stage of an insect, typically winged.
2. In biology, the imago is the last stage an insect attains during its metamorphosis, its process of growth and development; it also is called the imaginal stage, the stage in which the insect attains maturity.
3. image
4. Psychoanalysis
   An unconscious idealized mental image of someone which influences a person's behavior.

Words fly into our minds when the unconscious is trying to speak to us.

Great horned owls are speaking to me now. All summer long they called to each other between dusk and dawn. Robins and chickadees mobbed them repeatedly and chattered from cottonwood trees, giving the location of the owls away. But the owls would not be deterred.

Last summer, Brooke and I were seated on the porch in a bit of an argument. He said that I was too immersed in politics—"obsessed" was the word he used—and that it wasn't healthy. He said I was preoccupied, "unavailable," and that I needed to step away and find "a balance." I looked at him and said, "I am preoccupied and you're right, it's not healthy. What isn't healthy is that the Endangered Species Act is under attack, what isn't healthy is that our public lands are under assault, with Bears Ears and Grand Staircase–Escalante National

Monuments gutted and open for business. Of course I'm obsessed. I understand what you're saying, but where's the balance against insanity?

"We have to keep fighting," I argued. "It's not just about our species—"

Just then, a great horned owl flew toward us—at eye level—and banked before it could strike my face. The ferocity and focus of the owl left us speechless and shaking. I looked at Brooke, his eyes brimming with tears.

I stepped off the porch. I had to find the owl. There she was—perched on the peak of the roof above us. Her large yellow eyes reflected the last light of day. She didn't blink, just stared—and then, she flew.

Imagine a place where wind carves rock into canyons of light. Imagine a place where time is told in the stratigraphy of stone. Imagine a place where sandstone arches dare ravens to fly through them. And if your imagination were an exercise in ground truthing, you would be standing in the erosional landscape of the Colorado Plateau. It is here where Utah, Arizona, New Mexico, and Colorado meet in a common boundary point known as the Four Corners. In the harsh arid heart of the American Southwest, one drinks deeply from this wellspring of wonder, especially in drought.

When the word "occupy" infiltrated our language from Wall Street to Washington, D.C., to our own town squares in the name of resistance, I thought about what it means to occupy a place—to take root and stay.

"How one walks through the world, the endless small adjustments of balance, is affected by the shifting weights of beautiful things," Elaine Scarry writes.

I recall a river trip I took down the Grand Canyon. This excursion was sponsored by the Utah Museum of Natural History. I was working there as curator of education and was on the trip as the naturalist guide. It was a group of twelve, some of whom I knew, most of whom I did not. The common denominator among the participants was a shared interest in learning more about the Grand Canyon and coming to a deeper understanding of geologic time.

The first group action was agreeing to take off our watches.

Three days into the trip, traveling downriver, we were about to encounter our first set of serious rapids. Adrenaline started flowing and our boatman began to yawn, a sure sign he was getting pumped for what was coming. We were told to sit low in the boat, tighten our life vests, and observe where the ropes were tied in for handholds should we need them when the raft entered the white water. We were also encouraged to keep our bodies loose, not rigid, and move with the flow of the water. The boatman and his swamper, both highly skilled, would guide us through.

We could hear the roiling waters up ahead and see mist rising from the rapids on what appeared like a ledge. The force of the river seemed to be gaining momentum, a swift-moving slipstream funneling into what is referred to as "the tongue" of the river, defined as "the smooth 'V' of fast water found at the head of rapids." The boatman at the back of the raft, maneuvering with the motor, was focused straight ahead, steering the boat down the center of the river until we dropped into the rapids, disappeared momentarily into deep holes, recovered, only to face immense standing waves that curled over us, drenching our screams. The boatman beautifully finessed the rapids and rock gardens we were racing through—and then, before any of us could grasp what was happening, one of the participants, a middle-aged man, call him Paul, stood up in the bow, made a cross with his arms outstretched on either side of his body, and tried to hurl himself into the dangerous white water. Several of those closest to him grabbed his life vest while others hung on to his ankles and pulled him back into the boat. He collapsed on top of us, heaving and crying. And then the rapids subsided, and we all grew quiet as the raft floated through the flat water.

Paul had tried to kill himself. We learned this sitting in a circle after dinner that night. He said this had been his sole motivation for coming on the trip. No one spoke, until a senior woman said, "That is your choice, but do it on your time, not ours. This isn't going to happen under our watch."

Every day for the next ten days, someone was by Paul's side, talking with him, listening, sitting with him on the boat, holding his arm gently as they walked up a side canyon. I watched the twelve participants taking care of one another, not just Paul. On the last night, he apologized to the group, saying how this had been an honest reckoning of his life and what a transformative experience it had been for him. It was transformative for all of us.

We will all be forgotten. This does not frighten me. What I do fear day to day is who am I forgetting.

I think back to that moment on the river often, reflecting on how important community is to our survival and the amount of work it takes to support each other—and what we lose if we don't. I think about the people who would have grabbed my arms or held on to my ankles if I had wanted simply to surrender to the rapids. My friends wouldn't have let me. They would remind me where I belonged: back in the boat, floating downriver. To belong to a place and a group of people saves our lives. Without that, we lose sight of this precious gift called life.

Every day, I am astonished by what I see, smell, taste, touch, and hear. What I have learned in the face of a flash flood is to seek higher ground. When the fires come, leave quickly. The only recourse we have living in these dynamic places of wild beauty is to respect them. The only agenda in the broken rubble of a collapsing sandstone wall is to let go.

But I don't want to let go.

The way of the world is telling us that our desire to protect wild places has gotten in the way of business. With a wholesale rush toward energy development, public lands in the American West are feeling the relentless pressure of oil and gas extraction, which includes all the infrastructure required: the razing of land, the building of roads, the apparatus for drilling and fracking, and the water raid needed for tar sand processing. Add the construction of compression and distribution centers, pipelines, and housing for fossil fuel workers, alongside a renewed interest in uranium mining and strip mining for coal—a dying industry in the era of climate change—and you begin to see a collapse of wholeness and health of the land that is taxing the integrity of our communities.

As Tim Egan wrote in *The New York Times* on March 30, 2019, "Almost twenty-five percent of American earth-warming emissions originate from industrial action involving public land or offshore leases."

The debate over the noblest and wisest use of our public lands, particularly the red rock wilderness in Utah, dates back to the New Deal. In 1936, Secretary of the Interior Harold

Ickes had a vision of protecting everything south of I-70 in the state of Utah, setting aside close to seven thousand square miles of crimson canyons, buttes, and mesas, and the desert rivers that drain into them—including the Virgin, the Dirty Devil, the San Juan, the Green, and the mighty Colorado, which now deposits close to fifty million tons of sand and sediment into the Lake Powell reservoir on a yearly basis. Ickes wanted to call it the Escalante National Monument; his bold visionary act would have expanded our nation's commitment to protecting our natural heritage for the generations to come.

But there was strong opposition. Those who opposed President Franklin D. Roosevelt's secretary of the interior cried foul, in the name of protecting not land but what the land is used for: mining, grazing, and commercial development. And then when World War II began, the conversation ceased in favor of national security.

But beauty has its own power, and it lives inside the minds of those who have been touched by its magnetic pull. Stewart Udall was among those who loved Utah's canyonlands. In 1961, President John F. Kennedy appointed Udall as his secretary of the interior, and Udall immediately picked up the banner of Ickes's cause. The uncommon grace of the sandstone canyons that held the confluence of the Green and Colorado Rivers in place became a priority for Udall's vision of expanding the national park service.

It's a well-known story where I come from, the stuff of folklore: Secretary Udall was at a meeting in Arizona with Floyd Dominy, the chief of the Bureau of Reclamation, who asked Udall if he wanted a ride to Colorado in a private plane. Udall said yes. Dominy instructed his pilot to take a detour along the Colorado River at ten thousand feet above the canyon country. He had a captive audience with the secretary. As they flew over the confluence of the Green and Colorado Rivers, Dominy turned to Udall: "This is where I want to build the next dam." Udall saw a national park.

Back in Washington, with the help of Bates Wilson, the superintendent of Arches National Monument and a longtime advocate for the creation of Canyonlands National Park, and local outfitter Kent Frost, Udall organized a five-day tour of the region with more than thirty people, including photographers and writers from *Life*, *Look*, and *National Geographic* magazines, to see these little-known lands. The Utah senator Frank Moss was also on the trip. A flotilla of thirteen motorboats carried the fact-finding party down the Colorado River. The party was quickly reduced to, or seduced into, a state of awe by such spectacular geographic features as the Doll House perched high above the river, where miles of red rock canyons, arches, and petrified dunes seemed to extend well beyond the horizon. The curvature could not only be seen but felt.

Frank Masland, Jr., the chair of the National Parks Advisory Board during that time, said, "I do not believe there was a person on the trip who was not impressed by the grandeur of the country, by its loneliness, its beauty and its form." He went on to say, "With complete unanimity all agreed that as a National Park it would rank second to none."

The group was eventually joined by the governor of Utah, George Dewey Clyde, who was opposed to the idea of the national park. Even so, together they explored the untrammeled desert by foot, by Jeep, and by helicopter, visiting such iconic features as the Maze and Island in the Sky. Finally, as they gathered in Chesler Park, the Needles rising in the background and immense sandstone spires piercing the clouds, one of the writers asked the governor how he could oppose protecting such scenery. Governor Clyde waved at the Needles and the vast expanse surrounding him: "What you don't know is that we are a mining state. We might need this as building stone."

Stewart Udall's vision of establishing a new national park in the canyon country was solidified. The group's short expedition might not have lived up to John Wesley Powell's trip down the Colorado River in 1867, almost a hundred years earlier, but it did prove to be historically significant. Udall ordered a study team to develop boundaries for the new national park. "I told them to be generous," he said. "We made it a million-acre park."

But politics intervened, as it often does when natural beauty is pitted against natural resources. The language of economics trumps the language of aesthetics and science. Senator Frank Moss was determined to carry the torch for Canyonlands National Park forward. But once the legislation was on the Senate floor, in order to keep it alive he had to compromise. The wilderness park shrank to one-quarter the size of Udall's original vision, with a provision made for a cattle company to continue grazing its cows within the national park boundary for ten years.

In the summer of 1964, three years later, Congress passed the bill creating Canyonlands National Park, the same year the Wilderness Act was also signed into law.

"If I was young enough," Stewart Udall said on the edge of Canyonlands National Park at Grand View Point on July 26, 2006, "I would work to expand Canyonlands National Park to its original million acres." He paused. "I have been saying for decades, the most beautiful scenic area in the world is the Colorado Plateau."

Stewart Udall passed away on March 20, 2010.

While the vision of an expanded Canyonlands National Park has continued to be held by those who care about this part of the world, an older, deeper, and wiser vision of these serpentine canyons and pinyon-juniper mesas has been sustained through the generations—not by the National Park Service or radical environmentalists—but by the Native People who live here. Two buttes known as Bears Ears rise from Cedar Mesa south of Canyonlands. These are sacred lands to the Navajo, Hopi, Ute, Mountain Ute, and Zuni Nations. This is where their prayers are made. This is where their ceremonies are held. This is where medicines are gathered from an array of healing herbs. This is the place where Native People in the American Southwest have convened for centuries.

Mark Maryboy, a Diné leader, remembers being a child standing next to his grandmother in the spring of 1968 when the presidential candidate Robert F. Kennedy visited the Navajo community near Monument Valley. On the old footbridge on the south side of the San Juan River, Kennedy asked the elders how he could serve them. Their request was direct: protect Bears Ears.

For the past decade or more, the tribes have made a renewed and impassioned plea to protect these lands. Allies within the conservation movement have joined them. On December 16, 2016, President Barack Obama heard the call of the indigenous residents of Utah, Colorado, Arizona, and New Mexico and established, by presidential proclamation, Bears Ears National Monument, 1.2 million acres located in the corner of southeastern Utah.

Wild lands and wild lives—rooted, finned, scaled, winged, and furred—everywhere on Earth—are becoming more precious ecologically and spiritually to healthy and whole communities. The living world is something Native People honor and do not forget.

But so many of us in the United States of America are suffering from amnesia, both forgetting and losing track of who we are and what we stand for as a nation. The American landscape becomes us. If we see our natural heritage only as a quarry of building blocks instead of the bedrock of our integrity and cultural identities, we will indeed find ourselves made not only homeless but rootless by the impoverishment of our own imaginations. The cruelty of our ambitions and the ruthlessness of our priorities are undermining the ground beneath our feet. We are in a societal rockslide. Our democracy is collapsing.

On December 4, 2017, President Donald Trump eviscerated Bears Ears National Monument by 85 percent, disrespecting the spiritual practices of First Nations and ignoring the cultural calls to protect Bears Ears made by the Inter-Tribal Coalition of Bears Ears. It was another betrayal to Indian people by the United States government. A promise made, a promise shattered. A different allegiance was served, one that privileges corporate interests over Native communities and the land, in this case the fossil fuel industries.

"I'm a real estate developer," Donald Trump said. "When they start talking about millions of acres, I say, say it again . . ." Protecting 1.2 million acres from development in the name of spiritual practices and Indian sovereignty as requested by the Bears Ears Inter-Tribal Coalition was unfathomable to our forty-fifth president, who has neither seen nor walked these lands.

This political debacle, draconian and shortsighted, in the service of the fossil fuel industry, is now in the hands of the courts. May justice rule on the side of deep time and a storied landscape that has been held in place by the roots of indigenous wisdom.

To discount the beauty of this desert landscape and the cultures that have emerged over time from its graceful bounty is to discount the birthplace of our humanity. Without a respect for origins, the human spirit falters.

"Attention is the holy grail," says the scholar David Strayer, who is studying nature's effect on human brain function. "Everything that you're conscious of, everything you let in, everything you remember and you forget, depends on it." Nature recalibrates the brain. "Our senses change . . . You notice sounds, like crickets chirping; you hear the river, the sounds, the smells, you become more connected to the physical environment, the Earth, rather than the artificial environment."

By paying attention to what is real and true and authentic, we come home to our self, the person we want to become. We remember what we may have forgotten. The world is so beautiful in spite of the troubles. We are alive again to the way desert sage brings our breath all the way down.

This is the bleached-bone veritas of the Colorado Plateau. We stand on the edge of an erosional landscape looking out. The curvature of the Earth becomes our home range. The silence before us is time. We feel how small we are in the embrace of geologic relief.

The ledgers of history revealed in the layered face of the Grand Canyon; moving through the fracture lines of the Fiery Furnace in Arches National Park; walking across the knife-edged ridge of Angel's Landing in Zion; watching light captured and held within the pastel pinnacles of Bryce

Canyon in shades of pink, orange, and yellow—all these weathered places show us we are merely humans, soft, humble, and temporary.

In the valley where we live, I have walked paths up nearby canyons dozens if not hundreds of times. I love the repetition of my steps, the familiar points along the trails, even down to the recognition of specific rocks in the dry riverbeds. This has been my solace. Now, in the past few years, a certain kind of vulnerability has seeped into my wanderings. I feel the press of the time, not geologic time, but a time of lawlessness, entitlement, and aggression that has emerged, particularly in rural Utah. My mind is not as free as it used to be. I wonder how long this particular canyon or viewshed or ecosystem will remain intact, knowing the velocity and record number of oil and gas leases that have been sold since the Trump administration came into power.

I anticipate the incursions.

The rigs popping up feel like a violence on the land, and my anger ignites alongside the gas flares that assault the night.

White men wearing red hats that read "Make America Great Again" are only part of this shift in acts of brawn and bravado. It feels more like revenge—this manic appetite for development and deregulation of all kinds—a blowback after eight years of Obama's presidency, which was more favorable toward the environment. The fury to strategically undo decades of environmental regulations and laws passed on behalf of ecological integrity and human health has been unleashed inside the Department of the Interior and the Environmental Protection Agency. Restraints on the fossil fuel industry have been lifted. Millions of acres have been opened up for oil and gas exploration, which includes more offshore drilling, with ongoing threats to the Arctic National Wildlife Refuge, and increased development along the edges of many of our national parks and monuments, Chaco Canyon and Yellowstone among them.

Many of the precautionary checks and balances placed to monitor levels of toxins and pollutants in our rivers, lakes, and oceans have been removed. Short-term gains have laid waste to a long-term vision of what our social and ecological obligations are to future generations. But our children are reminding us in our homes and on the streets that this is not acceptable. And we know through brave whistle-blowers like Joel Clement, who was the director of the Office of Policy Analysis at the U.S. Interior Department, that the anti-science bias of the current administration was not only affecting climate change policy, but was exacting disciplinary measures on the scientists themselves, not to mention the removal of climate change materials from government websites, with financial support for climate science severely cut.

Bruno Latour writes in *Down to Earth: Politics and the New Climatic Regime*:

> For the first time, climate change denial defines the orientation of the public life of a nation . . . There is no longer a shared horizon . . . We shall really have to decide who is helping us and who is betraying us, who is our friend and who is our enemy, with whom we should make alliances and with whom we should fight—but while taking a direction that is no longer mapped out . . . Everything has to be mapped out anew, at new costs. What is more, this is an urgent task that must be carried out before the sleepwalkers, in their blind headlong rush forward, have crushed what we care about.

What I care about is this beautiful, broken world. I live in the same house with love and grief as my twin sisters. We may very well have to "learn how to live in the ruins," as Anna Lowenhaupt suggests in *The Mushroom at the End of the World*.

Even as I open my hand and playfully move it along the waves and undulations set in sandstone millions of years ago, I feel the fragility of this place that for most of my life has been bedrock, solid and secure. Today, cracks in the rock wall become the widening schism between those of us who keep human exceptionalism alive, privileging people's needs first, and those of us who view humans as "Terrestrials," one species living among other species, all deserving respect.

We are eroding and evolving, at once.

What is real, given what we know? I trust what I see—in an erosional landscape such as this, weathering agents are real: water freezes and shatters stone; rocks fall from the force of gravity; new rapids appear in rivers. Storms gather and floods roar through dry washes, cutting and scouring a wider channel and changing the course of water. Perhaps this is what is happening to us—we are being worn down to our essence as we are forced to change course.

I find a piece of shale in the shape of a deer. One form changes into another. Shape-shifting occurs. For desert dwellers, water is more often a mirage than something that quells thirst. In drought, bones are exposed; so are the scars of all we have left behind, from sunken boats to mining pilings to plastic bottles and beer cans to the glowing waste of uranium still leaching into the Colorado River. How to restore and reconstruct some semblance of humility and humanity despite our extraordinary power to erase what has taken eons to create?

A canyon wren registers its complaint in descending notes that ricochet between sandstone narrows. Ravens gurgle river songs from memory as we tell stories of what has been lost.

There are many stories of people and place within the

United States of America. Before there were private lands, there were public lands, and before we had public lands, there were Indian lands belonging to more than five hundred sovereign nations in North America. Our country's attempts and successes at committing cultural genocide of Native Peoples remain a shameful gaping wound in our history. The story and struggle of Bears Ears National Monument offers a path toward healing, and it is at the heart of this collection of essays. I choose to believe the end of this story will not be one of fragmentation, but one of reunion, a remembrance of what indigenous communities have always known, and are increasingly willing to share—that we are one with the land, not apart from it.

We need not lose hope, we just need to locate where it dwells.

◆ **ODE TO SANITY**
*Desolation Canyon Wilderness Study Area*
*Colorado Plateau, Utah*

**#1**
Here is the stillness
of a sanity restored—

A slit of light torn in the cliff
is just enough to remind me

There is only despair
in the world we create.

Remote is the human world
not wilderness—

**#2**
The smallest stream
is feeding this canyon

Is it an aerial view
of a mighty river—

Or an interior view
of my own open vein—

What is blood but the life force
that cannot be pushed back.

#3
I wear fear
like a cloak of feathers—

Not the fear of terror
but the terror of annihilation and exhilaration.

A mountain lion
crouches—waiting, watching.

Before she strikes—hunger,
action, elegant eruptive death.

#4
Dusk in the desert,
fall before winter—

The percussive rue of crickets
longing to stay—

This, a house of guests
leaving their tracks in sand.

Our presence
ephemeral as smoke.

#5
Clouds as thoughts,
thoughts as storms—

A trickle of water
displacing rock.

I am nothing but flesh,
bones among stones.

Disappearance
is the work of wind.

#6
My husband of well-shared years
with tenderness says

"I am proud of the life
I have lived with Rio—"

These words as our basenji
dances on red cliffs and howls.

There are many ways to gauge a life,
but none more noble than joy.

#7
Sage, rub me
between your fingers—

So everything I touch
after words will remember—

The pungency of memory
awakens one deep breath.

Our dreams
sneak up on us.

#8
Can it be this simple
that an ode to sanity

Be written by hand
in a wilderness unknown?

Can it be that ambitions
rest in the indifference of stone?

The boundaries we set
are a madness of our own making.

#9
There is a brass bed
half-buried in sand.

Its headboard bent
by time and neglect.

But imagine the night
when two lovers conjoined

Decided in whispers,
walls must fall: here, now.

**#10**
Vermillion clouds
call turquoise home.

A little-known stream stirs
like a snake unseen—thirsty.

There is pain in beauty
because we know it will end.

The mesas are burning,
as we are burning—tonight.

**#11**
Velocity is a band of pronghorn.
They stop, turn, and stare.

Their world is witness.
Vision as prey is prayer enough.

**#12**
In the creases of buttes and mesas
time is held without thought.

We are waiting in the desert to kill our dog. That sounds harsh. Death is harsh. We can try and soften the reality of the cessation of life, but that is an illusion. We do not pass away, or move on, or meet our maker. We die. Our heart stops and we are pronounced dead. It's that simple. The afterlife we imagine exists in our minds. Perhaps that is enough. If it isn't, we turn to religion.

I am thinking about owls.

I am thinking about owls because they remind me of how they see what we fear, like death. It's what they do with a startling grace. Create death. They watch for it, wait for it in a stance of perfect stillness. And when death appears in the movement of a mouse or a vole or a cat—recognition triggers flight. In the grip of an owl, death bears wings.

In my religion, owls are destroying angels. They prey on myths like the one that says when dogs die they walk across a rainbow. When Rio dies, I do not believe he will be walking across a rainbow—I believe his body will be returned to Earth—but I do believe his nose may be sniffing the approach of death now. I can smell death when it comes, sweet just like you hear and, at times, sour like spoiled milk. It's not a particular talent I have honed, having a nose for death; rather, it has become a practice within the life I've been given. Death is a sleight of hand. Black magic. Now you see it, now you don't.

When death approaches me, I call for owls, and more often than not they answer. Great horned owls. Saw-whet owls. Short-eared owls. Long-eared owls. Screech owls, in both red and black variations, whose voices are a tease, stray Ping-Pong balls bouncing in the dark, until they eventually stop. Great grey owls and hawk owls are found in the north. Pygmy owls and flammulated owls inhabit the desert south. Barred owls hide in the east. Spotted owls own the west. And the owl who haunts my dreams night after night is the one owl I have never seen: the snowy owl, white as bones picked clean.

It's not easy to see an owl. But through the years, I have learned they can be seduced by the echo of their own voices. One can call them close through flattery. I don't see this as an act of trickery. I see it as ritual, calling the future forward like an oracle, like the ancient Greeks sought at Delphi. Owls are my midnight muse. They speak through their eyes, burning words into my mind, branding whole sentences in my brain. Once, I stared at a burrowing owl on the edge of Great Salt Lake and was given a curse of a phrase: "If I can learn to love death, I can begin to find refuge in change."

An owl's feathers are silent in flight because individual barbs zipper shut so no air can rush through like the sound of desert wind. Each time I find a feather, I brush its webbing like velvet against my cheek. Sometimes, I close my eyes and fan the air by my ear. I hear nothing, only feel a slight breeze.

It's been a peaceful day. The waiting. I can't decide if the vet is an angel or an executioner. And then, I realize, he is neither. We called for him, just as I am calling for the owls. Both bring perspective. Both bring relief. They are accustomed to making house calls.

I have been asked to write an essay on owls but I am focused on the death of our dog named after a river—Rio; our dearly beloved, impossible Rio—like the Rio Colorado—high water, low water, always a study in extremes. Or maybe we named him after our favorite wine, a Spanish rioja that we drank in Seville, when we had all the time in the world to wander inside the landscape of Lorca and the poetry of Andalusia, where the ground is red and rich like home, more sand than soil, sucking the grapes already dry from drought. But our Rio is more water than wine, because he never allowed himself to be tamed. I will say we named our fearless basenji after a wild running river, a red river like his coat that turns white from light reflected on the edge of water where he seeks his own reflection. Whatever he does is for his own insatiable hunger.

But today on this long, too short afternoon that will be his last, Rio is lying on the couch, his little dark eyes weary from age as he drifts in and out of his dog state of mind. I stare at his elegant, thin leg, his left leg that now hangs off the couch lifeless even as he continues to breathe. I think of his beautiful legs prancing between sage in the red rock desert for fifteen years, effortlessly, proudly; how I never stopped admiring his joyful gait and deriving such pleasure from his beautiful body, how strong he was, how driven he was, how his nose led the way for our walks. Rio lifts his head as if he knows he is being watched and he licks his front paw, overcorrects his body, and sidles closer to Brooke, my husband of close to four decades who is asleep from sorrow. Rio is his soul mate about to die.

Brooke and Rio, a man and a dog, both beautifully, impossibly, unspeakably wild. Once, when I had been away for three months learning how to make mosaics, upon my return Rio was sleeping on my side of the bed. He growled when I tried to move him. We both competed for Brooke's attention. Rio won. I stepped to the side. But late one night as we were driving home along the river road and Rio was standing on the console of the truck with his left paw on Brooke's shoulder, I said I needed to have my place in the bed back. Rio had to sleep on the couch. He's a dog, I said. Brooke looked at me as the truck seemed to be driving itself; hell, maybe Rio was driving it. "Rio isn't a dog," Brooke said. "He's a little boy in a brown dog suit."

Who will Brooke be without Rio? Who will I be without Brooke and Rio? I am lazy with grief lying on the other couch with our little Winslow Homer, a rescue chihuahua with a name bigger than he is, asleep by me. We find our allies.

I once met a baby owl in a barn in Milburn, Utah. The owner of that barn asked if I would take him away because he was terrorizing his chickens. I was with my grandmother, who was driving a gold-finned Cadillac. How we found ourselves in this man's barn is another story too long to tell; suffice it to say it had something to do with visiting a senior center and talking about birds. Anyway, I looked at my grandmother in her black pantsuit, who said, without my asking, "Only if you can put the owl in a pillowcase and put a seat belt around it." This I did and sat in the back seat of my grandmother's Coupe de Ville until we reached what seemed like a promising field of mice, pulled off the lonely road, and placed the baby owl in the tall grasses, hoping that this bird of prey who would have been shot would be fierce enough and lucky enough to one day become an adult great horned, guardian of the moon.

Rio is now sitting next to me. His ears are upright like a fox's, like a pharaoh dog's. He is thin, his shoulder blades look like sails. I can count the vertebrae down his back. His ribs are showing, his belly extended. He lays his head on his two front paws, which are hanging off the side of the couch. Flies break the silence of the living room that is a dying room, where we are attempting to be peaceful in the midst of this impending act. We knew this was coming. Just like I knew death was coming to my mother, my grandmothers, my grandfathers, my brother, my friend. Is the terrible surprise of a violent death, the death we call an accident, easier than a death brought home, where the passage of time reveals bone by bone the ravages of disease, the indignities of old age, and the grace of an injection?

I only know death by ritual.

We are home in the desert. The desert is red. The river is red. The globe mallow are in bloom and meadowlarks call to each other from the tops of sage. The doors to our house are open. Rio walks in and out as though he is visiting two worlds. We think he is ready—I must finish the sentence, we are responsible for his sentence—we think he is ready to die. But we have no way of knowing in the way some Native People say when Owl calls your name, death is near. I choose to believe Owl does not choose whose death is next, but merely asks "Who?" And we decide the moment of our dying.

I will know. I will choose. This I believe. I do not fear it. I just want it postponed.

My brother had two pictures on his dresser before he died: Jesus Christ and a great grey owl. I remember when he called me from the Moose-Wilson Road in Jackson Hole, Wyoming, to tell me he was face-to-face with the great grey, who was perched on a snag. He held the phone toward the owl. I not only heard the owl's silence, I felt its presence.

Death is visiting our home. There are no owls in view, but

I know they are outside, waiting, watching. If we placed Rio out on the desert at night, would they come for him? See him first, motionless, fly toward him, bank their wings, one, two, three, then decide which one would swoop down with feathered talons splayed to clasp his flesh, puncture his back between fur and muscle, and carry him away—relieve us of our terrible burden, our humane duty to kill our dog? Is there a place or a perch where Rio could sleep, not on our couch but on a rock, an altar, where he could be devoured in the dignity of darkness and gleaming stars, eyes of heaven looking down to receive another pair now closed but soon to open to infinity?

I have been asked to write an essay about owls that has become an essay about the death of our dog who is not a dog but an old man in a brown dog suit who is weary of this world, a world he once danced and pranced through and explored with his nose and devoured with his teeth and owned with his heart, as we wait for him to die by the hand of a human at our request.

We can pretend and say Rio told us he was ready, that on his last walk in the desert, he finally sat down on the trail and refused to get up. But that was his body speaking, not his spirit. When Brooke picked him up in his arms and carried him home, Brooke and I both knew the weight he was carrying was not Rio's weight but the weight of the decision to end his life. The weight we both carried was our attempt to balance the scales: does Rio have more life in him or is the life he has left followed by more suffering?

Rio was increasingly uncomfortable, restless. We worried he was in pain and that it would only get worse. Friends faced with this same agonizing decision told us they waited too long. He can no longer see us clearly through the clouds of his aging eyes, but he smells us. He stays close to us. We stay close to him. And for several days, all we do is take turns holding him, talking to him, rubbing his well-worn fur. We sniff him, he sniffs us.

Pain follows suffering like a scent.

Seven feet from where Rio and I are sitting, an owl carved out of pine stands on a table watching us. As I write this line, Rio leans into me and breathes harder. He looks up. I stroke his back. We were told the vet would come sometime between one o'clock and five. It is now 2:48. Brooke is restless. His mind is made up. He wants this ordeal over. He is done. He is done having to think about killing his dog. He is done fearing the loss of Rio. He is done feeling the knife thrust in his side each time he looks at his loyal friend who shared his solitude in the desert. He can no longer bear seeing Rio's shriveled body, his beautiful body that for more than a decade was all muscle and grit.

He can no longer live in denial, believing Rio is going to get better.

This may be the appropriate time to be honest: Rio could be a pain in the ass. He was unpredictable, not trustworthy with strangers. He bit people. Sometimes out of defense. Sometimes to protect us. And in the end, sometimes because he was confused. Dementia was settling in. I have a red chevron on the underside of my right arm. It looks like a scar I made in a dark moment. It was a dark moment when Brooke defended Rio when I wanted him to defend me. Rio bit a poet who tried to pet him in the middle of a dinner party. The dinner party ended. He later appeared in her poem. He bit a writer who was a hunter who taunted him with a piece of raw elk. That was the only time he drew blood.

He bit a jogger running in front of my sister-in-law's house shortly after her husband, my brother Steve, died. He bit a neighbor walking up our road, whom I didn't want to see. He bit a woman who came to our door late at night. He bit Brooke when he tried to lasso him out of a bloody deer carcass. And he tried to nip a deer's ankle, but the buck spun around so fast Rio didn't have time to run. He was kicked into the air like a football, landing on the sand dazed and disoriented. That was the end of Rio harassing deer.

Some of our friends called Rio a hoot. Whenever he heard "The Star-Spangled Banner," our barkless basenji howled. Mozart's Requiem, along with any operatic aria, inspired him to yodel. Most people kept their distance. A few forged their own relationships with him. But no one disputed his spirit. Rio was a dance upon the desert.

Here is a fact: we never witnessed an encounter between Rio and an owl, not once, nor did we often hear an owl's voice near the house, until the night we buried Rio under the full moon in May.

The vet came. He was kind and unobtrusive. Brooke held Rio. I held Brooke. The first shot was to relax Rio. Our friend Rick Bass had told us to give Rio his favorite meat at this point so his last memory was one of gluttonous joy. Brooke had cooked some wild salmon, Rio's favorite. Rio lunged for the pink meat in Brooke's fingers, jumped off his lap, and searched the ground for more. He always wanted more. He was true to his nature until the end. And the end came. The second injection from the vet stopped his heart. His stomach rose and fell, rose and fell, and then Rio was still. Our dog was dead. His body went limp. His spirit gone.

The vet left. We stayed on the porch. Brooke held Rio until after sunset. Pink clouds flooded Castle Valley with encore light. The rest will remain private, except to say, we wrapped his shrunken canine body in a white shawl and set him gently down on a favorite blanket of his that lined the grave that

Brooke dug. We buried him in the red earth, slowly, a shovel at a time, and then covered his grave with cobblestones from the river so the coyotes couldn't disturb him.

The moon rose between Adobe Mesa and Round Mountain. Would you believe me if I told you coyotes howled? They did. And just as we lit a candle on the small mound for a point of light to focus our love and grief, we heard a great horned owl calling from the cottonwoods, asking, "Who? Who-who-who-who?"

Brooke and I turned and looked up at the moon casting a blue glow across the valley.

The silence cut deep.

Paper. Rock. Scissors. For some, wilderness is a game to win or lose. Paper covers rock. Rock crushes scissors. Scissors cut paper bills to shreds. For others, however, wilderness is a place, a state of being where open spaces open minds. In the stillness of a red rock canyon, we hear what has been lost to us—windsong, birdsong, the hymns of rivers resounding. Coyotes call up the moon. We see what has been obscured—sandstone sculpted through time, a night sky of stars. No longer numb, we feel ourselves alive, awakened.

We make our choices and calculations in the form of gestures: an open hand; a fist; fingers moving up and down to cut. Wilderness as a game is played at our own peril. "One, two, three, go—" When both players choose the same gesture, the game is tied.

Our hands are tied today by Washington's special interests. Big oil translates to big profits. The development of public lands by the extractive industry is money made and delivered into the private coffers of corporations. The revenues from oil and gas, tar sands, and coal will continue to build the yellowcake roads paving the way to uranium mines, illuminating what we know to be true: our economy is more important than ecology; conservation is mocked by capitalism; what we consume matters more than what we contemplate. When it comes to wilderness, "the open space of democracy" drowns in the wake of greed.

Intimidation is key. The political terrorism of the Far Right inspires the militias, who back the ranchers, who refuse to pay what they owe to the American people for grazing on public lands. Federal agencies like the Bureau of Land Management care more about keeping the peace than protecting the public commons.

Paper. Rock. Scissors. The stakes could not be higher.

## Paper

The Wilderness Act of 1964 was conceived as an open hand, a gesture of peace on behalf of wildlands, a protection and a promise that what is wild will remain wild and free. On this piece of paper, the Wilderness Act brought the eloquence of the land into the elegance of language. On this piece of paper, these words stand as a definition of wilderness:

> A wilderness, in contrast with those areas where man and his own works dominate the landscape, is hereby recognized as an area where the earth and its community of life are untrammeled by man, where man himself is a visitor who does not remain . . . an area of undeveloped Federal land retaining its primeval character and influence . . . protected and managed so as to preserve its natural conditions and which . . . appears to have been affected primarily by the forces of nature, with the imprint of man's work substantially unnoticeable; has outstanding opportunities for solitude or a

primitive and unconfined type of recreation; has at least five thousand acres of land or is of sufficient size . . . and may also contain ecological, geological, or other features of scientific, educational, scenic, or historical value.

By honoring wilderness, we honor beauty. Beauty is not peripheral, but at the core of what sustains us. Awe and wonder ignite our imagination. We are inspired. We witness the magnificent and miraculous nature of creation. We are humbled. Wilderness becomes soul settling; a homecoming; a reminder of what we have forgotten—that where there is harmony there is wholeness. The world is interconnected and interrelated. Wild nature is not only to be protected, but celebrated.

On September 3, 2014, the Wilderness Act celebrated its fiftieth anniversary. How has our thinking about wilderness evolved in these five decades?

The reasoning behind the Wilderness Act has not changed, but intensified. It is doubtful that the act's authors could have foreseen the levels of "increasing population, accompanied by expanding settlement and growing mechanization" that now threaten to move wild lands from the place of protection to the place of extinction. Climate change was a concept unknown to them, climate crisis unthinkable. Now these words are being used to redefine why wilderness matters in the twenty-first century.

As the Earth heats up, wilderness offers a cooling of the senses, a storing of the waters, and a bank of biodiversity where carbon is held, not spent. Wilderness becomes an insurance policy against ecological disasters caused by desertification, acidification, and mindless development that also leaves the land bare of beauty and vulnerable. Erosion becomes the story; dust, the narrative; and a scorched stratigraphy in the

American Southwest beyond, drought that creates a desolation unimaginable except in stories of apocalypse.

The Wilderness Act of 1964 became an act of restraint in 2014. The Wilderness Act, fifty years after its creation, remains an act of wisdom.

Did Howard Zahniser and Olaus Murie, the chief architects of the Wilderness Act, consciously create a definition for wilderness that would project us into the future?

The importance of wildness keeps expanding as our need for wilderness increases. "Scenic wilderness" helps us appreciate nature's grandeur. Wilderness that is ecologically and geologically diverse must now be folded into our society, which is equally diverse, allowing us to see the natural world as a web of fascinating and complex interconnected systems. And now, the idea of solitude in wilderness becomes the seminal gift at a time when we are on the verge of letting the noise of our own technologies drown out the sound of life itself.

The Wilderness Act of 1964 has not changed, we have. We read the landscape of our lives differently. Our connection to the world is virtual, not real. An apple is not just a fruit but a computer. A mouse is not simply a rodent but a controlling mechanism for a cursor. We have moved ourselves from the outdoors to the indoors. Nature is no longer a force but a source of images for our screensavers. We sit. We stare. We text on our iPhones and type on our keyboards, and await an immediate response. Patience is an endangered species. Intimacy is a threatened landscape.

Wilderness brings us back home to our bodies. We remember what it means to be challenged physically and stretched emotionally. We watch the weather and wonder if danger is near. It thunders. Lightning strikes. It rains. We are cold. We keep going in the midst of adverse conditions. The rain stops.

We dry as the land dries. A rainbow arches over the horizon. In wilderness, time is not measured in money but in miles, in the hours spent walking on a trail. The wealth of a day in wildness is measured in increments of awe.

The outer wilderness mirrors our inner wilderness. Our adventurous nature is intrinsically tied to wild nature. A freedom of spirit depends on big, wide open spaces, the same spaces that gave birth to our nation and were home already to hundreds of other nations of indigenous people for generations. If we destroy what is outside us, we will destroy what is inside us. Something precious and original is lost. The "home of the brave and the land of the free" disappears. Madness fills the void. Wilderness is a stay against insanity. The Wilderness Act of 1964 is a prescription. "We need the tonic of the wilderness"—Thoreau knew this two centuries ago.

Do we?

### Rock

The Wilderness Act originally covered rock and ice: nine million acres were to be protected, from the mountains in the Sierra Nevada to the Bridger-Teton National Forest to the Boundary Waters of Minnesota. The Wilderness Act signed into law on September 3, 1964, by President Lyndon B. Johnson became an act of generosity, an honoring of a communal wealth to be held in a public trust. These wildlands are not owned by a single species but shared with a community of species, so all might flourish. To designate wilderness is to honor the natural order of a place free from the hands of humans. Yet, the Wilderness Act is not without its irony. It was through human hands that this law came into being. And it will be through human hands that wilderness will continue.

Wilderness designation is "in the highest tradition of our

heritage as conservators as well as users of America's bountiful natural endowments," said President Johnson. "The wilderness bill preserves for our posterity, for all time to come, 9 million acres of this vast continent in their original and unchanging beauty and wonder . . . Americans have wisely and have courageously kept a faithful trust to the conservation of our natural resources and beauty."

Earth First! raised the clenched fist that defined the wilderness movement in the 1970s. "The idea of wilderness needs no defense, it only needs defenders," wrote Edward Abbey. And defenders we have. More than fifty years later, over 110 million acres have been added to the list, honored and protected by designation with more than 800 wilderness areas secured in all fifty states. And wilderness bills in Utah, New Mexico, and Montana are slow but ongoing.

Wilderness is a place where we experience the quiet and sometimes violent unfolding of nature, where the natural processes of life are sustained and supported. It is where we feel the rightness of relationships, where we sense our true place, a part of, not apart from, the forces of life. Wilderness is harmony revisited with adaptations unexpected and surprising like the first shining organisms that shimmered toward life, emerging from that steamy primordial swamp. And just like every other creature, we are selected for and selected against. Wilderness returns us to this one simple fact: we are animals. Unlike the world of humans, who trade on greed, scarcity, and selfishness, nature functions on frugality, abundance, and altruism. Nothing wasted. Yes, there is a brutality to the wild, but there is also resiliency in the renewal of each day.

Wilderness is akin to love, flush with chemical reactions hormonal and pheromonal, a firing of synapses in our brain that is integral to our survival. We are propelled by the currents of connection. Isolation is quelled. Fear is replaced by awe. We recognize wildness as creativity in the extreme. We are not in control. We surrender to solitude. We sit on the edge of a canyon looking out—and in the marvel of a moment far beyond ourselves, we inhale, exhale, relax, and swoon.

## Scissors

Scissors are a singular object made plural through language: a pair of scissors is one tool where two blades of metal are pivoted so the sharpened edges slide against each other in a common purpose. They can cut, slice, stab, or wound depending on whose hand directs them. To leave a pair of scissors open is to flirt with superstition that a fight will ensue. To open and close scissors mindlessly is to call in bad luck.

But in the game of paper, rock, scissors, the rock beats scissors every time. The clenched fist has supremacy over the first two fingers extended and touching. The rock of resistance can crush the political scissors of bureaucracy that threaten to destroy the paper bills that protect wilderness, even the Wilderness Act itself, so eloquently drafted by Howard Zahniser with friends on the porch of the Murie cabin in Moose, Wyoming.

These pragmatic visionaries who believed as Thoreau did that "wildness is the preservation of the world," made a commitment to the future. They saw wilderness not as the haunt of the elite, but the domain of everyone, regardless of race, class, or gender. Wildness is central to the cause of humanity. They built a foundation from which to care, a platform where humility embraced an intelligence of the wild. Nancy Newhall wrote in *This Is the American Earth*: "Wilderness holds the answers to more questions then we yet know how to ask."

They passed this rock on to us as we now pass it on to the next generation, who will pass it on to the one that follows them with the long-standing view that wild lands and wild lives deserve our respect. Wilderness protection is a generational embrace. This rock has been rolling through the halls of Washington for five decades with its own solid momentum. Conservation is a prayer and a practice for the life that is to come.

Wilderness is not a game. We must change the rules of engagement. Paper can be used for a map. A rock keeps the map in place. And the scissors can be retired. We have cut enough wilderness out of the heart of the American landscape. The Chinese believe that if you give a pair of scissors to someone you cut ties with them. We need to restore our ties to wild nature. It is time to draw up a new map of wilderness that is more inclusive, not just of our species, and with a broader understanding that we are living in a time of climate confirmation: the Earth is heating up. The remaining wild places can guide us and protect us as we move toward an uncertain and evolving future.

### Evolution as a Strategy

There is a revolution, an evolution, occurring on our public lands. There are those who want to sell them, abuse them, and write them off as a collective takeover of our individual rights and freedoms by the federal government. The Bundy standoff in 2016 at Malheur National Wildlife Refuge showed us where this leads. There are others who see our public lands as a public trust in the name of future generations and the life that is to come—be it a child or a wolf pup or a canyon wren singing in the desert.

This revolution is taking place primarily in the American

West, where it can be viewed as a battlefield or as a turning point in how we choose to live. Revolution inspires evolution, and we see the fear it is awakening in the bloodshot eyes of angry white men—star-spangled Americans who feel their power and influence slipping away. Blinded by their own sense of privilege, they fail to see how their patriarchal foundation built on guns, gas, and American exceptionalism is the very obstacle to the future they say they are fighting to protect. Their ideological cornerstone is crumbling.

How many shenanigans must we endure alongside the posturing, the posing, and the polemics that precede the actual destruction ensuing from their fear of a changing world. The "sagebrush rebels" who reincarnate each decade will bulldoze another road in the wilderness to show the wilderness has been tamed. Men with loaded guns wait and watch. Militias preparing for war stand guard. And now we have another cry of hysteria: "Build that Wall!" It is a wall against not only immigrants and asylum seekers, but wildlife and butterfly sanctuaries and corridors. If wilderness teaches us anything, it is that borders need to be fluid, not fixed.

Meanwhile, America's public lands, our national parks and monuments, have become places of pilgrimage, landscapes loved and cherished, most of them bordered by wilderness. Gateway communities to our parks are thriving. And the outdoor industry is a burgeoning business, one that may be contributing to the risk of loving these lands to death as more and more people seek solace in nature. Reservation systems at our parks and wilderness areas are becoming more common, despite the resistance. The revolution is coming; it just might not be what the old guard is planning.

Here is a prediction: the decade ahead will be one of the

most crucial breakdown or breakthrough moments in the history of our species.

It is not a game of paper, rock, or scissors.

Wilderness offers us a template to an enlightened citizenship. Instead of only caring for ourselves, we are invited to care for species other than our own. We are encouraged to look to the roots of things. "Care" is tied to the German root word *chara*, which means "to grieve" or "to lament." To care about wilderness is to grieve over what we have lost. To care about wilderness is to fall back in love with the world and lament how lost we are, and how lonely we have become. We are losing our minds. It is time to return to our senses and recognize that the bedrock of our sanity lies in every square inch of wilderness that remains.

Designating wilderness in the twenty-first century must include designating wider access for diverse communities to engage in wild nature. Issues of racial diversity, equity, and engagement must be woven into the fabric of protecting wildlands, while at the same time we must understand that these lands hold not only the natural histories of plants and animals, but human histories, varied and oftentimes violent histories. The complexity of these landscapes must be named and honored, not hidden as it has been in the past, with the erasure of Native Peoples from our national parks. We can begin to see wilderness in broader terms, a place where ecological health is sustained and environmental justice is maintained for all species.

For marginalized communities to feel supported in wilderness, not alienated from it or at risk, the separation narratives of a wilderness without people must cease, so that our survival and the survival of the planet can be woven together into a story of wholeness and planetary health.

Clean water and clean air are human rights. By its very nature, wilderness safeguards an intersectionality of concerns. Wildlands that frame our communities contribute to sustainable economies through recreation and tourism. Wilderness fosters a peace of mind that affects our physical and mental health. Forests are a vital source of carbon sequestration. These gifts are not just for us, but are meant to be extended beyond ourselves, beyond our own time.

The biologist E. O. Wilson advocates protecting the planet's remaining biodiversity in his book *Half-Earth*. He maintains "that the situation facing us is too large to be solved piecemeal and a solution commensurate with the magnitude of the problem is needed: dedicate fully half the surface of the Earth to nature." Much of that open space will be wilderness.

Wilderness is a necessity, not a luxury. Our experiences with the wild strengthen us and provide us with uncommon insights capable of moving us toward an evolutionary grace that enables us to be in relationship with all beings.

We have been with students on a sandstone bluff looking west across Utah's Sweetwater Reef, a proposed wilderness area near Canyonlands, surrounded by a dense quiet, watching. They are not looking for something in particular, not places for cows to graze or junipers to be bulldozed, or trying to see how many gallons of oil might be pooled and plotted for a cross-country pipeline. They are simply looking out to where the Earth curves—beyond a symphony of time.

"Wildness is evolution," says Michael Soule. As a conservation biologist, he sees wilderness as the place where all elements are working in concert as a natural system that has one goal: passing life on to the future. As humans, we not only evolved in wilderness, but we continue to evolve in wilderness. Wilderness ensures possibilities. Saving wilderness is about saving ourselves, as well as protecting the evolutionary integrity of all other life forms on the planet. An open hand and a clenched fist will be required, along with a generous heart that dares to feel enough to grieve and lament what we are watching disappear and try to slow down the destruction we have set in motion.

Evolution is about adapting to changing conditions. But climate changes are occurring faster than we can biologically evolve or adapt. Because we humans have so quickly modified the planet's ability to support life, we must call on different forms of evolutionary adaptations, conscious and deliberate, diverging away from anything we've yet been able to perceive. What if at the individual level, wildness takes the form of imagination? Imagination leads us to creative acts. Wilderness in the twenty-first century is not a site of nostalgia for what once was, but rather the seedbed of creativity for what we have yet to imagine.

◆ **A TOTEMIC ACT**
*The Endangered Species Act*

The Endangered Species Act celebrated its fortieth birthday on Saturday, December 28, 2013. As the year drew to a close, it's safe to say, no one reported the good news of saving a wee wildflower or included it on any year-end list of big moments in Utah. A small wildflower that grows in the Kaibab Formation in Washington County, known as a Gierisch mallow (*Sphaeralcea gierischii*), was finally granted protection under the federal Endangered Species Act. Only eighteen populations or communities of these rare plants, approximately five thousand to eight thousand individuals, remain on Earth. This vibrant orange crepe-petaled flower with yellow stamens can be seen squeezed between Interstate 15 and the Virgin River.

Some may say, "So what?" But if we look at the success story behind the 1973 Endangered Species Act, and where wild creatures stand today, we may be impressed by what a single law with vision can do. Species who are facing decreasing numbers as the result of various factors have legal protection under this prescient act. Birds like the bald eagle, peregrine falcon, and California condor were on the path to extinction in the 1960s because of such pesticides as DDT.

Today, the bald eagle population is vulnerable but stable; same with the peregrines. Both have been taken off the endangered species list.

The California condor was on the brink of extinction in 1987, with only twenty-two individuals left in the wild. Now, still "critically endangered," it has been successfully introduced in the Grand Canyon and Zion National Park through a captive breeding program. When their immense wings, spanning eleven feet, cross over you, casting their shadow as they soar effortlessly across the chasm at the South Rim, you feel the temperature drop. These are regal birds of prey that harken back to the Pleistocene. Each time I hold a condor in my binoculars, I am reminded of what care has been taken to keep their ancient spirits alive. It is reported that close to five hundred California condors are now living in the wild or captivity. From Baja California to Big Sur to the mountains of Ojai to the red rock desert canyons, they continue to animate the American landscape thanks to legal protection.

Since 2018, Senator John Barrasso from Wyoming and Senator Mike Lee from Utah, motivated by the belief that the Endangered Species Act is bad for business—for the fossil fuel industry and for some ranchers in rural areas—have been determined to introduce legislation that will fundamentally weaken the ESA. They are also minimizing the role of science, making it much more difficult to offer protection to endangered and threatened species.

Roughly sixteen hundred plants and animals have been listed on the endangered species list, with petitions for the addition of new species yearly by scientists and conservation groups, alongside those species being considered for delisting. It is a highly political process dependent on who holds the power in Congress.

"The Republicans are pushing bills to divert protection funding, prioritize corporate land development, and sidestep science," says Representative Raul Grijalva, a Democrat from Arizona. "These are blatant efforts to place corporate interests over species survival." In fact, since 2017, more than twenty-five bills have been sponsored by Republicans to "skirt, defang, weaken or undermine" the Endangered Species Act, says the National Resources Defense Council.

It is important to remember that America was the first country in the world to condemn human-caused extinction of other species and deem it illegal. John Dingell, one of the authors of the Endangered Species Act in 1973, said: "Protecting this Nation's wildlife and our public lands should never be a partisan or political issue; it should be about common sense . . . Living wild species are like a library of books still unread. Our heedless destruction of them is akin to burning that library without ever having read its books."

Every species on the endangered register has its own beautiful, threatened story.

The gray wolf was listed as an endangered species in 1974, having been shot, poisoned, and trapped to near extinction. In 1995, wolves were reintroduced to central Idaho and Yellowstone National Park from Canada. Thirteen years later, given their success, the gray wolf was delisted by the federal government. In the American West, controversy follows the wolf as surely as its howl calls up the moon. A lawsuit was filed immediately by Earth Justice on behalf of twelve conservation groups, challenging the decision to delist the gray wolf in the Northern Rockies. In July 2008, a federal court reinstated federal protections under the Endangered Species Act just in time to stop wolf hunting that had been implemented in Idaho, Montana, and Wyoming. This delisting and relisting dance in the courts around wolves continues seesawing between the politics and policies of each administration. Finally, on December 17, 2013, during a public comment period, roughly one million American citizens stood up and called for the protection of the gray wolf. It was one of the largest outcries on behalf of any species.

But old myths die hard, especially when it comes to wolves. Etched deep into our psyches are tales we heard as children that the wolf is the devil's dog dressed up like our grandmothers. Descriptions like "bloodthirsty, vicious killers" are commonplace in some western towns. And on occasion, wolves kill sheep. This doesn't help their reputation.

On March 7, 2017, the Washington, D.C., Circuit Court of Appeals stripped Endangered Species Act protections from wolves in Wyoming. The panel of three judges issued a ruling in *Defenders of Wildlife, et al. v. Zinke, et al.*, reversing a district court decision that had restored protections for the Wyoming wolves. These legal battles are far from over, yet the story of the gray wolf returning to the American West remains an uplifting one—the story of a threatened species' recovery through impassioned individuals working with the science and conservation communities with vigilance, creativity, and care.

And then there is the Utah prairie dog. It is no secret how much I love them. Call them America's meerkats; they are a keystone species that creates habitat through elaborate tunneled towns that traditionally stretched for miles, offering more than two hundred species, from rattlesnakes to burrowing owls to black widows, a home. They are also a vital food source for raptors, coyotes, foxes, and badgers. These communal creatures declined to perilous numbers due to the politics of livestock that continues to claim prairie dog burrows are hazardous and can break the legs of horses and cattle. An aggressive poison campaign in the 1960s and '70s, alongside indiscriminate long-range target shooting, plague, and drought, has almost done them in. In 1972, fewer than two thousand Utah prairie dogs remained. They appeared on the original roster of protected species on the 1973 endangered species list. Names like "pop-guts" and "varmints" still follow them into their burrows. My own family must be responsible for killing hundreds of them. As a child, I became a devoted advocate of prairie dogs because I saw so many of them slaughtered as they ran between clumps of sagebrush fleeing from my brothers' shotguns. In college, I lobbied the Utah State Legislature on their behalf. Instead of lending their support, these largely male lawmakers handed me their wives' recipes for prairie dog stew.

In 2000, *The New York Times Magazine* listed the Utah prairie dog as one of the ten species least likely to survive the next hundred years. My heart broke. I wasn't alone. Such organizations as Wild Earth Guardians, Defenders of Wildlife, and the Center for Biological Diversity led successful campaigns to educate the public on the plight of prairie dogs and took the federal government to court for their lack of protection. In 2013, the tide turned in favor of Utah prairie dogs when the Utah Nature Conservancy bought eight hundred acres through what is known as the School Institutional Trust Lands Administration (SITLA); lands that belong to the state can be sold with proceeds benefiting Utah schoolchildren. A Utah prairie dog sanctuary in Garfield County near Bryce Canyon National Park was created.

Today, the Utah prairie dog population is close to twenty thousand individuals, still less than 15 percent of its historic numbers, but we have the Endangered Species Act to thank for saving these wondrous creatures. Education matters and

A TOTEMIC ACT 53

breaks down prejudices. In some instances, Utah prairie dog habitat is now being restored by the very ranchers who opposed them decades earlier. Financial incentives like paying ranchers to restore some of their private property for prairie dog habitat has helped. And the law has upheld their right to a dignified life.

Even so, the fate of prairie dogs—like wolves—is still marked by frontier thinking. In 2018, the U.S. Supreme Court declined to hear an appeal from a group called People for the Ethical Treatment of Property Owners of Cedar City, from a small rural community in Utah, that has challenged endangered species protections for Utah prairie dogs for decades, insisting they are overrun by these rodents. In a film made by the group, a particularly sinister scene showed a prairie dog stealing flowers from the grave of a newly buried resident, implying that this patriarch's death was brought on by the stress that prairie dogs caused him. The soundtrack was straight out of a horror movie. The Trump administration has been sympathetic to this cause and is moving to loosen the rules that have prevented people from shooting, poisoning, or transporting prairie dogs to other locations. My faith and solidarity remain with the Utah prairie dogs. They stand outside their burrows as small beacons of hope.

The 1973 Endangered Species Act has been more than 99 percent successful at preventing the extinction of species under its watch. Scientists credit the ESA for saving 227 species from going extinct.

To honor, uphold, and anticipate celebrating the anniversary of this noble decree into its centennial year in 2073, it is worth remembering that on December 28, 1973, when Congress passed the Endangered Species Act into law, it was truly a bipartisan bill. The vote in the Senate was 92 in favor,

0 opposed; in the House, it was 355 to 4. This seems miraculous, bordering on the impossible, given the rancor in Congress today.

President Richard M. Nixon spoke these words when he signed the Endangered Species Act into law:

*Nothing is more priceless and more worthy of preservation than the rich array of animal life with which our country has been blessed. It is a many-faceted treasure, of value to scholars, scientists, and nature lovers alike, and it forms a vital part of the heritage we all share as Americans.*

A journalist from Washington, D.C., recently asked me, "Who is the most powerful individual in the American West right now?"

"Sage grouse," I answered.

"I'm serious," he said.

"So am I," I replied.

In the Interior West, where sagebrush covers the landscape like a sea-blue haze, sage grouse are controlling the conversation around oil and gas development. The Bureau of Land Management projections show that nearly ninety-six thousand new oil and gas wells will be drilled over the next twenty years in six states: Colorado, Montana, North Dakota, South Dakota, Utah, and Wyoming. Oil wells could fragment 11.8 million acres of sagebrush and grassland habitat, an area larger than the state of New Hampshire. Development, as planned, could affect the greater sage grouse populations by 19 percent.

Historic populations of sage grouse once numbered sixteen million, as they were part of the prairie ecosystem that included millions of bison and prairie dogs and pronghorns. Today, the population may be less than half a million, with many local populations in the vicinity of oil fields being drawn down to extinction.

One male sage grouse standing his ground on his ancestral lek against Shell Oil is akin to the lone man in China facing down a tank in Tiananmen Square.

Sage grouse are the latest bellwether species sounding the call for restraint on America's public lands. The bird was a "candidate" for listing in 2015, and amendments were madly written by every western state, including Utah, which recognizes the economic stranglehold this bird could have on the future of fossil fuel development. States were highly motivated to come up with a reasonable plan that could manage the sage grouse outside of the perceived constraints of the Endangered Species Act.

On September 22, 2016, Sally Jewell, secretary of the interior during the Obama administration, signed a historic document on behalf of the greater sage grouse, stating that "the charismatic rangeland bird . . . does not need to be protected under the Endangered Species Act," maintaining that through "strong Federal, state, and private collaborations . . . we can successfully conserve landscapes and save species while providing certainty to rural communities."

It was a bold compromise, with conservationists such as myself skeptical—but looking back, I admire Jewell's belief and her commitment to the process. The Fish and Wildlife Service worked with more than eleven hundred ranchers in eleven western states, with strong bipartisan leadership from the governors of Colorado, Wyoming, and Montana. Ninety-eight natural resource management plans detailing how various communities and states would protect grouse habitat were

completed in collaboration with scientists, ranchers, conservationists, and local politicians. In the end, seventy million acres
of public and private western rangeland were placed under
protection.

Not surprisingly, two years later, this historic conservation
initiative was largely undone by Sally Jewell's successor, Ryan
Zinke. Secretary Zinke called for a review of the Sage Grouse
Management Plans. *The New York Times* reported that the
Bureau of Land Management "intends to consider amending
all or some of the land use plans finalized under the Obama
Administration." It was another sleight-of-hand move on behalf
of the oil and gas industry.

On December 6, 2018, newspaper headlines across the
country read "Zinke Moves to Weaken Landmark Greater
Sage Grouse Conservation Plan." It was his last act as secretary of the interior, "a fine feather in his cap," his defenders
said.

Nine days later, on December 15, 2018, Ryan Zinke sub-
mitted his letter of resignation as secretary of the interior to
President Trump, citing "vicious and politically motivated attacks" on his character. In truth, the White House pressured
him to do so. He left under a cloud of questions surrounding allegations of corruption and conflict of interest, some of
which were reported to be the subject of Department of Justice investigations. David Bernhardt, a former lobbyist for the
oil and gas industry, has taken Zinke's place as secretary of
the interior. One month after his appointment, the Bureau of
Land Management began auctioning 758,198 acres of public
land for new oil and gas leases, including thirty-one parcels in
Wyoming that biologists spoke out against with great urgency,
saying that these lands up for bid contain "the highest sage
grouse density on Earth." The sage grouse will now resume its

power in the courts as national conservation groups petition the U.S. Fish and Wildlife Service for the iconic bird to be listed as an endangered species.

It is not simply the future of the sage grouse that is imperiled by America's drive for oil independence, it is the entire sagebrush steppe ecosystem. For someone like me, who grew up in the Interior West where sagebrush was as ubiquitous as wind, the thought that this landscape, with its resident grouse, pronghorn, black-footed ferrets, and prairie dogs, would be threatened is unfathomable. It was not just common, it was our "sagebrush ocean," which stretched from the badlands of the Dakotas to the high plains and plateaus of Montana, Wyoming, and Idaho to the Great Basin playas of Nevada to the pinyon-juniper grasslands and red rock deserts of Utah, New Mexico, southern Colorado, and Arizona. Sage flats exist in California, as well.

This is the totemic power of the sage grouse, who joins the ranks of other species who have changed the course of public policy, local power structures, and the landscape itself, within western towns and cities. Consider the spotted owl and the salmon in the Pacific Northwest, which saved millions of acres of ancient forests from being felled. Add the gray wolf and the grizzly as species now defining the Greater Yellowstone Ecosystem. The mountain bluebird showed us the cascading effects of DDT; the black-footed ferret and its relationship to prairie dogs illuminated its role in vibrant grasslands; and the willow flycatcher and the wound fin minnow are measures of the health of the Colorado River. And there are so many more—from the Everglade kite to the monarch butterfly to the Preble's meadow jumping mouse, to hundreds of plants and creatures who are having a profound impact on how we understand what is integral to the integrity of natural ecosystems.

The beauty of the Endangered Species Act is that it is a federal act of empathy, put into writing and upheld by law. It is an enlightened act of mind and heart that is both visionary and inclusive. It proceeds from our Declaration of Independence and portends a Declaration of Interdependence. It gives us an opportunity to exercise our conscience and consciousness on behalf of all species.

The great consequence of the Endangered Species Act, over time, is that it ensures that we, as a species, will not be alone. We will remain part of a living, breathing, thriving community of vibrant beings with feathers, fins, and fur; roots, petals, and spines; trunks, branches, and leaves. It promises that creatures that walk with four legs or scurry on six or crawl with eight will move alongside upright *Homo sapiens*—our humanity walking side by side with our humility. Wild beauty sustains us. A wolverine becomes more than a thought; it makes each of us an heir to wonder.

The plants and animals are asking us for respect and restraint. The Endangered Species Act, designed in the late twentieth century, promises them that we will try. When my friend from Washington, D.C., asks me again about where power resides in the American West, I will ask him to accompany me in the spring to smell the sweet fragrance of sage after rain. And in that moment of reverie, just maybe we will hear the drumbeats of sage grouse rising above the oil rigs on the horizon.

The Endangered Species Act has never been more relevant and never been more at risk. As a conscious and conscientious citizenry, may we rededicate ourselves to its survival, especially as we face the future with climate change. Congress will need our support. So will the plants and animals.

We must be creative. We must be collaborative. And we must exercise our compassion on behalf of all species. Empathy moves us to action.

When I was writing the book *Finding Beauty in a Broken World*, I made the decision to link the plight of Utah prairie dogs with the Rwandan genocide. It was met with harsh criticism from human rights activists and literary critics. "You cannot compare a rodent to a human being," one individual said. But I would argue that they missed the point. The loss of a species and the loss of a people are both predicated on the same qualities of prejudice, cruelty, arrogance, and ignorance, ultimately creating the seedbed of war. We need a new conscience and consciousness in our relationship with the Other. And this has everything to do with cultivating peace.

The Endangered Species Act is both a policy and a prayer, in both forms calling out what Albert Schweitzer called the three most important words we can embrace: "Reverence for life."

Last month, I was invited to meet a lynx held in captivity while it was healing from a broken leg at a wildlife rehabilitation center in Idaho. I have never seen a lynx in the wild, but on that day, our eyes locked and I could not walk away. Finally, my name was being called. The people I came with were leaving. I left the lynx and then, at the last minute, I told my friends I had forgotten something. In truth, I needed more time with the lynx. I returned. Our eyes met again, neither of us blinked—something passed between us—and then, the lynx began to nod her head.

I will never know what this gesture implied, nor what the lynx was actually thinking. But for the rest of my life, I will remember her—believing that the animals among us are nodding their heads, waiting for us to respond to this moment in time. We are all endangered species on an endangered planet.

What is required of us is love. The Endangered Species Act is an act of love.

## ❖ DANCING IN PLACE

WITH JOANNE DORNAN

In the spring of 1974, Joanne Dornan and I were driving up to Jackson Hole, Wyoming, after our ornithology class in Salt Lake City at the University of Utah. We stopped to watch a large gathering of sandhill cranes dance in their courtship ritual outside the fields of Cokeville. Suddenly, without warning, they all flew at once without any visible trigger. What did they see that we couldn't? What did they know that we didn't?

Forty years later, we are still wondering about the wisdom of birds. Having both been naturalists at Grand Teton National Park who took visitors on bird walks, we have watched the encroachment of the Jackson Hole airport on the ancestral leks of sage grouse. Following the decision not to federally list the greater sage grouse as an endangered species on September 22, 2015, by Secretary of the Interior Sally Jewell, but to protect it locally, state by state, we made a commitment to visit a lek we knew and sit in place.

❖

A clearing. A clearing among the sage, silver-blue. We are sitting in two lawn chairs north of the Jackson Hole airport, west of the runway, east of the Teton Range. For as far as we can see, we are surrounded by sage.

We can draw a circle with our eyes by simply following the circumference of the yellow-braided grasses lit up in afternoon light. It is as if an invisible fence has kept sage out. In truth, the dancing feet of grouse through time has tamped out any seedlings from taking root.

Six months from now, this ancient lek will be the stage for the amorous display of greater sage grouse, where the flamboyant males will be vying for the females' attention. Together they will dance, ensuring that another generation of grouse will flourish.

Where are they now?

❖

JD: *We sit at grouse level, twelve to eighteen inches off the ground. The grasses, golden in this late afternoon light, create a clearing in an otherwise sagebrush sea that stretches across the Jackson Hole valley from the flanks of Sleeping Indian to the terminal moraines of the Tetons.*

*This lek, at the end of the Jackson airport runway, has been used as a mating ground by a lineage of sage grouse since before anyone kept records of such things and long before there was an airport. "Site fidelity" is characteristic of greater sage grouse, and it intrigues me, draws me to them. Who would remain loyal to a place whose silence was broken by the nearly incessant thrust of jet engines?*

❖

*With my binoculars, I can see a large red sign with white block letters—VOC CRITICAL AREA, NO STOPPING—facing the runway, preceded by NO TRESPASSING signs attached to the metal fence. I don't know what "VOC" means. I will later learn from the FAA Aviation and Emissions Primer that "unburned or partially combusted hydrocarbons (also known as volatile organic compounds (VOCs)), particulates, and other trace compounds. . . . are considered hazardous air pollutants. . . . local air quality pollutants or greenhouse gases . . ." About 10 percent of aircraft emissions are produced during landing and takeoff.*

TTW: As if the sage grouse don't have enough to contend with during a sixty-five-decibel rise and onslaught of incoming and outgoing jets. One study revealed that a volume of sixty-five decibels affects memory and the recall of auditory information. For a greater sage grouse, this could mean the difference between life and death. It is memory that brings them back to their ancestral leks each year. It is the sound of booming air sacs during courtship that ensures the next generation.

The clouds today are small and dome shaped and I see them as sage grouse flying low above the sagebrush steppe buoyed by the wind—but that spell is quickly broken by the sound of a propeller, a small plane driving down the runway until it becomes airborne like the birds themselves.

The soundscape of Grand Teton National Park is as threatened as the sage grouse. We have grown used to the intrusion of noise: the propellers of planes, the engines of jets, the screeching brakes when a jet comes to a halt. Close to four million visitors come to the park each year, many by air, and I wonder how many see the incoming planes as a disturbance. Politics placed the airport here.

JD: *This was once a place of deep silences, especially in winter, until spring was heralded by the ritualized courtship dance of the grouse. With their white-feathered collar turned up, their spiked tail feathers splayed like a fan, males would strut themselves in front of the females, led by their inflating yellow air sacs that popped out from their breasts like an old-fashioned camera flash after each picture snapped.*

TTW: Whenever I witness this enduring grace, I am brought back into the heart of wildness and my ongoing faith in nature's cycles.

❖

JD: *I admire these birds for their passionate dance. Using their own bodies as instruments and with every feather aquiver, the males stamp their feet and shake their booty in precise and rapid rhythm. The urge to dance as part of courtship is something we share with birds—perhaps they taught us. Native People of the sagebrush steppe—Lakota, Omaha, Blackfeet, Cree, Oglala, Crow—danced with gratitude, ceremony, and merriment in honor and imitation of grouse and prairie chickens. It was an act of love. In the Omaha language, the word for "dance" is the same as the word for "love."*

*I admire these birds because they drum an original score. At mating time, on leks such as the one we are on now, males face into a circle. The music begins with foot drumming, accompanied by a low, faraway sound like the rustling of silk. The neck stretches, the body bobs up and down, and the long, white-feathered collar inflates. A percolating sound emerges, followed by a loud popping or hooting delivered by a pair of inflatable yellow throat pouches. Indian dancers imitate this sound with drums. Whether played by humans or grouse, the drum is an instrument of power and its rhythm is the rhythm of the entire universe, the heartbeat of all creation.*

*The voice, the heartbeat, the measure of health of the sage-covered American West—all 186 million acres of it—is the greater sage grouse. Today, wildlife biologists estimate that the bird's population, once in the millions, has been reduced to as few as two hundred thousand. This reduction is the direct result of habitat loss caused by: oil and gas development in Wyoming, sod-busting in Montana, invasive conifers in Oregon, invasive annual grasses. Roads. Lights. Houses. Fences—everywhere. Sage grouse cannot tolerate habitat fragmentation; they perish. Without sage we have no grouse, no Brewers sparrows, pronghorn, or pygmy rabbits; and most heartbreaking of all, we lose that pungent smell that rolls across the West to greet us after a rain.*

*In 2007, the U.S. government, ranchers, oil and gas developers, private landowners—everyone close to the story—saw the listing of the greater sage grouse as an endangered species coming. To forestall this decision, the U.S. Department of Agriculture in 2010 initiated a voluntary, incentive-based program aimed to mitigate the threats to sage grouse. Based on only five years of this multipartner program, the U.S. Fish and Wildlife Service decided in September 2011 that the greater sage grouse does not require protection under the Endangered Species Act.*

*Like elephants, sage grouse have a low reproductive rate that makes them slow to respond to positive environmental change. Sagebrush, once plowed up, takes fifty years to come back. As promising as the collaborative efforts have been, it is still too early to call the situation a "win-win" for grouse, ranchers, agriculture, and industry. The economic predators of the sagebrush steppe are enormous and powerful. The number one protection against these predators is policy. We all must remain vigilant as we insist that our government create and enforce policy that ensures these unique and magnificent birds don't go the way of passenger pigeons and bison.*

TTW: "Sage Grouse Surge at Jackson Hole Leks," the headline reads in the *Jackson Hole News & Guide*. "The sage grouse population in the Snake River basin took off this year. Numbers of male birds displaying to attract females in some places were at historic levels this spring," the article reports.

I hope this is true. But on a day like today, in the crease between fall and winter, where we are never out of range of the roar of our own kind, I am not so sure. Everything here feels compromised—too many planes—too many cars—too many concessions where commerce is favored over contemplation. What if it is only through the deep sustained silences that precede and follow love that life can be brought forth in all its fullness?

Now, the alarm of a backhoe reversing its direction.

Now, the stream of traffic mimicking the sound of rushing water.

Now, the sound of another jet overhead scribbling the sky with contrails.

And then, in between the pause of decibels rising, I hear the greatest disturbance of all: the noise of my own mind.

JD: *The sagebrush steppe is called the "big empty." If this is true, I find it the fullest empty I've ever known. As we sit in silence, our own breath and beating hearts are indistinguishable from the living, breathing landscape that pulses with sensations, memories, and the very real awareness that what happens to these birds happens to us.*

*What will it take for us to change so that other species like the greater sage grouse, the grizzly, the wolf, and the wolverine can live and thrive in peace? What will it take for us to honor what they need, instead of what we want?*

*A quiet landscape.*

TTW: We are now walking the straight and paved runway at our own peril. What if the NO TRESPASSING signs meant to protect the landing strip of the privileged few were posted to protect the fancy dancing of the strutting grouse?

There is a momentary silence—we can hear the thundering feet of the grassland birds inviting us to create ceremony.

We awoke before dawn and dressed like duck hunters in a palette of browns, beiges, and grays. The attire was a hopeful gesture, the hope of not being seen even inside a bird blind. We were on a pilgrimage to see the great migration of sand-hill cranes along the Platte River in Nebraska. It was a spring ritual, both human and wild. More than half a million cranes descend along this meandering river through marshes and cornfields. Thousands of visitors come to watch.

Tom Mangelsen, the legendary wildlife photographer known for his imprint, Images of Nature, was our guide. Mangelsen grew up on the Nebraska prairie, sandhill cranes have always been part of his weather system. Now he returns each year with the cranes and shares this spectacle with others in his family's decades-old duck-hunting blind on the edge of the Platte.

We left the Mangelsen cabin an hour or so before dawn and snuck out to shore, barely a hundred yards away. We didn't want to disturb the roosting cranes nearby, some on the sandbar, others standing in the shallows. Tom took the lead walking the well-worn path through the willows and grasses wet with dew. We followed him single file, quiet and attentive to the early sounds of birdsong, red-winged blackbirds among them.

Once inside the wooden box, roughly four feet wide and eight feet long, four of us gingerly unpacked our gear—scopes, tripods, binoculars, cameras, notebooks and pencils, thermoses of hot tea—and prepared to settle in for the morning. Our breath visible, we took our designated spots, each with an ample slice of view, just as the first line of light appeared on the water. Tom and the two others quickly began setting up their equipment. I sat. The tools of a writer are not only simple, but primitive: a stick of sharpened lead and pieces of paper, bound, small enough to slide into a back pocket.

The damp smell inside the blind—musky and oiled, like dried fish laced with mosquito repellent—reminded me of being in the bird blinds at the Bear River Migratory Bird Refuge as a college student studying ornithology. The blinds I sat in at dawn and dusk were also designed for duck hunters, as were many of the structures that dot our sanctuaries, refuges, and parks today, blending into the landscape, seemingly as natural as a stand of willows. They were small, five feet by five feet, camouflaged with cattails and bulrushes. Some were made out of concrete, others were simply a platform made of plywood flush with the water; some offered a bench or chairs to sit on, while the simplest blinds required you to squat or sit on the floor, or turn over a discarded five-gallon drum for a makeshift chair. When the ducks flew overhead, you leaped to your feet and shot away. Or in my case, stood and pointed a camera or raised a pair of binoculars, not a gun.

I find peering through bird blinds somewhat voyeuristic, akin to spying on neighbors through their well-lit windows when our lights are off; they can't see us, but we can see them. The intimacy felt is not earned, because it is not shared. It is different from when I stand on the edge of the marsh, still as a heron, and when a great blue heron arrives, she stays because she does not perceive me as a threat. Yet the benefit of a bird blind is more than invisibility; it is also about comfort. It's warmer inside than out, especially in weather best suited for watching waterfowl—cloudy with winds on the verge of rain, when birds fly fast and furiously in all directions, looking for cover. On a hot summer day, songbirds, waders, and waterfowl settle between cattails, in grasses, or on small protected ponds, difficult to find, hard to see. A blind provides protection while you practice patience.

In that blind on the Platte, the growing light drew my attention to what was taking shape before me: the shrouded silhouettes of sandhill cranes, multitudes, standing stoically in the shallows looking like a Chinese scroll of tall, statuesque birds.

And then, in a flurry and cacophony of sound, primal and singular, the guttural cries of the cranes shattered the darkness like wildness itself, with hundreds of thousands of birds lifting up the landscape with their wings. Everything was in motion: the water, the grasses, the cornfields, the sky. Flock after flock of cranes rising from river, higher and higher, flying above the Platte in all directions, some of the cranes crisscrossing each other like long undulating strands of calligraphy, writing themselves against the pages of a pastel sky. The outstretched wings of the sandhill cranes with their finger feathers extended are the farthest reaches of hope against the press of modernity. Their return is our assurance that the world is still fit for beauty. Nine million years of perfection resides in the bones of these birds that bear witness to the wisdom of evolution in its adaptive grace. Generation after generation, the memory of cranes landing in Middle America to feed and breed on the banks of the Platte River allows their story to continue.

I am the pupil of the bird blind, an eye squinting for insight beyond my own kind. The cranes slowly float back to Earth, descending like angels, only to rise and fall and rise again in the amorous play of lovers, leaping and bowing to the embodied knowledge that the future depends on each gesture granted to the other. In response to one of the oldest dances on the planet—the kind of mastery only evolution can perfect—we, also, rise to an awakened state of being for having witnessed the ongoing nature of grace.

We were close to the birds, close enough to be touched by the majesty and presence of these gray-feathered elders standing tall on the prairie with their beaks pointing upward as they danced and bowed to one another. Through the open window framing and focusing our attention, we saw what survival looks like in the shimmering light of awe.

*March 11, 2014, the* Samba *Sets Sail*
Today begins a ten-day sojourn in the Galápagos Islands with dearest friends, including my husband, Brooke, who visited these "Enchanted Islands" in 1983. Thirty-one years later, we are fulfilling his vow to return. We are with members of our chosen family, including Doug Peacock, whom I met on the trail in Glacier National Park in 1982. His wife, Andrea, and his daughter, Laurel, whom I have known since birth, have accompanied him. Rick Bass is here. (We met in 1989, when I picked him up hitchhiking en route to Ed Abbey's wake in Arches National Park.) Terry Osborne and M.K. Beach are friends from Dartmouth College who have joined us with their children, Hillary Beach and Jacob Osborne.

"We are in the middle of the world," says Juan Salcedo, our naturalist aboard the *Samba*, a seventy-eight-foot motor-sailer yacht built in Holland in 1966. Juan is a Galápagos native, born on the island of Santa Cruz. He comes to the naturalist gaze by way of his father, Jose Miguel Salcedo, a well-known expert on the Galápagos, having penned and illustrated a monograph of the islands for local high school students. As a boy always by his father's side, Juan lived and breathed this archipelago. By the time he was nine, his father was letting him lead tourists. Twenty-two years later, sharing the natural history of the Galápagos remains his passion.

Juan gives us our schedule in the language of military time: At 15:45 we will experience "a wet landing" on Las Bachas beach; at 18:30 we will be back on board the *Samba*. Dinner will be served at 19:30, an evening lecture will begin at 22:00, and at 23:00 we will begin our navigation to the island of Genovesa, traveling the open seas throughout the night. At 05:30 the next morning we will be walking on a new island; at 09:00 it's snorkeling in open water.

"Pace yourself," a friend said to me before we left for the Galápagos. She had visited the islands, and returned home invigorated but exhausted. I would be balancing choices of withdrawal alongside choices of engagement; such is the nature of being an introvert. One-on-one encounters sustain me. Groups do not. But community is something different: a group of people interconnected, interrelated, respecting one another's place within a shared landscape. The *Samba* quickly became a community, each person finding their niche, occupying their space on deck. The ecology of experience began on the boat with hypnotic hours spent simply staring out toward the rolling horizon.

### March 11, Las Bachas

We leave the *Samba* on schedule and file into the small Zodiac that motors toward the island in view. Once we step out of the ocean and onto the beach, my feet tell me all I need to know. I am on solid ground, even if it is shifting sands—white, like flour.

We follow Juan beyond mounds of green sea turtle eggs, freshly laid and buried in the sand, to a mangrove pond. Five flamingos, perfectly spaced in an embrace of green, meet us. The long-legged birds, pink with vermillion feathers, fan the humid air. Defying the stereotype of stolid lawn ornaments, they feed peaceably in paradise—walking slowly, with their small heads and black beaks submerged, only briefly coming up for air. And when they do stand in full view, their yellow eyes, like topaz, catch ours. It is a bejeweled moment of exotica in the tropics, a water-colored landscape saturated in light.

Watching the flamingos beneath a lapis sky, it becomes clear that the Galápagos are not a bow toward silence or solitude but an ongoing conversation with a multitude of species. The mockingbird has a Galápagos accent, a subtle variation of the call of those living in North America. And variation is the key even for a bird skilled in mimicry. All around us we are being asked to discern familiar yet different narratives in the wild. This is no longer about facts and field guides, but a saturation of the senses: salt, sea breezes, the touch of sand, stones, and shells.

Everywhere we turn, life is present. A marine iguana's silhouette against the lava rocks looks both sinister and seductive. The collision of sea lions barking on the beach is an exercise in dominance. A female sea lion lies on her side purring, a pup is nursing; the sucking of milk is fast and fluid.

Sanderlings skitter directly in front of us—we yield. A ruddy turnstone is doing just that: turning stones. Ghost crabs appear and disappear like a seaside magic show. It becomes comical, species on cue. A theater in the round. Foreground, background, and peripheral; it is a steady state of joy.

I catch Doug's eye—we begin laughing. Brooke is bent over, examining a dragonfly. Laurel is photographing an iguana in the surf. Andrea is watching an oystercatcher. Jacob is crouched near hermit crab tracks, while Rick takes notes on stray pieces of paper. M.K. and Terry are walking ahead, eyes focused on something we cannot see.

Hillary, tall and elegant, enters the rising waters of the sea. She is human radiance bathed in gold light in the descending heat of day. Each of us follows behind her and falls back, floating between the oscillations of the tide, arms outstretched, looking upward.

### March 12, Genovesa Island

*Pajaro pirata.* Pirate bird. Black crossbows are launched against a field of blue. Great frigate birds crisscross the sky, avian mercenaries bombing swallow-tailed gulls for the mackerel in their bills. They steal midair from boobies, from shearwaters, from any bird in flight carrying fish home.

When sailors saw these "man-of-war" birds, they knew land was near; on the cliff face of the island of Genovesa, hundreds of them gather in colonies, quivering for attention. Males perch on branches or nestle in the sand, inflating their gular sacs, like clowns blowing up red balloons, before indifferent females that circle above them. Long neck plumes of green iridescent heat flame and flare nuptial intent.

Hours pass as I watch the spectacle of desire through my binoculars. The intensity and solipsism of courtship humbles the male thief birds into amorous desperation. Their voices rise as a collective rattle and wail. Eventually, a soaring female descends upon the partner of her choice, mounting the male as he pants, his outstretched wings trembling. The next generation is ensured. It is dusk. Everywhere I look, the sky is a script of wings I am just beginning to decipher.

### March 13, Marchena Island

Collapsed lava tubes become secret waterways for fur seals on Marchena Island. The lava rocks scorch our feet. The water is warm. We are snorkeling in an igneous pool, a blue eye lined in black. This is where Juan learned to swim as a boy. Curiosity is the great teacher. He simply watched fur seals wheel in the water—inquisitive, playful, and buoyant.

Little has changed. Underwater, the seals glide, spin, and turn abruptly—some just missing a brush with our bodies. I want to touch them, but resist. Can intimacy exist between two species? Or only longing?

A baby fur seal erupts in front of my mask and blows bubbles in my face. I surface—no fur seal in sight. I submerge once again, swim ahead to find him. He nips my arm from behind. I turn—nothing. Suddenly the baby is back, suspended in the water, floating upside down. He is staring at me. I stare back. Curiosity is the great teacher. His large opaque eyes are a wilderness.

### March 15, Punta Espinosa, Isabela Island

The hand of the iguana is my hand. The only difference I see between my fingers splayed on the lava and hers is one of scale instead of skin. Her eye blinks as my eye blinks. Her chest inhales as mine exhales. She is wary of my presence, and I am in awe of hers. I could choose to see this marine iguana as something alien to myself, more dinosaur than human, but that would be to discount and deny the very tail that remains in me as a remnant of our shared evolution. The coccyx. I fall hard on the rocks as a swift reminder that my family tree is not as neat and tidy as my kin would have me believe.

The Bible tells us the Earth was created in seven days. The

marine iguana tells me this is a myth. Here is another: nature is tooth and claw. What if the survival of the fittest is the survival of compassion? The tenderness I feel is as unnerving as the spines that highlight her back. I move closer. She hisses. The hairs on my arm stand. Multitudes of marine iguanas leap off the ledges into the sea at sunrise.

### March 16, Pacific Ocean

We are snorkeling, breathing, looking below. A raft of golden cownose rays is fanning the waters—hundreds of them, like an order of brown-cloaked monks that has retreated to the sea. Schools of creole fish, Moorish idols, parrot fish, puffer fish, angelfish, and eels swim through the pastel reefs. Masked, our human eyes focus on movement as much as color. Hammerhead sharks are in the distance. Blue starfish, purple anemone, and buried stingrays inhabit the sandy bottoms.

I am following Jose Ricardo, our captain, a black man wearing white fins, at home in the sea, agile and elegant as he dives deep and surfaces, graceful as a sea lion. He takes my hand in his and points with the other: octopus.

It appears as a purple-veined orchid camouflaged against the coral. And then the eight tapered legs—long, white, and suckered—are suddenly wrapping themselves around the captain's taut arm as he reaches toward the unearthly creature now crawling across his chest, latching onto his back. I think I detect a struggle between man and beast—or is it play? I can't be certain, but the eyes of both are wild and intense, two minds locked. And as the captain tries to grab the legs and pull the shape-shifting octopus off his body—poof! A cloud of red ink, not blood, envelops us—the octopus is gone. We float in suspended disbelief.

### *March 17, Fernandina Island*

If there is an underlying melody heard throughout the Galápagos—on all islands in all habitats in all hours of the day—it is the song of the yellow warbler. I hear them singing at the airport on the island of Baltra. I hear them singing from the bow of the boat when we are close to shore. When we walk across a bleak lava bed, their voices accompany us as a hymn against the heat. And the flashes of joy foraging in the poison apple trees of Fernandina sing in spite of the shadowed landscape.

The voice of the yellow warbler is an oracle and a bow to the power of small things. With my eyes closed, the bird is singing in the red rock canyons of Utah. Perhaps this is the grace note that binds us together. Earth is our shared home, no matter where we live. Endemic, native, migrant, or accidental, the yellow warbler reminds us: we are not the only species that flies around the world. The yellow warbler is the relentless voice of the joyous traveler.

### *March 18, Santa Cruz Island*

Time. The evolution of time in the Galápagos. A time of unexpected interludes, incantatory moments with fellow species that live somewhere on the edge of an evolving planet witnessed by a party of friends. In the beginning it is about love. In the end it is about relationships. I want to follow. I want to follow what I can never understand, a love that is wild. Cradled in the boat with a lullaby of stars, I am being rocked to sleep.

I am following my thoughts. *Creation is not an act but a process.* What is the process? The world is a wobble. We are animals subject to the same laws of natural selection.

Has anyone been face-to-face with evolution? The other day I was eye-to-eye with a Galápagos tortoise that had spent three months walking from the top of the volcano down to the sea to lay her eggs at night on the island of Isabela. In the slow, deliberate nature of her world, she upholds twelve million years of perfection. Beauty is the origin of wonder. What enables her to live eighteen months without food or water? Does a fast predicated by drought or famine become spiritual? What can we do for the tortoise? Step to the side. Give her the right-of-way. Kneel.

## ❖ THE TELLURIAN

We smelled them before we heard them. We heard them before we saw them. And when we saw them we disappeared in
the eyes of kin.

Tellurian: of Earth. In the Virunga Mountains of Rwanda,
we walked with mountain gorillas. We followed them. We followed them through a wet bamboo forest, ducking and sliding
as they moved powerfully, gracefully, deliberately through the
landscape. It was a family of twenty-one individuals. We were
a family of four with two guides. When they crossed over a
stone fence, jumping down from the piled rocks of lava, we
did the same, until we found ourselves standing on the steep
slopes of potato fields.

The silverback turned toward us. We froze. My eyes looked
down. Our guide Frances Ndagijimana knew him by name.
Kwitonda. He is the dominant silverback. He sets the direction and the pace for the day. All females follow him. There
are three other silverbacks, two blackbacks, the juveniles and
babies, all moving through the rich black furrows of exposed
potatoes. Our guide tells us that this is a hopeful story of how
local communities from Ruhengheri to Kinigi have become

conservationists and work with the gorillas. Everyone benefits. The economy is growing.

It does not feel hopeful to me. It feels crowded and precarious. The bleeding of forest into field conceals a great wound. We never see the wound. But I smell it, familiar. Dressed in their bright batiked kitenges, the women with their hoes in hand scatter.

The silverback sits down and leans his great black body against the trunk of a tree and looks out over the expanse of quilted hills far into the Congo where he and his clan once lived. The Congo is at war. Women are being raped. Forests are being burned. Gorillas are being killed. Charcoal is being sold. Kwitonda and his clan fled to the mountains of Rwanda in shrouds of smoke. Now they are refugees. Exiled.

In the past ten years, more than 160 rangers charged with protecting the gorillas have been murdered within the Virunga National Park in the Congo. Most were killed by the FDLR (Democratic Forces for Liberation of Rwanda), the rebel militia, reported to include perpetrators of the Rwandan genocide in 1994. The rangers protect the endangered mountain gorillas who stand in the way of charcoal production. The guerrillas want the gorillas gone, so they can cut down the forests, cook the trees, and get on with the illegal business of selling charcoal, a $35 million industry that has benefited the FDLR as they illegally continue to smuggle much of the charcoal into Rwanda, where it is used by rural households for cooking fuel. How much wood does it take to make charcoal? The carbonization ratio in Central Africa ranges from 5 to 12.6 tons of wood for 1 ton of charcoal.

Conservation begins with crisis.

In this "land of a thousand hills," there is not a square inch in this war-torn country that has not been bled on or bled over. In the decades since the 1994 genocide, Rwanda is a nation reconstructing itself in peace.

Meanwhile, Rwanda is thirsty for oil, and appears to have found it on the flanks of Virunga National Park. Kwitonda is now sitting on reserves of oil.

There is a gorilla in the room. What is it? The American artist Walton Ford's painting of him hangs in the room of the Paul Kasmin Gallery in New York City. It is large and harrowing and easily mistaken for a cartoon. But it is not a cartoon, nor a parody. It is a portrait of King Kong. And he looks a lot like us.

Another artist, Ben Peberdy, has created a collage titled *The Giant Buddha* that hangs on the rippled wall of the Main Street Museum in White River Junction, Vermont. Hurricane Irene ripped and flooded the town in 2011. *The Giant Buddha* is another gorilla, only six inches tall, who holds a dancing atom serenely on his lap, captive to our atomic, demonic visions of the future. Neither Ford's nor Peberdy's portrait shows this beast in its rightful place of a bamboo forest.

Of place: Tellurian. Forgetting our place. Distellurian.

Displacement is my concern. Disappearance my fear. There is no home for those who are native, of Earth, inhabitants of Earth, anymore. "Tellurian" is an endangered word that every endangered species hides inside. We are all on the run, human and wild. Exiled. Endangered. Refugees.

I smell the wound and it smells like me. This wound will not heal and is spreading as an infection. Stabbed by our illusions and legacies of grandeur, we stagger through our forests of consumption. We are lost. We are in pain. And we don't know the cause or the cure of what is making us sick. We long for something more, when what we have is more than enough. We are becoming blind. We are becoming deaf. We are hobbling along the path of distractions, trying to find our way back or forward or sideways to a place of dreams as we bleed from the wound of longing.

What are we longing for?

I wish there was a gorilla in every corner of our imaginations to remind us what we are choosing to harm and ignore. I wish we could smell them, hear them, see them for who they are in place, and know them by name: the most gentle of creatures, with strength and power.

But there are no gorillas in the rooms we inhabit: the boardrooms, the bedrooms from which we populate the world. Inside our sitting rooms, inside the halls of political power and public policy—there is only talking, endless talking that ends in schemes to dominate the world because we are entitled to "the American Dream." There is only our flimsy mythology of King Kong, of a man in a gorilla suit, plucking airplanes from the New York City sky.

Terror is in the air.

We have forgotten what is true.

We have forgotten the difference between fear and terror, because to face the gaze of a gorilla is a privilege.

This is my third trip to Rwanda in six years. I can recall only one instance when a Rwandan told me of encountering a gorilla. It was a woman, now a long-distance runner, who fled the Interhamwe during the genocide by escaping up the flanks of the Virunga Mountains. She told me that as she was running up the steep slopes of the forest, she saw a silverback flash by in her peripheral vision. She did not stop, nor did she look back.

I have the privilege of looking forward and I have the

privilege of watching mountain gorillas, not simply as a wild-life experience, but as part of an understanding of how Rwanda as a country is changing in its postgenocide reconstruction and reimagining of itself. The development of an ecological ethic is following economic development as part of a sustainable vision of people living in place with other creatures.

Frances tells us that there are now 480 mountain gorillas in Virunga National Park, with one-third of them living in the Rwandan mountains. When Dian Fossey was doing her fieldwork at the Karisoke Research Center from 1966 until her death in 1985, there were half that many gorillas.

Though the gorilla population has doubled, the human population in Rwanda has also doubled, more than doubled. In 1983, the population was five million. Today, it is eleven million people. Four million people live within walking distance of the Virunga National Park. Add millions of tourists like me each year and the pressure on land in this tiny country barely the size of Vermont—to cultivate it, develop it, use the forests for fuel as much of the soil exposed in deforestation erodes downriver—is enormous.

My family and I had one hour with Kwitonda's clan of mountain gorillas foraging among the bamboo shoots, leading us from the forest into the fertile fields of Rwanda, these dignified refugees from the Congo struggling to find their place.

As a writer, must I write a hopeful story? Or an evolving one?

### ❖ THE COUNCIL OF PRONGHORN

I strongly suspect a big part of real art-fiction's job is to aggravate
this sense of entrapment and loneliness and death in people, to
move people to countenance it, since any possible human
redemption requires us first to face what's dreadful, what we
want to deny.

—DAVID FOSTER WALLACE, *Review of Contemporary Fiction*, 1993

What I want to deny is that fossil fuels are killing us. What
I want to deny is that living in the state of Wyoming is living
in the heart of denial. And if we want to see "entrapment and
loneliness and death," all we have to do is go out and visit the
oil patch in Sublette County or Sweetwater County or Gillette, more commonly known as "Razor City," in Campbell
County, Wyoming.

The "dreadful" truth is that if Wyoming were a nation, it
would be among the largest coal-producing countries in the
world. Since 1996, more than 7.7 billion tons of coal have been
produced, most of it coming from the Powder River Basin.
Trains leave Gillette twenty-four hours a day carrying coal
from our state to yours. We live in a rectangle that borders Utah,
Idaho, Montana, South Dakota, Nebraska, and Colorado, all

part of the fossil fuel boom in the Interior West. This is a ravaged landscape and few see it, even those who live here.

In 2007, I accepted an invitation to become the first "writer in residence" at the University of Wyoming's creative writing department. The students I worked with were extraordinary. Many of them were local, but others were not. The students—poets and nonfiction and fiction writers—decided they wanted to do more than examine themselves on the page, they wanted to go outside. They wanted to get a glimpse into the state of the state of Wyoming and believed storytelling could open a door to what a sense of place really means, a gauge and a guide to what folks in Wyoming were thinking.

Together, we created a program called "Weather Reports." It would be simple, direct, and nonthreatening: "What's the weather like in your town?" Students created a road map. We would visit seven communities in the state that were being impacted by oil and gas and coal-bed methane gas development from Pinedale to the Powder River Basin to Rawlins, Riverton, and the Wind River Reservation.

The "Weather Reports" took place on Friday evenings, when we would gather at a library or arts center, a politically neutral zone, and invite the community to gather in the name of storytelling. On Saturday, we would offer a writing workshop to those in attendance who were interested in developing their stories on the page.

The format was always the same: A student would read a story they had written, then invite those in attendance to tell their own. We would form a circle and begin with one question: "What keeps you up at night?" No one was prepared for the emotion or depth of sharing that followed.

Our first "Weather Report" took place in the town of Pinedale, elevation 7,182 feet, located at the base of the Wind

River Range; population 1,865. It is also a boomtown, 32 miles north of the Jonah Oil Field, which is estimated to contain 10.5 trillion cubic feet of natural gas.

It was standing room only in the public library. Residents talked about poisoned water, the elevated benzene levels related to the oil and gas development, the ozone alert that was posted for the first time in their history on that very day. We listened to senior people, primarily women, talk about "Project Wagon Wheel." In the 1960s, during the Cold War, the Atomic Energy Commission planned to extract Wyoming natural gas with five underground nuclear explosions. The women who protested that action rose to tell their history and it was personal. "I'll be damned if they were going to blow up our backyard, sage or no sage," one of the women said. They recounted a straw poll in Sublette County on the presidential election day in 1972 that showed 970 people were opposed to Project Wagon Wheel, 279 were in favor, and 105 were undecided. This was a revelation to the hundred-plus residents in the room. A young man stood up and said: "If you could stop five nuclear bombs, we can hold these gas companies accountable."

One story of courage followed another until well after midnight. The librarian stood in the back of the room. Her words closed the evening: "One day, I think I'm going to wake up and Wyoming will just be one giant hole in the ground with everything we love, gone."

In the town of Gillette, elevation 4,556 feet, population 30,560, a mother stood up and said, "What keeps me up at night is the health of my children. My five-year-old son has a rash on his legs and our well water is red." She paused to control her emotions. "Is anyone else experiencing this?" One by one, other mothers stood in solidarity and shared similar stories, and then two nurses took the floor: "Can anyone tell us why we can't keep enough chemotherapy in this town to treat all the cancers in Campbell County?"

When we arrived in Casper, the financial hub of the state, elevation 5,118 feet, population 57,814, it was a different story. The state senator Kit Jennings showed up in his shiny black cowboy boots, wearing his sport coat, a bolo tie, and Levi's held up by a belt with a silver buckle shaped like an oil rig. Everyone knew who he was and everyone knew he was in the pocket of the coal-bed methane industry now following our every move. They didn't like people talking. Wyoming is a state of big distances with few occasions to assemble. People were isolated and the oil and gas companies liked it that way. The industry had gotten to Jennings, and Jennings was going to get to us.

The senator might as well have entered the room with a loaded shotgun, so violent was his rhetoric and so personal—but a circle had been created and a space of respect had been established. The woman seated next to him handed him the microphone.

"What keeps me up at night is thinking I have to show up to a hippie-dippie circle like this . . . You say there is a direct correlation between the rise of crystal meth and rise of rigs in our towns, well that's bullshit, what do you know"—he was addressing his remarks to me—"you're an outsider from Utah."

We listened. It was his turn to tell his story. When he finally realized there would be no confrontation, no conflict, no heated exchange of words, he simply paused and said: "I was raised on the oil patch as a kid—people looked down on us, called us white trash." And with that the combative senator began to tell the truth of his life.

We witnessed the art of storytelling and story receiving.

Senator Jennings had tried to shut down the students' "Weather Reports" and pressure the president of the University of Wyoming to fire me. But President Buchanan defended our program. Freedom of speech. What's wrong with telling stories and listening to one another? What's wrong with gathering as a community to consider where we live, what we love, and what is at stake in the twenty-first century?

What lawmakers fear most, especially those financed by the energy industry, is the art of independent thinking, *the arc* of creative thinking. What power tries to control is the story, especially the story that sees the world as a complicated whole. What the oil and gas companies know is that if they can keep people isolated and the story fragmented, keep as little known as possible, and in some cases lie, then they can go about their business without protest or accountability.

But the most revelatory of all our "Weather Reports" took place in the bars in Riverton, elevation 4,951 feet, population 11,058, adjacent to the Wind River Reservation, home to the Northern Arapaho and Eastern Shoshone tribes.

Riverton, Wyoming, is famous for having sixteen drinking holes in a two-mile stretch. The bars are segregated. We went to a roughneck bar and an Indian bar. The roughnecks were making big money at big risk with long days, where a little meth went a long way to carry them through what is known as "a tower"—twelve-hour days for fourteen days straight and then a week off to rest. We learned Wyoming has the highest worker fatality rate in the nation, three times the national average. The men know this. And one young oil worker after another told stories of death by "trippin' pipe" or "throwing chain" accidents, or incidents where the drilling mud caught fire or the actual rigs blew up. But their stories always had the same tagline: "It was the guy next to me." At age twenty-one, many of them saw themselves as invincible. "The sick thing is the family whose boy got chewed up on the rig received a check for ten thousand dollars from the worker compensation fund. And what's really fucked up is that the company only got fined six hundred and twenty-five dollars for the chain tong mess-up."

The stories told in the Indian bar where the Arapahos and Shoshone hang were not about jobs on the rigs at all, they were about no jobs.

Their stories were about poverty, missing women, and bison being killed once they crossed the boundary of Yellowstone National Park. Some of the men were blunt enough to ask why we were hanging out in the "wrong bar." Then it got real.

The students came to understand that story engages the whole person. People lean forward. Words matter and cut through race, class, and politics. Stories move us and move through us, become the conscience of a community.

It is difficult to get a man to understand something when his salary depends upon his not understanding it.
—UPTON SINCLAIR, *Oil!*

A year after the "Weather Reports," I set out on a road trip with two artists, Felicia Resor and Ben Roth, to witness the oil and gas development in Wyoming. We wanted to go deeper than we were able to go with our "Weather Reports." We wanted to see for ourselves how the fossil fuel economy was impacting the state physically, something that was largely invisible to its citizens, because of either lack of interest or lack of access. Felicia was born in Teton County and raised on a ranch. She was a recent graduate of Yale, with a major in the humanities. Ben was native to Colorado, a metal artist, now living in Jackson.

We had received funding from a foundation called Invoking the Pause, by an anonymous donor who asked that we reflect on some aspect of climate change through an art project and how this work might enter into the public conversation. The grant was designed as a two-year project. The first year, we were to investigate what a climate change art project might look like, do some ground truthing, then "pause" to reflect as a team on the information we had gleaned. During the second year, we would begin to collaborate and create something out of that pause.

We formulated our project with the knowledge that Wyoming was the largest coal producer in the country, responsible for more than 90 percent of U.S. coal. Our road trip would bring us into proximity with the sources of Wyoming's coal, oil, and gas. We wanted the abstract to become real. We were aware of our complicity behind the wheel, the gas we were using (Wyoming is not a small state), but short of riding horses, this was our means of traversing the "Cowboy State," visiting such far-flung towns as Spotted Horse, Buffalo, and Ten Sleep. We were committed to thinking about what we might do as artists to "move people to countenance it," the "it" that was not yet known to us.

We made visits to the Jonah Oil Field, to the man-camps in Sweetwater County, to the Halliburton Hilton in Pinedale, to the coal mines in Gillette, to the ranches in the Powder River Basin suffering from the "split-estate agreement" that says residents might own the surface rights to the land, but the federal government owns the natural resources below the land. We witnessed coal-bed methane pumps in the front yards of ranch houses; water-quality issues associated with hydraulic fracking; boomtowns where locals are few and roughnecks are many. We became acutely aware of our nation's thirst for oil and the hidden costs that remain invisible to most of us.

When we asked our guide at the Jonah patch about the decline in air quality in Sublette and Sweetwater Counties, he said it was a result of the geysers in Yellowstone National Park spewing "god knows what" into the atmosphere. There was no discussion to be had. He was the industry's public relations man. "Those who say the ozone is up don't have any baseline studies to support their claims."

That night, we stayed at a friend's cabin beneath a sky of stars now noticeably obscured by the lights of a twenty-four-hour workforce on rigs lit up like Christmas trees. A decade ago, this was a night sky of only stars, not construction lights and gas flares dotting the sage flats from one horizon to the next. We talked about how these same lights fuel our economy, pave our roads, and pay for free in-state college tuition for any graduating high school senior in Wyoming who wants to go to the University of Wyoming in Laramie, the state's only university. Residents benefit from its natural gas, oil, coal, and coal-bed methane in tangible ways. Wyoming is a rich state because of its rich resources—and a well-educated one.

We drove from Pinedale to Cora and traveled across Union Pass in the Wind Rivers through a forest of lodgepole pines, once green, now red. It was a long, dry, and dusty road, eerie, even, for those of us who had lived in the American West all our lives. The expanse was so vast, we almost got used to the red forests, a result of local warming that has created a double life span for pine bark beetles, who cut through the bark of the trees to the cambium layer and kill the pines. We saw ghost forests of white bark pines and we imagined hungry grizzlies searching for their autumn food source of pine nuts and not finding them—at risk of entering hibernation in a state of starvation. We witnessed more split estates of mineral rights, above ground and below, that have torn up the hearts of ranches and ranchers in the Powder River Basin, where coal-bed methane operations have ravaged what ranching families believed was their rightful land passed down through the generations. And we witnessed the enormity of the black open-pit coal mines in Gillette, a town where there is so much money, local kids have learned to stand in front of the open doors of bars to catch twenty-dollar bills as they fly out of the saloons or pick them up in the desert snatched by the fingers of sage.

Throughout our wanderings, there was one constant: pronghorn. They were present wherever we went, four-legged witnesses to the environmental stresses in the sagebrush plains. We would see the antelopes watching, not running, as they sat on the edges of the Jonah Oil Field between the rigs and the man-camps, between the roads and the burning slag ponds. Their legs would be hung up in barbed-wire fences as they tried to escape the oil reservations. Many of them, defeated, just sat directly on the oil patches, lethargic, emaciated, fenced in and trapped, their ancestral sage flats now crisscrossed with roads looking like black asphalt scribbles on the whiteboard of winter.

As we drove the long distances, we saw pronghorn antelope standing behind the barbed wire, frozen in fear. And then, in the Big Horn Basin, we saw them running with the wind. And then they would stop and turn, as if looking over their shoulders for what was chasing them. They haunted us. And their large black protruding eyes never left us, as we wondered what they were seeing that we could not.

Pronghorn antelope are uniquely American, found no-where else on Earth, part of an ancient family, Antilocapridae, that has been roaming North America since the Pliocene era, with fossil records dating back five million years. It is one of the only mammals to have survived the Ice Age.

For almost two million years, the pronghorn's primary predator was the cheetah. They still run with a memory of this Pleistocene cat with speeds of up to eighty miles per hour. The Arapaho and Shoshone call the pronghorn antelope "Wind-horse." With their remarkable peripheral vision, the pronghorn can see in a radius of 360 degrees and spot intruders for up to three to four miles.

The herds we saw in Sublette County around the Jonah Oil Field migrate from Grand Teton National Park in the fall back to Pinedale in the winter, in a hundred-mile seasonal journey returning to the Tetons in the spring. This path of the pronghorn is the longest ungulate migration in the lower forty-eight and has been intact for more than eight thousand years. Now, with the intrusion of development, it is more difficult for them to manage their ancestral trek.

No matter where we seemed to go in the state, the pronghorn were present. Their white geometric markings on tan fur and their black hooked horns create the most stunning of animals. Averaging three feet tall at the shoulder and seventy-five to a hundred pounds, pronghorn are barrel-chested animals with a huge heart and expansive lungs, perfectly adapted with their short buoyant legs to fly across the high plains.

As we drove through the miles of open range, another pronghorn would appear on the side of the barbed-wire fence, white fanny flared as danger was noted. I remembered a Polaroid of my three brothers, Steve, Bob, and Dan, each holding up by the horns the pronghorn they had shot as a rite of passage in the 1970s—their boyhood pride exhibited.

We returned home from our road trip with a sobering perspective. The oil and gas companies had created a wide and gaping wound across Wyoming. As U.S. citizens, it can be said, we are all the beneficiaries of America's oil independence, but there are social and environmental costs and the price is being paid by small rural communities. In Pavillion, Wyoming, with a population of roughly 250, the EPA warned residents in 2011 that they could no longer drink, bathe in, cook with, or farm with their water. Why? No one was saying exactly, but everyone suspected it was contaminated by fracking, by the chemical soup injected into the substrate to release the natural gas. The very company that had fouled their water, Encana, the Canadian company responsible for drilling more than two hundred natural gas wells in the area, donated $1 million to provide water cisterns "to impacted residents" and fund a state study, all the while repeating to the community, "We are not responsible for the problem."

When we sat with these images over the next year, reflected on them, and digested all the information we had gleaned from our summer of witness, we discussed how our ideas as artists might contribute to the conversation surrounding climate change.

What emerged from the "pause" was the overriding presence of the pronghorn.

The pronghorn as witness. What were they seeing? What were they saying to one another? What would they say to us from the vantage point of the Pliocene?

The three of us imagined "A Council of Pronghorn," a circle of witnesses: twenty-three pronghorn antelope standing in a circle representative of the twenty-three counties in Wyoming. We imagined their skulls floating above weathered fence posts—an homage to the ranching culture—each secured to an iron base repurposed from the gas fields.

We saw each skull not only representing a county in the

state, but a voice heard, a story told, a perspective felt. We gathered antelope skulls from hunters, from local collectors, and many from roadkills left behind on the shoulders of lonely straightaways, cleaned meticulously by Felicia and her sister, Avery. The posts were made of lodgepole pine and spoke to the obstacles the animals face, whether fences, roads, or oil rigs. Most of these posts came directly from the Resor ranch. The metal bases made of discarded machinery disks were salvaged from the oil patches, addressing our industrial footprint. We believed these various elements could tell a story:

Animals bear witness to a changing world, a changing climate. The fate of the pronghorn is our own, holding us accountable for what has been taken and for the beauty that remains.

Over the next six months, Ben created the twenty-three Pronghorn Witnesses. Their skulls did float above the spines of weathered ranch posts, each one secured in an iron base. The Council appeared. My task as the writer was to create a poem that would animate them. We imagined lines, words, written in black calligraphy across their skulls.

But once we saw "The Council of Pronghorn" fully articulated in their circle, it became clear to us that they did not need the imposition of our words. A secret language was held within their presence. Their power was gleaned from place.

The poem would simply appear as a bookmark, located on a stand to the side of the circle.

Here's how the words came to me: I lived with one of the skulls. Wherever I was sitting in our house, the skull sat with me. If I was writing in my study, the skull was on my desk watching me. If I was cooking a meal, the skull was by my side preparing the food. If I sat on the porch, the pronghorn skull accompanied me.

After a month, I felt comfortable with our relationship. I slept with the skull.

Brooke was away—and that night, I placed the pronghorn skull on the pillow next to me. I cannot tell you where my dreams took me that night, only that when I awoke, the words were fully formed.

> We, The Council
> of Pronghorn
> have convened
> as witnesses
> to this moment
> in time
> when our eyes
> wish to peer
> into the hearts
> of humans
> and ask
> what kind
> of world
> are you creating
> when we can
> no longer
> run as Windhorses
> but are relegated
> to watching
> behind fences
> dreaming, dreaming
> of Spirit
> Migrations?

*The Council of Pronghorn* made its first appearance in the courtyard of the Center for the Arts in Jackson, Wyoming. They circled the square as a disturbance. Visitors had the choice of standing next to pronghorns as part of the circle; inside the circle enduring the horned witnesses' gaze; or outside the circle as observers. Most people stood outside the circle. The children, however, wanted to build a fire in the center and dance.

And then, *The Council of Pronghorn* received an invitation to participate in an international exhibit on water at the Cathedral of St. John the Divine in New York City. Ben Roth agreed to drive the pronghorn across the country in his van. What he couldn't have known at the start of his journey was that the day he arrived in Manhattan, August 27, 2011, would be the day Hurricane Irene made landfall in New York. It took him approximately six and a half minutes to get the twenty-three pronghorns from one end of the island to the other, to get to the cathedral. The city had been evacuated—there were no cars, no buses or taxis or people on the streets. Since this was Ben's first trip to New York, he didn't realize the rarity of this moment.

*The Council of Pronghorn* arrived at the Cathedral of St. John the Divine just as the Arapaho describe them, "Windhorses." One by one, Ben brought *The Council of Pronghorn* into the cathedral, which was now a pop-up shelter for the homeless where people could weather the storm.

The pronghorn were placed stoically in a spacious circle inside the nave of the cathedral as the wind roared outside. They told the story of fracking in the American West, of a boom-and-bust economy and contaminated water in towns like Pavillion, Wyoming. They stood as witnesses to the costs of a fossil fuel economy. They haunted, frightened, instructed,

and inspired each visitor with their dignity and stark beauty—
many who came to see them had never encountered a pronghorn antelope before.

*The Council of Pronghorn* came to be known as "The Eighth
Chapel" and remained in the Cathedral of St. John the Divine
for almost a year, so compelling was its aura. It is still there,
now a semipermanent installation on the grounds of the cathedral on 114th Street in Manhattan, bearing witness to a
city and state that continue to face and to fight against their
own fracking future.

2

Soon it would be too hot.

—J. G. BALLARD, *The Drowned World*

### ❖ WHAT LOVE LOOKS LIKE: EROSION OF SAFETY
*A Conversation with Tim DeChristopher*

From the moment I heard about Bidder #70 raising his paddle inside a BLM auction to outbid oil and gas companies in the leasing of Utah's public lands, I recognized Tim DeChristopher as a brave, creative citizen-activist. That was on December 19, 2008, in Salt Lake City. Since that moment, Tim has become a thoughtful, dynamic leader of his generation in the climate change movement. While many of us talk about the importance of democracy, Tim has put his body on the line and has paid the consequences.

On March 2, 2011, Tim DeChristopher was found guilty on two felony charges for violation of the Federal Onshore Oil and Gas Leasing Reform Act and for making false statements. He refused to entertain any type of plea bargain. On July 26, 2011, he was sentenced to two years in a federal prison with a ten-thousand-dollar fine, followed by three years of supervised probation. Minutes before receiving his sentence, Tim DeChristopher delivered an impassioned speech from the courtroom floor. At the end of the speech, he turned toward Judge Dee Benson, who presided over his trial, looked him in the eye, and said, "This is what love looks like." Minutes later, he was placed in handcuffs and briskly taken away.

When I asked Tim about his thoughts concerning prison, he responded, "All these people are worrying about how to keep me out of prison, but I feel like the goal should be to get other people in prison. How do we get more people to join me?"

In fact, in the past decade, thousands of citizens have followed his lead and chosen to commit acts of civil resistance in protest of mountaintop removal and the construction of the Keystone XL pipeline and other pipelines across the country, as well as resisting the practice of fracking. These engaged citizens, call them climate justice activists, recognize that we can no longer look for leadership outside ourselves. And that if public opinion changes, government changes.

On May 28, 2011 (two months before he was sent to prison), Tim DeChristopher and I had a three-hour conversation in Telluride, Colorado, during the Mountainfilm Festival. We talked openly and candidly with one another as friends. No one else was in the room.

TERRY TEMPEST WILLIAMS: The first thing I want to say to you, Tim, is thank you. Thank you for what you've done for us, as an act of protest, an act of imagination, and an act of true civil resistance.

TIM DECHRISTOPHER: Well, thank *you*.

TERRY: So let's talk about your mother.

TIM: [Laughter.] Okay.

TERRY: You know, when I saw your mother, I had a better sense of who you are.

TIM: Why did you have a better sense of who I am?

TERRY: I watched her during the trial. And I imagined what it must be like for her, who loves you so much, who gave birth to you, who's raised you—what that must have been like for her to have to sit there, not speak, you know, watch how political this was, watch your dignity, knowing what the consequences might be and, in fact, are going to be. And I never saw her waver. I mean, the only person that I saw with as much composure in that courtroom as you was your mother. You couldn't see her—she was sitting behind you—but she *never* wavered. Her spine was like steel.

TIM: Yeah. I think that's definitely what I've gotten from her. I only have vague memories of when she was fighting the coal companies, when I was a little kid, in the early days of mountaintop removal—I don't know if they were really my memories or stories that I've heard from the family. But I think a lot of my activism has been shaped by that. I remember hearing about when this coal miner stood up at this hearing and said, "My grandfather worked in the mine, my father worked in the mine, and I worked in the mine, and you people are telling us we can't do this, and blah blah blah." And my mom just fired right back and said, "And if you start blowing up these mountains, you will be the last generation that is ever a miner in West Virginia. You will kill the family tradition if you try to mine this way."

TERRY: And how old were you?

TIM: I was really young. We moved away when I was eight.

TERRY: And so was this in the seventies?

TIM: No, it was in the early eighties.

TERRY: And you were born?

TIM: Eighty-one.

TERRY: And what was the trigger point for your mother?

TIM: I don't know. But then, as I got older, she got out of activism. She told me once that she pulled out of all the political stuff to focus on raising me and my sister. And I think that's always been something that I carried with me. You know, that she had this role in the political sphere in our community, and she stepped out of that to put it into me. So I've always felt like I had somewhat of a greater responsibility to pull not just my own weight, but that extra weight that she put into me.

TERRY: And you were the oldest?

TIM: No, I'm the youngest. My sister's two years older.

TERRY: And is it just the two of you?

TIM: Mm-hmm.

TERRY: And what town in West Virginia?

TIM: I was born in a town called Lost Creek. And then when I was really little we moved to West Milford.

TERRY: And has anyone in your family been in the coal industry?

TIM: My dad worked his whole career in the natural gas industry.

TERRY: So you and I have that in common.

TIM: Yep.

TERRY: In what venue? Was he laying pipe?

TIM: He was an engineer, involved in the transmission side of things. And then rose up and became a manager and an executive.

TERRY: And what would you say the ethos in your home was?

TIM: You mean like politically?

TERRY: Yeah, and spiritually. You know, if there was a DeChristopher credo . . . I mean, in our family I'd say it was "work." That was my father's credo. That was his religion. And so it became ours.

TIM: I'd say in my family it was "knowledge," or "logic." It was very intellectual.

TERRY: So a typical conversation around your dinner table would be?

TIM: Around political issues. Local issues. My parents definitely identified as liberals or progressives. And I think especially when I was younger, they were rather free-thinking. But then got comfortable. As I got older.

TERRY: How so?

TIM: They started making more money.

TERRY: And how did that impact you?

TIM: Well, certainly in some good ways. I mean, they were able to help me with college and that sort of thing.

TERRY: Did you have a religion growing up?

TIM: No.

TERRY: So was there a particular spiritual tradition in your home?

TIM: No, more atheist, or humanist.

TERRY: And yet one of the things that's been so impressive to me, Tim, is not only have you had this intellectual grounding—which you say comes out of your family—but you have had this very strong spiritual basis with the Unitarian Church, with your own sense of wildness or landscape. This is a rumor, but I want to ask: I heard you were, like, a born-again Christian?

TIM: At one point, yeah.

TERRY: Talk to me about that.

TIM: I became that way when I was eighteen. My senior year of high school. I'd always been a jock. That was my identity. And then I had this shoulder problem for a couple years, and I finally went to the doctor and he told me that I'd broken my scapula two years earlier.

TERRY: You were a wrestler.

TIM: Yeah. And I played football.

TERRY: Talk about that.

TIM: Oh, I don't know. That's not very interesting.

TERRY: I think it's really interesting. You know, high school's a big deal. It helps form you. Wrestling is a contact sport—not unlike politics. You were really good at it.

TIM: It's *combat*, more than contact.

TERRY: And it's also mental.

TIM: Mm-hmm. I mean, it bred a very combative mind-set for me. Something that I struggled against for a while. It took me a while to recover from that.

TERRY: How so?

TIM: It taught me to look at things from a combative perspective, and a somewhat violent perspective. It was a part of myself that I really hated when I was in high school. I didn't really like who I was.

TERRY: As a wrestler?

TIM: As a person.

TERRY: Was it anger? I mean, I've got three brothers. And I watched them go through adolescence. And what you do with that kind of physicality, power, strength, anger, frustration, you know what I mean?

TIM: Mm-hmm.

TERRY: I mean, was it that?

TIM: Yeah, somewhat. It was a lot of confusion around what power and respect are, that I think a lot of young males struggle with.

TERRY: And where were you living?

TIM: In Pittsburgh.

TERRY: So you'd moved at this point?

TIM: Yeah.

TERRY: And so you'd been told by the doctors that you had a shoulder problem.

TIM: Yeah, well, basically they took an X-ray and immediately the doctor said, "You're done. You're never going to wrestle again." Because I'd broken the back of my scapula that held my shoulder in place. And so it had been sliding out for two years.

TERRY: And you had to have been in a lot of pain, right?

TIM: Yeah. And all of the soft tissue in my shoulder had stretched out, so I had to have this huge reconstructive surgery; they basically replaced everything in my left shoulder. At the end of the day, for my whole high school career, I'd go to practice. That was what I did. And it was like the second day after I'd gotten this news from the doctor that after school I didn't have anywhere to go. I just sat in the senior lounge, and there were all these people kind of wandering around, and I had no idea what these people did with their lives. Then one of my teachers, who was a younger guy, sat down next to me and started talking. And the conversation drifted to a finding-meaning-in-life kind of discussion, and then we kept talking after that, and at some point that spring, we decided to do a religion study group kind of thing with me and a few other seniors. And so we were studying religion, and we were reading the Bible, and it was just kind of an informal thing. And then at some point I accepted it. I thought I'd found answers.

TERRY: You accepted what?

TIM: I accepted Christianity. And found something more meaningful than what I had before.

TERRY: Which was?

TIM: That, you know, there was this God who pays attention, and all that stuff. And when I went to college, I got involved with some Christian clubs in a small church. And then officially became a Christian after that, and was baptized and everything.

TERRY: Which church?

TIM: It was a nondenominational Christian church. It was kind of an Evangelical church.

TERRY: Was this in Arizona?

TIM: Yeah, in Tempe. It was a big part of my life there. And then, once I moved to the Ozarks and dropped out of school, I was just kind of continuing my own search. And I gradually started to see that religion was less about having the answers and more about finding those answers—that that search was more of a lifelong process than about saying, "This is it. I'm eighteen and done." [Laughter.]

TERRY: Was there a moment, a situation?

TIM: Around the time that I was leaving Missouri, I guess, was when I first admitted to myself that I wasn't a Christian anymore.

TERRY: And how? How did you know that?

TIM: Just looking at my own beliefs, you know, about Jesus and things like that, and saying, "I don't believe that in any sort of literal way. I guess that makes me not a Christian anymore."

TERRY: I think I understand what you are saying. You know, I was raised Mormon, and a belief in Jesus Christ was an important component of my upbringing—even though there are those religious scholars who say Mormonism is not a Christian religion. But for me there really was a moment. I was teaching on the reservation, steeped in Navajo stories. In doing my thesis research, I came across Marie-Louise von Franz's book *Creation Myths*. Among the many creation narratives, there was the story of Changing Woman in the Navajo tradition; there was Kali in the Hindu tradition; and then there was Adam and Eve. And I remember thinking, *That's blasphemous. Those are myths, but the story of the Garden of Eden is true.* And then I thought, *Really? Is that so?* And it led me down this path of inquiry, not so much for meaning, but for understanding: What are the stories that we tell? You know, what are the stories that move us forward culturally? What are the stories that keep us in place? What are the stories that actually perpetuate the myths of a dominant culture or the subjugation of women? In the Book of Mormon, indigenous people are referred to as "Lamanites." Suddenly, the doctrine I had been raised with was exposed as a form of racism. Or to say that African Americans were not worthy of the priesthood . . . issues of social justice rose to the fore. And I thought, *I cannot, in good conscience, believe this.* I felt like the scaffolding had been knocked out from under me.

TIM: Well, I think the powerful thing for me was when I got to the point of looking at Christianity and the Bible as more of a painting than as a photograph . . . that there were people who had this powerful experience with something bigger than themselves, and that this was their painting of it; this was how they articulated and painted that experience. But it wasn't a photograph. And there were other groups of people in other parts of the world that had this other powerful experience with something bigger than themselves and they painted their picture of it. And, you know, we might have the same kind of experience, or have an experience with the same thing, and paint two very different pictures of it.

TERRY: A while back I was reading Albert Schweitzer's book on historical Jesus. Do you see Jesus as a historical figure in terms of leadership?

TIM: Yeah, I do view him as an example of a revolutionary leader.

TERRY: How?

TIM: Well, he was saying very challenging things both to the people who were following him and to the dominant culture at the time. And it led to some radical changes in the way people were living and the way people were structuring society.

TERRY: What would you view as the most radical of his teachings?

TIM: Turning the other cheek, I think, is one extremely radical thing. That, I think, is his powerful message about civil disobedience. And the other, which might be even more radical, is letting go of material wealth. That's so radical that Christians today still can't talk about it. I mean, he said it's easier to pass a camel through the eye of a needle than for a rich man to get into Heaven. And he told his followers to drop what they had, to let go of their jobs, to let go of their material possessions. Even let go of their families. If they wanted to follow him, they had to let go of everything they were holding on to, all the things that brought them security in life. They had to be insecure. That's pretty radical.

TERRY: And when you look at religious leaders, when you look at St. Francis—certainly he came to that recognition. When you look at Gandhi, certainly. Thoreau was advocating simplicity. And if you look at those two tenets you just brought up, moving from the Old Testament "eye for an eye" to the New Testament's teachings of Christ offering the alternative action of "turning the other cheek," you see that this idea of letting go of materialism is tied to charity and love. These are two tenets that you address frequently in your speaking, right?

TIM: Mm-hmm.

TERRY: Yesterday, weren't you saying that rich people don't make great activists?

TIM: Yeah. In front of a very wealthy audience.

TERRY: But people understood what you were saying. I mean, we're all privileged, right? Especially as predominantly white Americans sitting in a film festival in Telluride, Colorado.

TIM: Yeah. I also think that's why we're bad activists. That's why the climate movement is weaker in this country than in the rest of the world. Because we have more stuff. We have much higher levels of consumption, and that's how people have been oppressed in this country, through comfort. We've been oppressed by consumerism. By believing that we have so much to lose.

TERRY: In John de Graaf's film *Affluenza*, you see what a methodical, slow process that really was to turn American culture into a culture of debt through consumption. In the 1950s, as a country, we shunned credit cards. That was not part of the frugal mind of an American. And now, not only is our national debt skyrocketing, but our personal debt as well.

TIM: Yeah, it keeps people controlled.

TERRY: By our own appetites? By our insecurities? By whom?

TIM: By those who succeed in our current system. I think our economic model, in a big sense—our whole economic system—protects itself by making people dependent upon it. By making sure that any change, any departure from that system, is going to be hard. And it's going to lead to hardship, both individually and on a large scale as well. We can't change our economic system without it falling apart, without things crashing really hard. Just like as an individual you can't let go of your job and all that stuff without crashing pretty hard.

TERRY: In personal terms, your life has been in limbo for the last two years. And that's my word, not yours. But is it fair to say you haven't known what your future is going to be? Because you didn't know when you were going to go to trial, or whether you'd be convicted. How has that felt?

TIM: I think part of what empowered me to take that leap and have that insecurity was that I already felt that insecurity.

I didn't know what my future was going to be. My future was already lost.

TERRY: Coming out of college?

TIM: No. Realizing how fucked we are in our future.

TERRY: In terms of climate change?

TIM: Yeah. I met Terry Root, one of the lead authors of the IPCC report, at the Stegner Symposium at the University of Utah. She presented all the IPCC data, and I went up to her afterwards and said, "That graph that you showed, with the possible emission scenarios in the twenty-first century? It looked like the best case was that carbon peaked around 2030 and started coming back down." She said, "Yeah, that's right." And I said, "But didn't the report that you guys just put out say that if we didn't peak by 2015 and then start coming back down that we were pretty much all screwed, and we wouldn't even recognize the planet?" And she said, "Yeah, that's right." And I said: "So, what am I missing? It seems like you guys are saying there's no way we can make it." And she said, "You're not missing anything. There are things we could have done in the eighties, there are some things we could have done in the nineties—but it's probably too late to avoid any of the worst-case scenarios that we're talking about." And she literally put her hand on my shoulder and said, "I'm sorry my generation failed yours." That was shattering to me.

TERRY: When was this?

TIM: This was in March of 2008. And I said, "You just gave a speech to four hundred people and you didn't say anything like that. Why aren't you telling people this?" And she said, "Oh, I don't want to scare people into paralysis. I feel like if I told people the truth, people would just give up." And I talked to her a couple years later, and she's still not telling people the truth. But with me, it did the exact opposite. Once I realized that there was no hope in any sort of normal future, there's no hope for me to have anything my parents or grandparents would have considered a normal future—of a career and a retirement and all that stuff—I realized I have absolutely nothing to lose by fighting back; it was all going to be lost anyway.

TERRY: So, in other words, at that moment, it was like, "I have no expectations."

TIM: Yeah. And it did push me into this deep period of despair.

TERRY: And what did you do with it?

TIM: Nothing. I was rather paralyzed, and it really felt like a period of mourning. I really felt like I was grieving my own future, and grieving the futures of everyone I care about.

TERRY: Did you talk to your friends about this?

TIM: Yeah, I had friends who were coming to similar conclusions. And I was able to kind of work through it, and get to a point of action. But I think it's that period of grieving that's missing from the climate movement.

TERRY: I would say it's also missing from the environmental movement.

TIM: Yeah. That denies the severity of the situation, because that grieving process is really hard. I struggle with pushing people into that period of grieving. I mean, I find myself pulling back. I see people who still have that kind of buoyancy and hopefulness. And I don't want to shatter that, you know?

TERRY: But I think that what no one tells you is, if you go into that dark place, you do come out the other side, you know? If you can go into that darkest place, you can emerge with a sense of empathy and empowerment. But it's not easy, and there is the real sense of danger that we may not move through our despair to a place of illumination, which for me is the taproot of action. When I was studying the Bosch painting

*The Garden of Earthly Delights*, I was really interested in finding the brightest point in the triptych. I remember squinting at the painting and searching for the most intense point of light. To my surprise, the brightest, the most numinous point was in the right corner of Hell. That's where the fire burned brightest. And that was something I recognized as true. My mother had just died, my grandmother had just died, my other grandmother had just died. You know, there's a Syrian myth of going into the underworld, and when you emerge, you come out with what they call "death eyes"—eyes turned inward. I had been given "death eyes." I had been changed. I had a deeper sense of suffering but I also felt a deeper sense of joy. Hard to explain, but I remember someone saying to me, "Terry, you're married to sorrow." And I said, "No, I'm not married to sorrow, I just refuse to look away." You stay with it—we are stronger than we know. But it isn't easy. And you don't have any assurance that you're going to find your way out. And there've certainly been days where I've wondered . . .

TIM: Mm-hmm. And the other powerful thing that was happening in my life in 2008 was that I was coming out of the wilderness. I mean, it had always been a big part of my life growing up. All of our family vacations were in the wilderness.

TERRY: Where?

TIM: West Virginia. New Hampshire. Montana. Wyoming. Everywhere we could go. And so it always had an important influence on me. I remember when I was seventeen? Sixteen? I was struggling with all this teenage angst, and being overwhelmed with the world, and I had this feeling that I just wanted things to *stop* for a while so that I could catch up. And I told my mom at one point that I was going to pretend that I was crazy and get myself checked into a mental institution so that I could spend a few weeks where people wouldn't expect me to do anything other than just stare out the window and drool. And she convinced me that that was a bad idea [laughter], with some potentially long-term consequences—like a lobotomy. And she said, "You need to go to the wilderness."

TERRY: Wow.

TIM: We were living in Pittsburgh at the time, and she sent me down to West Virginia, to the Otter Creek Wilderness, in the Monongahela National Forest, which was a place that I'd been to several times. And I spent eight days alone there. And it was a really powerful experience that led to my formation as an individual. I mean, it was the first time that I ever experienced myself without any other influences. Without any cultural influences, any influences from other people. And it was terrifying to experience that—I mean, I really thought I was *actually* going crazy at that point. But it allowed me to develop that individual identity of who I was without anyone else around. And then it continued to play a bigger role in my life once I went to college. I started an outdoor recreation and conservation group my freshman year. And I spent every weekend out in the desert somewhere in Arizona. Then I dropped out after two years to go work with kids in the wilderness, in the Ozarks. And did that for three years, and then came to Utah to work for a more intense wilderness therapy program—with troubled teens. And during that time I was fully into the wilderness. Especially when I moved to Utah, I was out there all the time. That was where I lived. And I did feel like I had escaped, in a lot of ways. I felt free, I felt like whatever shit was going on in the world didn't affect me. I didn't watch the news, I didn't know what was going on in the world. And I didn't think it mattered to me.

TERRY: And what effect would you say the Utah wilderness had on you as a young man?

TIM: Well, it put me in perspective. I think especially the western landscapes have done that for me because they're so big and so open. You know, when you spend all your time in a little room, you feel very big and very important, and everything that happens to you is a big deal. And when you're out in the desert, you see that you're really small. And that's a very liberating sense—of being very small. Every little thing that happens to you isn't that big a deal. Going to prison for a few years—it's not that big a deal. But also just my views on how to live, and what actually makes me happy; how to form a little community out there with a few people; how human actions really work when there isn't a TV telling us what to do—that all formed out there. And I think that's part of why some people fight against wilderness, fight to extinguish all of it. I mean, I think there's definitely a lot of folks who don't understand it, and have never experienced it. But I think some of the opponents of wilderness really do understand it. They understand . . .

TERRY: Its power.

TIM: That it's a place where people can think freely. Tyranny can never be complete as long as there's wilderness. But eventually I wanted to come back. And that's where I see one of those lessons of Jesus going out to the wilderness for a long time and then coming back and being an activist. What I experienced when I came out of the wilderness and went back to school was just outrage with society. And complete intolerance for the world. Just constantly saying, "How the hell could people live this way? How the hell could people accept this as being okay?" So many things about our society, I just kept looking at them after being in the wilderness for so long and saying, "How the hell could people accept this? This is outrageous." And I think that's one of the things that the wilderness does for us, you know, it allows us to live the way we actually want to live for a while. It puts things in the perspective of "Wait, this isn't inevitable. It doesn't actually have to be this way. And this isn't the way I want to live. It's not okay." I think activism at its best is refusing to accept things. Saying that this is unacceptable. And I felt that so strongly sitting there at the auction, watching parcels go for eight or ten dollars an acre. I mean, that's why I first started bidding—just to drive up the prices—because I had this overwhelming sense that this is not acceptable.

TERRY: I remember having a conversation with Breyten Breytenbach, who wrote *The True Confessions of an Albino Terrorist*, who spent time in prison in South Africa for being antiapartheid. We were in a bus driving to Mexico City, and he said to me, "You Americans, you've mastered the art of living with the unacceptable." And that haunted me. For decades, his statement has haunted me. From that point forward, I've kept thinking about what is unacceptable. And that's what I hear you saying: that it was unacceptable from your standpoint that these public lands, these wild places that you knew by name and in a very physical, spiritual way, were being sold for eight dollars an acre.

TIM: Mm-hmm. There's so much acceptance. And, I don't know, I think tolerance is the enemy of activism.

TERRY: That's interesting. Because if you talk about empathy, and turning the other cheek, then tolerance takes on another definition. Doesn't it?

TIM: I don't know. I wouldn't consider turning the other cheek "tolerating violence."

TERRY: What's the difference between tolerance and compassion? I don't mean *tolerating* a situation, but really practicing tolerance.

TIM: The compassion actively works to undermine injustice and violence. For me, that's kind of the misinterpretation of the whole turn-the-other-cheek thing, that it's about tolerating the violence. I mean, to me it's about actively ending the violence. It's the most effective weapon we have against violence: turning the other cheek.

TERRY: But what about racial intolerance? Or intolerance toward another species, like prairie dogs—if you turn that word around?

TIM: Yeah, but if you're tolerating prairie dogs, it's because you don't like prairie dogs. I mean, I don't like the idea of *tolerating* other races. I don't like the idea that it's something we put up with. The idea of tolerating different people, to me, is not something that I'm comfortable with—and when I look at the modern environmental movement, to bring it back to that, I think it's defined by what we accept. By what we speak out against, but ultimately accept. You know, we'll sign a petition, or even do an action, or even get arrested for a day, but ultimately we're gonna go back to our normal lives. Ultimately, we're going to keep participating in this system.

TERRY: You know, it was interesting, I was listening to Robert Pinsky speak, and he was talking about the word "medium." Like, what is the writer's medium, what is the poet's medium? And he was saying that a poet's medium is his body, or her body. And that *medium* is "in between." So that *immediacy* is "nothing in between." And I hadn't thought about that . . . that there are so many words where we don't know what the root is, and knowing that could help inform our discussions. You know, what is an activist's medium? I mean, what would you say your medium is? If a poet's medium is his or her body—because it's voice, it's breath, it's animating language, it's sound—what would an activist's medium be?

TIM: I would say it's the same as a poet. I would say it's my body or my life. It's that which I use to reach other people. It's the interaction between me and society.

TERRY: I mean, you are laying your body down. You sat your body down, right? In the auction.

TIM: I raised it up. [Laughter.]

TERRY: So tell me about that moment when you picked up the paddle and then started winning. You know, when you were bidding them up, but you weren't really bidding to win. At the trial, Agent Love was saying, "And, if you looked, he was looking over his shoulder! Here's the photograph that shows there was a deep conspiracy as he kept looking into his bag, you know, looking to see who else was in the room."

TIM: Well, so many of the things he brought up were to try to frame me as, like, this shady character.

TERRY: And a medium for a bigger interest, right?

TIM: Yeah. Like the fact that I was looking over my shoulder, and they have this photograph. I remember that moment so clearly. I was amazed when I first saw that picture—I could see by the look on my face that that's when I was looking at Krista [Bowers], who was on the other side of the room. And she was crying.

TERRY: And you knew her through the Unitarian Church?

TIM: Yeah. And it was so clear to me that she was over-whelmed by the heartlessness of this whole scenario. And, you know, when you see a woman crying, you feel like you have to do something about changing the situation that's causing that.

TERRY: Was it really just an act of chivalry? Or when you saw her tears, were they really your tears, too?

TIM: She was clearly feeling it as sadness. But for me, it was going into outrage. I was turning it more outward, where she was turning it inward—but the depth of her emotion justified the depth of my own emotion, and was something that pushed me to act. When Agent Love—

TERRY: Not to be confused with Bishop Love, from Abbey's *Monkey Wrench Gang* . . .

TIM: Exactly. No, but when Agent Love was talking about how I was looking at my phone, he said that I was sending text messages. But I'd never even sent a text message at that point. What I was doing, once I was winning parcels, was pulling a phone number out of my phone and writing it down on the back of a business card and handing it to my roommate, who was sitting next to me, and saying, "You need to go call my friend Michael and tell him that I need help."

TERRY: Paying for these.

TIM: Yeah. [Laughs.]

TERRY: Did you think about the consequences?

TIM: Yeah.

TERRY: And it was worth it.

TIM: Mm-hmm.

TERRY: So you were there because of the wilderness. Was climate change part of it? Or did it become a larger issue afterward? Because I'm interested in how stories change, evolve.

TIM: It was much more climate change than the wilderness. For me, the wilderness was the third most important issue. The first was climate change, the second was the attack on our democracy, and the fact that people were locked out of the decision-making process with this. And, you know, something I realized last year, when I was on a panel with Dave Foreman and Katie Lee, and they were talking about their motivations for protecting wilderness, doing this for the coyote, and all that stuff. And I realized that I was coming from a completely different place than them. I would never go to jail to protect animals or plants or wilderness. For me, it's about the people.

And even my value of wilderness is about what it brings to people. I have a very anthropocentric worldview.

TERRY: And do you think that goes back to your basic spiritual perspective that set you out on this path with Christianity?

TIM: I don't know. I don't think so.

TERRY: Because that is a much more human-centered philosophical starting point.

TIM: Yeah. Well, I think it goes beyond that. I think it's just what I've learned to value in my life. I've spent a lot of time with people, and I've spent a lot of time with animals and the wilderness, and it's the people that I really value, at a totally different level than anything else. And that's when I started wondering whether I was actually an environmentalist. [Laughter.]

TERRY: Again, we go back to language. What does an environmentalist mean, anyway? What does a Christian mean? What does an activist mean? I mean, if we took away all these loaded words, or even stopped using war terminology . . . I'm aware of the aggression of language, of "fighting" or "combating" or "war." How do we take the violence out of our language? How do we become less oppositional and more inclusive in how we talk about these issues? I don't know. This is what I struggle with. Because I would say that your approach is confrontational.

TIM: Mm-hmm.

TERRY: And yet, you're asking that we sing songs. That it not be confrontational.

TIM: No. That it be more effective confrontation. That it be stronger confrontation than what violence can do.

TERRY: But the organization that you and Ashley [Anderson] began—Peaceful Uprising—I love those two words because they're paradoxical, right?

TIM: Are they?

TERRY: Well, what I hear you saying in Peaceful Uprising is "We will create an uprising, but it will be peaceful." You know, "We will create a confrontational presence, but we will do it singing."

TIM: Yeah. And I think that's a strategic decision, rather than a moral one.

TERRY: How so?

TIM: I mean, my commitment to a nonviolent movement ultimately comes down to the fact that it's more effective.

TERRY: And how did you come to know that?

TIM: I think the reality of the climate crisis—and all the other crises facing us as humanity today—justify the strongest possible tactics in response. Demand the strongest possible tactics. And I think that requires nonviolent resistance.

TERRY: Is violence ever justified?

TIM: Well, it's justified. But that doesn't mean it makes sense. I mean, if you're talking moral justification, yeah—to prevent the collapse of our civilization, and the deaths and suffering of billions of people, it's morally justified. But violence is the game that the United States government is the best in the world at. That's their territory.

TERRY: And when you talk about growing up, it was your own confrontation with the violent part of yourself that was most problematic for you.

TIM: Mm-hmm.

TERRY: And so you've had to figure out how to use that anger or rage constructively.

TIM: Yeah, I mean, that's something I struggle with: the common liberal mind-set that says, "Oh, we don't want those negative emotions like anger and outrage and fear." To me that doesn't make sense—that those are negative emotions.

TERRY: In the same way we don't allow ourselves to grieve.

TIM: Those are real emotions. Those are part of human nature. We evolved with those emotions for a reason. Because all the people who were threatened, and didn't feel fear, or whose children were threatened, and they didn't feel outrage—those people all died off. And now that we're facing these very real threats to ourselves and our children, if we don't feel and find a way to constructively use anger and outrage and fear—

TERRY: And indignation.

TIM: —we should expect to meet the same fate as all those dead-end roads of human evolution.

TERRY: But if it's true, what Terry Root first told you—that there is no hope—then what's the point?

TIM: Well, there's no hope in avoiding collapse. If you look at the worst-case consequences of climate change, those pretty much mean the collapse of our industrial civilization. But that doesn't mean the end of everything. It means that we're going to be living through the most rapid and intense period of change that humanity has ever faced. And that's certainly not hopeless. It means we're going to have to build another world in the ashes of this one. And it could very easily be a better world. I have a lot of hope in my generation's ability to build a better world in the ashes of this one. And I have very little doubt that we'll have to. The nice thing about that is that this culture hasn't led to happiness anyway, it hasn't satisfied our human needs. So there's a lot of room for improvement.

TERRY: How has this experience—these past two years—changed you?

TIM: [Sighing.] It's made me worry less.

TERRY: Why?

TIM: It's somewhat comforting knowing that things are going to fall apart, because it does give us that opportunity to drastically change things.

TERRY: I've watched you, you know, from afar. And when we were at the Glen Canyon Institute's David Brower celebration in 2010, I looked at you, and I was so happy because it was like there was a lightness about you. Before, I felt like you were carrying the weight of the world on your shoulders—and you have broad shoulders—but there was something in your eyes, there was a light in your eyes I had not seen before. And I remember saying, "Something's different." And you were saying that rather than being the one who was inspiring, you were being inspired. And rather than being the one who was carrying this cause, it was carrying you. Can you talk about that? Because I think that's instructive for all of us.

TIM: I think letting go of that burden had a lot to do with embracing how good this whole thing has felt. It's been so liberating and empowering.

TERRY: To you, personally?

TIM: Yeah. I went into this thinking, *It's worth sacrificing my freedom for this.*

TERRY: And you did it alone. It's not like you had a movement behind you, or the support group that you have now.

TIM: Right. But I feel like I did the opposite. I thought I was sacrificing my freedom, but instead I was grabbing on to my freedom and refusing to let go of it for the first time, you know? Finally accepting that I wasn't this helpless victim of society, and couldn't do anything to shape my own future, you know, that I didn't have that freedom to steer the course of my life. Finally I said, "I have the freedom to change this situation. I'm that powerful." And that's been a wonderful feeling that I've held on to since then.

TERRY: Are you surprised by this?

TIM: Yeah. And I think that's where some of that lightness has come from. And also seeing that it's having an impact.

That it's firing some other people up, that it's embarrassing the government. I mean, one of the great things about the trial was seeing how vulnerable the U.S. attorney felt. He was freaking out all the time. And he was terrified. I mean, the government was terrified just that people showed up for the trial. They were terrified by the fact that all these other people are worrying about how to keep me out of prison—

TERRY: I'm one of them.

TIM: [Laughs.] I feel like the goal should be to get other people in prison. How do we get more people to join me? Because that's where the liberation is, that's where the effectiveness is.

TERRY: Is that the only alternative?

TIM: No. [Pause.] But it's one that feels good.

TERRY: For you.

TIM: Yeah.

TERRY: So what are some of the alternatives for those who maybe don't have that option? Maybe they've got children. You know what I'm saying?

TIM: Well, everybody has a reason why they can't.

TERRY: But I was aware when I was arrested in front of the White House, protesting during the buildup to the Iraq war, that when I looked around, it was a lot easier for me to be arrested than others, you know? I didn't have a traditional job, I didn't have children. I mean, some people have more at stake than others. And you're right, there's every reason not to. But I'm just playing devil's advocate. Civil disobedience is one path. It's a path I've personally chosen at times—certainly not with the stakes as high as they are for you. But it's an act that I powerfully support and believe in and have subscribed to. But what about other alternatives?

TIM: If people aren't willing to go to jail, there are alternatives in which they can be powerful and effective. But if people feel they've got too much to lose—they've got all this other stuff in their life, and they might be risking their job, or their reputation, and things like that—I don't think they can be powerful in other ways.

TERRY: So you can't be powerful as an organizer or as a support person behind the scene? Or as a teacher or educator?

TIM: You can, but I don't think people are going to realize their power as revolutionaries if they feel like they've got all this stuff to lose.

TERRY: If there's only one way—which is arrest—then I would argue that you sound like a true believer.

TIM: No, I'm not saying that's the only way. I'm saying that the *willingness for that* is what's necessary. That willingness to not hold back, to not be safe. People can do it without getting arrested. But people can't be powerful if their first concern is staying safe.

TERRY: Okay. So that's different than being arrested.

TIM: Yeah. I'm just using that as an example of that level of risk.

TERRY: What I hear you saying is breaking set with the status quo, pushing the boundaries of whatever venue we choose to be active in.

TIM: Mm-hmm.

TERRY: Because I think what is killing us is the level of comfort, this level of complacency. What you have said repeatedly is one person can make a difference, we *are* powerful, we *can* disrupt the status quo, right? Even at a multimillion-dollar oil and gas auction. And if the government isn't going to do it for us, if our nonprofits aren't going to do it, if the environmental movement isn't going to do it, who's going to do it? We can no longer look for leadership beyond ourselves.

TIM: Yeah, exactly. And I think our current power structures only have power over us because of what they can take away from us. That's where their power comes from—their ability to take things away. And so if we have a lot that we're afraid of losing, or that we're not willing to lose, they have a lot of power over us.

TERRY: And that goes back to your own sovereignty of soul—of really knowing who you are, knowing what your intention is, and having the strength to go forward. That's why I was so interested in what led you up to that moment, because in a way, your whole life prepares you for that moment, when you look your divine soul in the face and say, "Okay, do I have it in me to act now?"

TIM: Mm-hmm.

TERRY: Because, for most of us, it's not a planned thing—there is no choice to be made. It's just, this is the next step that you take, because everything prior to that moment has prepared you for that, you know? Mardy Murie once said, "Don't worry about your future. There's just usually enough light shining to show you the next step you're going to take." And then, when that perfect alliance comes, when your spirit is aligned with your destiny, then an action occurs that's revolutionary.

TIM: Something that I've related to through this is the Annie Dillard quote, "Sometimes you jump off the cliff first, and build your wings on the way down." That's how I felt in this whole process. First I didn't know what I was going to do at the auction, but I knew I was going to disrupt it. And then, after disrupting it, I had no idea who was going to support me and how that was going to play out. And no idea whether or not I could handle that role. I mean, I can't say I even had any understanding or expectation that it would put me in this kind of role. But even to the extent that I knew it would put me in some kind of role, I had no idea whether or not I could handle it.

TERRY: And how are you?

TIM: I feel like I'm perfectly suited for this.

TERRY: [Laughter.] I love your honesty! I mean, it appears so. Is that a surprise?

TIM: Yeah. I'd never given a public speech before this. And now I feel like I can just roll right into it anytime. And people are responding when I speak. I mean, I had no idea that that would be the case. And I don't even know that it ever would have been. I don't know if any of these skills or abilities ever would have been developed had it not been for the necessity of the situation.

TERRY: And that's where I would go back to intention. I think your intention was really pure. You didn't know what the outcome was going to be. It feels like you just keep moving. And when we talk about a movement, I think you're really showing us what that movement looks like. And I don't even like the word "movement." For me, it's: how do we build community around these issues?

TIM: Yeah. I mean, I gave a whole speech about that last fall, about the difference between a climate lobby and a climate movement. I talked about the need to build a genuine climate movement. But I like the idea of a community that supports people. I feel like that's what we're building with Peaceful Uprising.

TERRY: Each person has a role to play, according to what they do best. I love that you said, "I'm perfectly suited for this." There are other people that aren't.

TIM: Yeah.

TERRY: And so I think for each of us to find our own path

in the name of community, you know, if each of us finds our own niche, with our own gifts, each in our own way and our own time, change can occur. Radical change. And for me, Tim, this is how you have inspired me: we all need to take that next step, whatever that looks like, for the integrity of our own lives. And when I asked you, "How can I support you?" you said, "Join me. Get arrested." But it's easy to get arrested, really. I've done it more times than I can count. That's not my risk, at this point, as a fifty-five-year-old person. But the challenge that I heard was: what's the most uncomfortable thing you can do—the greatest risk, with the most at stake? And I can't answer that right now. But I'm going to be thinking about that, and figuring out what that next step is for me both as a writer and as a person.

TIM: I think what I was really trying to get across was the idea of not backing down. Because it's important to make sure that the government doesn't win in their quest to intimidate people into obedience. They're trying to make an example out of me to scare other people into obedience. I mean, they're looking for people to back down.

TERRY: Right. And I think democracy requires participation. Democracy also requires numbers. It is about showing up. And we do need leadership. And I think what your actions say to us as your community is "How are we going to respond so you are not forgotten? So that this isn't in vain?" And I think that brings up another question: we know what we're against, but what are we for? Our friend Ben Cromwell asked this question. What are *you* for? What do you love?

TIM: I'm for a humane world. A world that values humanity. I'm for a world where we meet our emotional needs not through the consumption of material goods, but through human relationships. A world where we measure our progress not through how much stuff we produce, but through our quality of life—whether or not we're actually promoting a higher quality of life for human beings. I don't think we have that in any shape or form now. I mean, we have a world where, in order to place a value on human beings, we monetize it— and say that the value of a human life is $3 million if you're an American, $100,000 if you're an Indian, or something like that. And I'm for a world where we would say that money has value because it can make human lives better, rather than saying that money is the thing with value.

TERRY: I think about the boulder that hit the child in Virginia. What was that child's life worth—$14,000? The life of a pelican. What was it—$233? A being that has existed for sixty million years. What do you love?

TIM: I love people. [Very long pause.] I think that's it.

TERRY: I think that's why people are inspired. Because I think they feel that from you. And I really feel if we're motivated by love, it's a very different response. Here's an idea that I want to know what you think of: Laurance Rockefeller, as you know, came from a family of great privilege, and he was a conservationist. And in his nineties, he informed his family that the JY Ranch—the piece of land in Grand Teton National Park that his father, John D. Rockefeller, set aside for his family—would be returned to the American people. This was a vow he had made to his father. And he was going to "rewild it"—remove the dozens of cabins from the land and place them elsewhere. Well, you can imagine the response from his family. Shocked. Heartsick. Not pleased. But he did it anyway, and he did it with great spiritual resolve and intention. He died shortly after. I was asked to write about this story, so I wanted to visit his office to see what he looked out at when he was working in New York. Everything had been cleared out, except for scales and Buddhas. That was all that was in there. I was so struck by that. And his secretary said, "I think you would be interested in this piece of writing." And she disappeared and she came back, and this is what she handed me: [Reading] "I love the concept of unity and diversity. Most decisions are based on a tiny difference. People say, 'This was right, that was wrong'; the difference was a feather. I keep scales wherever I am to remind me of that. They're a symbol of my awareness. Of the distortion most people have of what is better and what is not." How would you respond to that? The key sentence, I think, is "The difference was a feather."

TIM: Yeah, the difference is a feather. I guess that's why I believe that we can be powerful as individuals. Why we actually can make a difference. The status quo is this balance that we have right now. And if we shift ourselves, we shift that scale. I remember one of the big things that pushed me over the edge before the auction was Naomi Klein's speech that she gave at Bioneers in November of 2008. She was talking about Obama, and talking about where he was at with climate change, and the things he was throwing out there as campaign promises, you know, the best things he was offering. And she was talking about how that's nowhere near enough. That even his pie-in-the-sky campaign promises were not enough. And she talked about how, ultimately, Obama was a centrist. That he found the center and he went there. And that that's where his power came from. She said, "And that's not gonna change." And so if the center is not good enough for our survival, and if Obama is a centrist, and will always be a centrist, then our job is to move the center. And that's what she ended the speech with: "Our job is to move the center." And it was so powerful that we actually got the video as soon as we could and replayed it at the Unitarian church in Salt Lake, and had this event one evening where we played that speech and then broke up into groups and talked about what it meant to move the center. And what I came away from that with was the realization that you can't move the center from the center. That if you want to shift the balance—if you want to tilt that scale—you have to go to the edge and push. You have to go beyond what people consider to be reasonable, and push.

TERRY: I think that's so true.

TIM: And that's what I thought I was doing at the auction—doing something unreasonable.

TERRY: Rather than just standing outside with placards, you came inside.

TIM: To make the people standing outside with placards look reasonable.

TERRY: Which was Earth First!'s tactic early on, right?

TIM: Yeah.

TERRY: You know, with Breyten Breytenbach, going back to that comment, "You Americans have mastered the art of living with the unacceptable," my next question to him was "So what do we do?" And he said, "Support people on the margins." Because it's from the margins that the center is moved.

TIM: Yeah, that margin—that's the feather. I mean, with climate change, the center is this balancing point between the climate scientists on one side saying, "This is what needs to be done," and ExxonMobil on the other. And so the center is always going to be less than what's required for our survival.

## ◈ OPERATION SAVE AMERICA

With dirt under my fingernails, I dug a grave for a thrush—
the morning hermit thrush who had been singing me awake
this spring. I came home after being assaulted by antiabortion
activists lined up on the highway who proclaim my friend a
murderer. I know my friend is a doctor who honors the choice,
the voice, of women who have a right to make decisions over
their own bodies. It was a visual, brutal assault to drive by
their gauntlet of torn-apart babies and hear their vitriol spoken through a traveling microphone planted in front of the
doctor's clinic. There is only one doctor in Utah who is known
publicly to perform abortions. I went about my business, sickened, haunted by the images. On my way home, I had to drive
through their bloody billboards again; this time, I pulled over,
got out of my car, and tried to speak to one of them. The man
I approached was wearing a red baseball cap with JESUS sewn
on it. When I asked him if we could have a conversation, he
simply said, "Are you for murder or not?" There was no conversation to be had. I learned he was from Kansas and they had
come to stop "the abortionist." They are part of Operation Save
America. He walked away from me and continued his yelling at
motorists. I called two friends and warned them not to come

to town. Once home, I went to open the back door, only to find the hermit thrush that had been singing hymns each morning in the aspens, dead on the threshold of our porch. She had hit the glass window and died. I felt responsible. And I panicked, thinking her beautiful voice in the world is gone. All I could do was hold her small, feathered body in my hands and feel her warmth even in death and apologize, apologize for the rancor of the world, my world, that has become so treacherous. And I cherished her cinnamon tail feathers, olive-brown body, and white speckled breast. With my finger, I touched the one drop of blood held in the closure of her beak and marked the window for other birds. Then, I buried her in a nest of last year's leaves. I buried her with a prayer and a vow that I will not be silenced by intimidation or grief.

We were in the Arctic. It snowed. The snowstorm turned into a blizzard. For days, we were confined to our tents, peeking out just long enough to see we had zero visibility.

And then, one night after too many to count, it cleared. We walked out of our tent and stood beneath a shimmering aurora borealis and watched dancing streamers of light—green, blue, red, yellow. A sound akin to Tibetan singing bowls emanated from the north.

Above a jagged toothlike peak silhouetted against the display of northern lights was a circle of rotating red flares. My partner and I saw it at the same time and wondered what it could be. We went back to our tent to retrieve our binoculars: a helicopter, no; a plane, no; not a satellite; what was it? It rose up, moved laterally as if run by some kind of astro-geomancy, and vanished.

That night, you might say, I was abducted. It wasn't as if I was taken by green men into a spaceship. Not at all. But it was like being inhabited by an alien being. It felt as if I was dreaming and being visited inside my body at once.

A specific entity spoke to me: "You've got it wrong. It isn't oil your kind should be following. It's too crude. [Please believe me when I tell you that I am not making this up.] Follow the paths of the caribou in the north and the prairie dogs in the west. Their migrations and settlements follow energy lines. But it isn't the kind of energy you think it is—"

The visitor who inhabited my body began to recite a list of place-names from around the world, from Perth, Australia, to a trio of towns in Russia to Aneth, Utah. I was madly taking notations with my left hand in my small notebook that is always by my side where I sleep. Even as my eyes were closed, I was recording the site names of these subtle energy lines that were being given to me.

And then, the encounter was over.

When I awoke the next morning, the experience was still alive in me. I walked out of the tent into the snow. The sun was just rising above the white peaks. The shadow I cast on the frozen ground was not mine.

What has been guarded must now be shared.

All that is hidden is now being revealed.

This is what happened.

I have a map.

## ❖ A PUBLIC BENCH MADE OF WHITE BARK PINE

WITH BEN ROTH

White Bark Bones bear the borings of beetles their script on wood is written in the heat of our own carbon ambitions.

Ghost Trees now haunt the crags, their listless limbs bare to haunt and hamper the hibernating dreams of bears.

### ❧ THE PEOPLE'S MARCH
*New York City, New York*
*September 22, 2014*

They just kept coming in waves, in torrents, a river of people convening on the streets of New York City in the march for climate justice. They just kept coming, hundreds of thousands of individuals, indigenous, black, white, brown, yellow, and red, a rainbow of colors winding through the canyons of Manhattan.

This movement of climate justice is no longer segregated, is no longer privileged, is no longer young or old, or the radical fringe moving toward the center. Instead, this movement resides in the core of a collective concern: Earth has a fever. There is no Planet B. What we witnessed yesterday on Sunday, September 21, was four hundred thousand individuals standing in the center of this crisis with love.

At one o'clock, the river of the People's March became quiet, silent in a haunting moment of stillness. And then, a rolling cry of care rose from the street with undulating momentum like an animated heat wave blown by the wind that electrified the crowd like thunder and lightning, followed by a rain of voices.

The written language of hand-painted signs created its own poetry:

> Save the Earth, Heal the Spirit
> I can't swim—
> Let our voices rise, not the sea
> I can't swim—
> Divest from fossil fuels
> If the Rockefellers can do it, so can we—
> I am building a community that runs without fossil
>     fuels
> No more oil, no more coal—
> Keep our future in our soil
> It is raining, it is pouring
> We are all Noah now—
> Wall Street Corporations are junkies
> Renewables bring peace—
> People and the Planet, over profit—
> Please
> Love your Mother—
> We have to make peace with Nature—
> Care now, you might be coming back
> Quilters for the Planet—
> Chefs for Climate Change—
> Howling for the future—
> Earth First!
> Abbey was right—
> Frack Off!
> Hey, Obama, Don't need no fracking drama!
> Protect me—
> I can't swim—

Hi, I'm a friendly, sociable scientist—
Come talk to me—
Clean water is a right
Not just for the rich and white—
I am Water
I am Earth
I am Fire
I am Air
We are engaged in a crisis of breath
We can overcome—
Our planet has a fever—
We know who is responsible
Look out the window, U.N.
The Debate is over
The Facts are in
The Evidence is clear
The next flood won't be biblical
Stop the Fossil Fuel Octopus—
Stop the tentacles of tar sands and oil shale—
Apathy kills
Our planet, our patience, our future—
Interfaith Power & Light—
Why not?
What's next?
The future of all life depends on our mindful steps—
We are the people
Walk with the river
This is what love looks like—

Activists are flooding Wall Street. The present is now lock-
ing hands with the future.

We can be grateful for the organizers who mapped out the territory of our engagement.

Last night inside the Cathedral of St. John the Divine, with a great phoenix rising above the congregation, the Reverend Serene Jones said, "We have a soul-size work before us."

Something has been set in motion. With throbbing feet, we are river-walking.

Castle Valley, Utah—My husband, Brooke Williams, and I recently bought leasing rights to 1,120 acres of federal public lands near our home in Utah. The lease gives us the right to drill for oil or natural gas. We paid $1,680 for it, plus an $820 processing fee.

We put it on our credit card.

I hadn't planned on leasing these lands when I attended an auction run by the federal Bureau of Land Management, a government agency that manages hundreds of millions of acres of public land across the West. I was there to protest the leasing of these lands to oil and gas companies planning to drill for fossil fuels.

But I unknowingly ended up in the shorter line to get into the auction, the one for people registering as bidders. So I signed a registration form and was given the number nineteen. I followed the other bidders and found a seat in the front row.

My husband entered with the protesters, who were assigned to a separate space set aside for them.

As people filed in, a BLM agent approached me and asked, "Are you aware that if you have misrepresented yourself as a

legitimate bidder with an energy company you will be prosecuted and you could go to prison?"

His tone moved from inquiry to intimidation to harassment.
"I am asking you, are you aware . . ."

I said I was aware of what happened to Tim DeChristopher,
who attended a similar auction in 2008, where he bid up prices
and ended up with 22,000 acres, worth nearly $1.8 million,
that he had no intention of paying for. He was doing it to
protest the auction. He was sentenced to two years in federal
prison on felony counts of interfering with the auction and
making false representations.

"As an American citizen," I told the agent, "I have a right
to be here and witness this auction and decide if I am going to
bid or not on these leases on our public lands, correct?"

"I am saying, if you choose to misrepresent yourself . . ."

"But I have this right . . ."

"What energy do you plan to develop?"

"You can't define energy for us. Our energy development is
fueling a movement to keep it in the ground."

"You will be prosecuted if . . ."

We were interrupted as the auction began. Parcel after parcel was sold to the rhythmic bantering of the auctioneer until
voices in the back of the room began singing, "People got to
rise like water . . ."

The singing became louder and louder until the bidders
could no longer hear the auctioneer. The auction stopped. The
protesters were told to be quiet. They kept singing. They were
asked again. They sat down. The auction continued.

"Two dollars, two dollars, do I hear two twenty-five, I hear
two twenty-five, two fifty, three, four, five, are you in, are you
out, do I hear five, I hear five, do I hear six, six dollars, do I
hear seven, seven. Sold! Bidder number fourteen."

And so it went.

Then the protesters began to sing again. This time, they were escorted out by the police. They offered up words of protest as they departed, ending with "Keep it in the ground!"

The doors were closed. The auction continued as the singing of protesters echoed from the stairwell.

"Come on, men, are you in, are you out, or are you stayin' home—this is a lot of scenery going to waste," the auctioneer joked when no one bid on a parcel.

As the auction closed, we were told that if we wished to lease parcels that had not been sold, we could go to the BLM office and purchase them "over the counter" at a discounted price. Call it a fire sale.

Which is exactly what my husband and I did. We were interested in buying leases within the county where we live specifically, on land where oil and gas exploration might threaten sage grouse, prairie dogs, and other wildlife. We met the qualification: we're adult citizens of the United States.

With maps stretched out before us, we found what we were looking for. The two-dollars-per-acre base price had been reduced to one fifty. We took out our credit card and sealed the deal. The land sits adjacent to a proposed wilderness area. When we visited, we were struck by its hard-edge beauty and castle-like topography.

We have every intention of complying with the law, even as we challenge it. To establish ourselves as a legitimate energy company, we have formed Tempest Exploration Company, LLC. We will pay the annual rent for the duration of the ten-year lease and keep whatever oil and gas lies beneath these lands in the ground.

———

Those resources will remain there until science finds a way to use those fossil fuels in sustainable, nonpolluting ways. After ten years, we will lose our lease if we haven't drilled.

We're not suggesting that everyone who feels as we do about the exploitation of our public lands should do what we did. We aren't going to be able to buy our way out of this problem. Our purchase was more or less spontaneous, done with a coyote's grin, to shine a light on the auctioning away of America's public lands to extract the very fossil fuels that are warming our planet and pushing us toward climate disaster.

Out here in the Utah desert, we are hoping to tap into the energy that is powering the movement to keep fossil fuels in the ground. Some thirty-two million acres of lands managed by the BLM have already been leased to energy companies to drill for oil and gas, even as some climate scientists tell us the world needs to keep most fossil fuels in the ground to avert a catastrophic future of runaway global warming.

The energy we hope to produce through Tempest Exploration Company is not the kind that will destroy our planet, but the kind that will fuel moral imagination. We need to harness this spiritual and political energy to sustain the planet we call home.

Staring from the tundra through a gray scrim of clouds was the bird of my dreams. Yellow eyes were anchored in a sea of fog. White feathers tinged with brown were indistinguishable from the arctic landscape. A snowy owl was standing on a tussock. It was my sixtieth birthday.

On this day, age felt foreboding. When the fog lifted—the white owl was standing in front of a forest of tall white crosses made of wood. It was the cemetery of Inupiak elders buried on the outskirts of Kaktovik, Alaska. We were on the edge of the Beaufort Sea with the Brooks Range, snow-covered, stretching east. The owl flew. She dropped a feather. I fixed my eyes on the location where it fell, found it, and slipped the white down between the pages of my journal.

That night, I heard gunshots. We had been warned: three gunshots at night means a polar bear in the village. The next day, we saw the great white bears scavenging among the scattered bones of a bowhead whale.

The bears were immense. Hungry, intense, and focused. We watched them emerge from the waves, quick and agile. When they shook themselves, it rained, but they remained dry down to the guard hairs beneath their outer fur. I was not prepared for their predatory silhouette, the small head at the end of a long graceful neck, the muscular body, the massive haunches and large furred feet acting as paddles and rudders with black claws. The bears were beautiful among the bones.

Polar bears, *Ursus maritimus*, the largest of bears, weigh an average of one thousand pounds, but there are some on record weighing up to two thousand pounds. From rump to nose they can measure up to nine feet long, six feet from ground to shoulder. When they stand, they tower ten feet tall. Their range circles the Arctic Ocean and its surrounding seas; they inhabit the edges of land that ring the freezing waters. They are rapacious carnivores preying on seals and fish, most often from the platform of ice.

We watched both males and females with cubs on Kaktovik, foraging near the "bone yard," where native hunters leave whale carcasses on a particular spit of land after they have taken what they need. As strong and formidable as the bears are, they are vulnerable. Polar bears can swim a hundred kilometers without rest. Now they must swim farther because the pack ice is melting. Hence many bears are moving inland to hunt, and there is a rise in bears walking into coastal villages.

In 2011, the International Union for Conservation of Nature issued a warning that there will be "a dramatic reduction" in polar bear habitat due to climate change. They have listed the status of the polar bear as "vulnerable" on their Red List of Threatened Species. Polar bears were included on the United States' endangered species list in 2008, where they currently remain. Estimates put the wild polar bear population at around twenty thousand animals. Their numbers are plummeting as the result of shrinking sea ice. Their habitat is melting. In the Arctic, global warming is not an abstraction.

When we walked along the gravel edge of the Beaufort Sea in searing arctic light, distinguishing between beached ice and bears was difficult. When the bears turned, we froze.

In the village, I met a woman named Marie. Marie was dancing, twirling-twirling—making circles in the middle of the road like a whirling dervish focused on the sky—spinning-spinning-spinning—until she collapsed. She got up and kept twirling-twirling—singing simultaneously. She saw me and stopped. She told me her family's fishing camp had fallen into the sea. She told me her family had spent summers there for generations and now it was gone. She told me she didn't know what to do and so she was dancing. "Things aren't right," she said. "The world is spinning out of control."

In Utah, things aren't right, either. Oil and gas development is out of control throughout the entire Interior West. Oil pumps like crows nodding up and down populate the landscape visible from highways. Where there once was darkness, well-lit derricks pierce the night sky, competing with stars.

In the fall of 2016, I was teaching a class called "Art, Advocacy, and Landscape" with Geralyn Dreyfous, a film producer; Tim DeChristopher, a climate activist; Dylan Schneider, a community organizer; and my husband, Brooke. We were working with fifteen students from the Environmental Humanities Graduate Program at the University of Utah, a program I cofounded with Robert Newman, the dean of the College of Humanities. We were in our thirteenth year and we had received a grant from the Compton Foundation. Our project was to explore and examine communities in Utah that were dependent on fossil fuel development. We wanted to view climate change through the kaleidoscopic lens of environmental humanities, where the arts and sciences are creating a more multifaceted conversation within these rural areas.

In the town of Vernal, we came to witness and explore the economic boom of fracking natural gas and a concurrent rise in infant mortality. We met with a midwife named Donna Young who believed the increasing number of deaths among the babies she delivered had something to do with environmental contaminants produced by the livelihood of many of the newborns' parents. Young, a mother of six, with a clientele of eighteen to twenty-five expectant mothers a year, blew the whistle. *Rolling Stone* magazine gave her a megaphone when no one in Utah would listen to her: "She stumbled onto the truth that an alarming number of babies were dying in Vernal— at least ten in 2013 alone, what seemed to her a shockingly high infant mortality rate for a small town of roughly ten thousand people. That summer, she raised her hand and put the obvious question to Joe Shaffer, director of the TriCounty Health Department: why are so many of our babies dying?"

The rise in the infant mortality rate in Vernal is commensurate with the rise of fracking in Uintah County. According to *Rolling Stone*, air pollution with winter inversions revealed "ground air fraught with carcinogenic gases like benzene, rogue emissions from oil and gas drilling." These gases, they said, lingered in the stale winter air, creating toxic conditions especially hazardous to small children and the elderly. We listened to Donna Young's story and her concerns about both the health and safety of her community and how she has been marginalized by her truth telling. We began to understand why she carries a pistol for protection in a small town ruled by oil.

We visited the first tar sands mine under construction in

the United States, 180 miles southeast of Salt Lake City, south of Vernal, located in the remote Book Cliffs on the border of Utah and Colorado. The mine sits on Ute lands. The Bureau of Land Management estimates that Utah's tar sand reserves could yield as much as 12 to 19 million barrels, producing up to 2,000 barrels a day. Tar sands operations use massive amounts of water, water Utah doesn't have, because of "extreme aridity," which scientists have said supersedes drought.

Among the oil and gas boosters, we found a growing community resistance to the tar sands mine, including much of the Native population, with some locals supporting the climate activists who, for several years, created an encampment at Pipe Springs across from the mine. News was filtering down from Canada that tar sands development in Alberta had meant an increase in rare cancer among residents, largely within First Nation communities, not seen prior to the mining.

The Tar Sands Resistance Group highlighted these claims, chaining themselves to the fences and equipment in protest, while other activists repeatedly created blockades to thwart entry to the site. Over the years, hundreds of arrests were made.

We held a community screening of the film *Profit and Loss*, part of the Sacred Land Film Project produced by Toby McLeod, which focused on the health risks associated with oil sands extraction in Alberta. The film played to a full house; Toby McLeod led the discussion with one of our graduate students, Carl Ingwell, a lifelong resident of Vernal. Questions were taken late into the night.

The community was beginning to see the physical and emotional costs of large-scale oil and gas production, not to mention the perils associated with a boom-and-bust economy. Many families spent beyond their means when money was flush and found themselves financially overextended, and with the economic downturn, house foreclosures were common.

We visited Dinosaur National Monument, where the Yampa and Green Rivers converge. Both are sites of excavation, one for oil and the other for bones—dinosaur bones. We met with rangers and ranchers who told us with great pride stories about the geologic and cultural histories of the region, and the conflicts between protecting the monument while still trying to sustain a robust economy of extraction.

We had similar encounters in Moab, Utah, where oil and gas development lights up the boundaries of Canyonlands National Park with gas flares at night. We listened to tribal leaders speaking on behalf of Bears Ears National Monument farther south, in San Juan County. They tracked the fossil fuel industry's stranglehold on the health and wealth of Native communities from a scorched history of uranium mining, leaving a legacy of cancer among the miners and their children who played in the tailings. They spoke of drinking from contaminated wells. And yet, they also spoke of how the Navajo Nation has benefited mightily from oil and gas royalties.

A complex landscape creates complex communities. We saw how there were no easy answers or quick solutions and multiple perspectives. Trusting the emotional register of art and using what they had gleaned from their fieldwork, students produced short films, performed acts of theater, wrote short stories and poetry, composed music, and created public rituals surrounding land art installations. Simple place-names on a map became personal geographies exposed through stories. The encounters we had as witnesses to life inside a fossil fuel economy lit soul-fires within our learning community. For some, it was disturbing; they wanted more data and turned toward science. Others saw facts as fuel for art. And there were those whose outrage transformed them into activists. We ended our course with a desert tea ceremony led by a local practitioner in Castle Valley.

After the semester, I traveled to Paris to participate in various activities surrounding the 2015 U.N. Climate Change Conference. Climate art was on display throughout the city. I became obsessed with *Ice Watch*—twelve free-floating icebergs weighing some eighty tons that were brought to Place du Panthéon by the Danish-Icelandic artist Olafur Eliasson. From December 3 through December 12, 2015, we watched them melt before our eyes. I visited them nightly with others—touching them as one would attend to the dying—as they morphed into strange abstract shapes, some resembling human corpses abandoned on the street. I thought of the snowy owl standing guard at the cemetery and the great white bears licking the bones of bowhead whales in the Arctic; the white crosses we are all carrying in our processions of resistance.

On the last day of the conference, a massive march began at the Arc de Triomphe and flowed like water to the Eiffel Tower. The atmosphere was spirited. Red banners were unfurled down the Avenue de la Grande Armée as symbols of the "red line"—a line that should not be crossed, setting a global commitment of 80 percent of fossil fuels being kept in the ground with a "just transition" to 100 percent clean energy by 2050.

My friend Rebecca Solnit and I carried bouquets of red ranunculus, taking great pleasure in giving them away to global activists along the way.

But after several hours of political theater, placards, costumes, and chants, I grew weary. I thought about home in the eroding desert, of real people in real places who were suffering from living in such close proximity to an oiled economy. The march turned a corner—the Eiffel Tower was in view. Instead of feeling the euphoria of this climactic moment, I withdrew. I stepped out of the collective current and sat down on the lawn, a football field away from the rallying finish.

I felt desperate to return home and do something tangible. Utah was my ground zero. The Colorado Plateau was my blood line in the sand. A large red banner with black letters reading KEEP IT IN THE GROUND, carried by a dozen or more indigenous people from South America, passed by me as a raised fist.

On February 16, 2016, a quarterly Bureau of Land Management oil and gas lease auction was set for 10:00 a.m. inside the Salt Palace Convention Center in Salt Lake City. Brooke and I gathered with hundreds of citizens downtown to protest the lease sales on our public lands. Many of our students had organized the protest with local community members. Activists went inside and disrupted the auction until they were forced by police to leave. By chance, I found myself inside the auction and stayed; I later described it in my opinion piece for *The New York Times*. The language used by the auctioneer with all its sexual innuendoes sickened me. They referenced the land as a woman, here for the taking, in the vilest of words. Only two women were present in this auction of men, myself and a surrogate for an oil company. My next step became clear.

The auction ended. Everyone slapped each other on the back and shook hands. The woman turned to me as she was leaving and said, "You are a fraud, you had no intention of buying a lease. You don't belong here."

I found Brooke outside and we both came to the same conclusion. We walked to the BLM office and in a "remnant sale" bought two oil and gas leases comprising 1,120 acres of public lands in the Book Cliffs, with one lease fourteen miles from Arches National Park and the other near a critical sage grouse habitat farther east.

My father, who had worked as a contractor for natural gas companies for more than six decades laying pipe that distributed natural gas to rural towns and cities in Utah, was at his house waiting for us. He was boiling beyond fury having heard what we had done. His words were direct: "You have made a mockery of our family business. For what? A political stunt?" His partner, Jan, who had been at the protest, had a meal prepared. We sat down in silence. At an emotional conversation around the dinner table, we told him we had filed for an LLC called Tempest Exploration Company. We said that we couldn't be more serious.

"You are so naïve, you don't know what the hell you are doing, I know these bastards, these oil and gas men will destroy you." He left the table.

The next day, the story of our leases appeared on the front page of *The Salt Lake Tribune*. It was the first time a layperson had legally bought an oil and gas lease outside of the fossil fuel industry. Eight years earlier, Tim DeChristopher had bid up several oil and gas leases worth $1.8 million dollars as an act of civil disobedience to expose the BLM's complicity with industry. It was his cry and call for a livable future. As I mentioned earlier, he served two years in a federal prison.

As we prepared to leave Salt Lake before sunrise and drive back to Castle Valley, my father, in his eighties and still more than six feet tall in his boots, was already dressed in his Levi's, a striped work shirt, and a down vest. He was standing outside next to our car. "Look, I know you have good intentions, but you are way in over your head. Somebody has to save your ass," he said. And he reluctantly agreed to be the CEO of our newly formed energy company.

Two weeks later, I found myself called into the office of the new dean of the College of Humanities with the University of Utah's lead attorney by her side. It went something like this: "We want to thank you for your service. We are giving you twenty thousand dollars and a platinum-pillow insurance policy and you are no longer teaching here."

Stunned. I was told I was out of compliance with Obama's Affordable Care Act, which made no sense to me. Then they switched to saying I was making too much money for doing too little compared to teaching fellows who were teaching several classes a semester, something like that. Never mind the successes and caliber of our students within the Environmental Humanities Graduate Program. In the midst of what felt like the mumbo-jumbo of an academic takedown, all I could think to say was "I'm not leaving."

"Excuse me?" I recall the dean saying.

"I'm not leaving. Deans come and go, but my bones will be buried here."

I managed to ask how much this had to do with purchasing the Bureau of Land Management's oil and gas leases.

At that point, both the dean and the attorney fell all over themselves assuring me that this meeting and their decision had nothing to do with the auction or my political views. I remember them saying that if this had anything to do with academic freedom, they would be defending me. I stopped listening. They wanted me gone.

The University of Utah depends on the Utah State Legislature for much of its funding, and state representatives are greatly influenced by the lobbyists from the oil and gas industry, not to mention that some of the university's largest donors come from the fossil fuel sector.

I fought to keep my job and position as the Annie Clark Tanner Scholar in the Environmental Humanities Graduate Program. Six weeks of private negotiations that included a pay cut and an understanding that I would teach three more years and then leave didn't bring a resolution. Our talks collapsed after the attorney emailed (two days before I was to sign a new agreed-upon contract) to explain that I was "out of compliance again," that I was a danger to the university and my students, "engendering resentment" regarding the nature of our field trips. The attorney reported I would be expected to teach within the four walls of a classroom on campus in Salt Lake City. Any future field trips would require proper oversight and paperwork. I sought support from the director of the EH Program. He simply said, "Terry, these decisions are made in much higher offices than mine."

I recognized the straitjacket I was being handed.

My letter of resignation to the dean was published in *The Salt Lake Tribune*. Here is an excerpt:

> What I have realized in these six weeks is this: I can no longer work in an institution or program that privileges compliance over creativity; that values the language of bureaucracy over relationships and respect; and that is more concerned over issues of insurance than the assurance of emancipatory curriculum that benefits our students . . . Throughout these negotiations, fear and scarcity seem to be driving the discussions. My fear is that universities, now under increased pressure to raise money, are being led by corporate managers rather than innovative educators . . .

If we say the Environmental Humanities Graduate Program encourages our students to think "out of the box" and engage in creative and collaborative approaches, if we agree it is our responsibility to explore the pressing issues of our time, especially regarding the work of advocacy, which we have identified as a core value of the program, in the name of environmental issues, social issues, and issues of climate justice—then shouldn't we have flexibility in our curriculum and with our faculty to accommodate this? It has been sobering, indeed, to have witnessed first-hand the box I have been placed in repeatedly with the new administration within the College of Humanities, as I have tried to secure my contract that has otherwise been supported and renewed for the past twelve years.

Although the dean and the University of Utah's attorney said adamantly that Brooke and my purchases of the BLM oil and gas leases on February 16, 2016, had nothing to do with my forced and early retirement in this program, even as the dean's email to me was delivered on February 29, less than two weeks after our action—I am left with many questions.

Life surprises us. One bold action sets other actions in motion. In the end, both our BLM decision and my decision to leave the University of Utah are decisions about energy: how we choose to define it, where we feel we receive energy and where we feel energy is being drained. It is not without sadness.

The weather system has changed.

And the weather continues to change.

Here is what I have learned: my leaving the University of Utah, whether I was basically fired or chose to resign, is not the essential story, but the one that leads up to it. The bigger story I wish to tell you isn't about the cowardice of institutions or my unwillingness to conform; the story I am grappling with and trying to understand now is the story of change and the unraveling of the self, my self. I wish this were a story about wisdom. I believe it is, instead, a story about disruption and failure.

From the very beginning, my life's work has been as a teacher in Utah. I have taught in elementary schools, middle schools, and high schools and at the University of Utah since 1983, where I received my undergraduate and master's degrees and an honorary doctorate degree in 2003. I thought I would continue this work in my home state until I died. My soul had other plans.

What we experience as heartbreak, the loss of a job or a marriage, or illness, or another disruption in the life we had planned for ourselves, may be our liberation—an open door to growth. I couldn't see it at the time, but I certainly realize it now. There were solitary steps I had to take along the way, alongside the support from my family and the community that embraced me outside the university.

Brooke and I were lucky to have saved enough money to be able to take six months off and sit with what had happened. I grieved. I sat with my failures and wondered how I might have done things differently. How might I have been more attentive to my students? Was I too hard on those who complained? Had I become too lax with rules and regulations? Or was it more than that—actual contempt for the bureaucratic mind? Was the safety of our students at risk? Or were these institutional tactics to undermine my confidence and justify the administration's actions?

I no longer trusted myself. I read every public comment published online in *The Salt Lake Tribune* after the articles appeared regarding my resignation from the University of Utah and those that followed the political debacle that ensued. I read them all, hundreds of tough, brutal comments that sent me into a tailspin of self-doubt and a sharp-edged awareness. I wasn't prepared for the public backlash. But mainly, I was just sad. Grief comes in many forms. I had lost a job that I loved, a key piece of my purpose and identity.

You can't take on the powers that be in Utah with your pen—from the Mormon Church to politicians to the fossil fuel industry—especially as a woman, without offending at least half of your hometown. In my case, it felt like more than half. I did not regret my actions, but the consequences were painful. I don't remember the supportive letters, but I memorized the hateful ones. I plummeted into depression and retreated.

Time passed slowly. There were some job offers, which I appreciated but ultimately declined, knowing I was not yet capable of being present with students, that I would simply be going through the motions. I couldn't do that. I wrote articles to make up the difference financially between our savings and my lost salary. I needed these months at home to reflect on what had happened and what I wanted and needed next. This open space was a privilege and a terror. I knew that without this time to embrace my own brokenness—which Alexandra Fuller says "every writer must do if she is to be any good: Court eviction from the tribe that raised you, and later from any tribe that seeks to co-opt you"—I could not bring my full self to whatever would come next. I needed a time of undoing.

One night I awoke to the light of the full moon pouring into our bedroom. Its brightness called me outside. It was November, cold in the high desert. I got up, put on my parka, and walked out the door. The full face of the moon shone above me. Under the immensity of the night sky, I addressed the moon as if I were speaking to my mother and grandmother. I bared my soul—a lament and a longing. I don't remember the words; I only recall feeling in that moment that I had dared to tell this celestial body what my spiritual body desired: a deepening—a new way to understand and serve the world.

I didn't want to become afraid or bitter or smaller than I was. "Use me," I said.

It did not feel indulgent. It felt urgent and true.

I needed a sign—something, anything to acknowledge I had been heard and had not completely gone mad. Almost instantaneously, a rooster started crowing. I laughed. I was hoping for a chorus of coyotes or one lone owl calling in the creases between darkness and light.

But a rooster!

I felt my sense of humor returning with that rooster. I went back inside. Brooke was still sleeping. I lit a candle and wrote what had just happened in the pages of my journal so that when I came to my senses, I would remember and, most important, trust this encounter with the moon. The panic of not having a job was quietly replaced by my faith that one would come. Something had been released. The noose of grief had been loosened.

———

Krista Tippett writes, "A mystic is anyone who has a gnawing suspicion that the apparent discord, brokenness, contradiction, and discontinuities that assault us every day might conceal a hidden unity."

A hidden unity is what we cannot see until we are shattered and shamed, split apart by uninvited change. My beautiful undoing began with being evicted from Utah, the only home I have ever known. I am seeing my place more clearly. Physically. Spiritually. This is the erosion of self. Brooke and I bought the leases for 1,120 acres in the Book Cliffs near our home for one simple reason: love. We didn't matter, the consequences didn't matter; the moment when we agreed to put our love into action did. It was not an act of courage. It was a statement of belief that the world can change if we are willing to risk our own change first. Shortly thereafter, the Bureau of Land Management made a policy decision to do away with in-person auctions and offer only online auctions with tightly controlled entry specifications. The public was cut out of public land auctions for oil and gas leases. Our leases were revoked by the Bureau of Land Management nine months after we purchased them, on the grounds we had no intention of developing them for oil and gas. Neither did the other companies who bought leases that day. It was simply an investment, a speculation, a gamble. The only plan they had for their leases was to sit on them until the price of oil went up. Like us, they were waiting. But our waiting had a more permanent purpose. The climate crisis was before us.

What we know from a Freedom of Information filing with the BLM is that since the Mineral Leasing Act of 1920 was established, no individual, company, or corporation has ever been denied a lease they have purchased. In close to a century, our leases were the first to be denied by the federal government. We are appealing the decision with the Department of the Interior's Land Board of Appeals. It has been three years since October 2016, and still no word, no decision.

All the times I have stood on the edge of the Needles Overlook in Canyonlands, holding that view of a vast broken landscape, blood-red, in my heart, I didn't know how it was sculpting my imagination the way wind sculpts stone. Nor could I have imagined the way this landscape fuels the fury and passion of engaged students and inspires them to make beautiful, radical change in the world, which is what I believe many institutions fear most. Weathering breaks things down. Erosion carries them away.

There is no sanctuary from the warming Earth; there is only change and an eroding future where we are twirling-twirling-twirling and collapsing into finely honed humans who dare to fall and fail in the name of love.

## ◈ THE LOST DAUGHTER OF THE OCEAN

The cure for anything is salt water: sweat, tears or the sea.
—ISAK DINESEN

### Sweat

It is hot. Alisha Anderson and I have just passed Golden Spike National Historic Site on our way to the *Spiral Jetty*. Alisha is a former student of mine from the Environmental Humanities Graduate Program at the University of Utah. She is now a dear friend, a woman also in love with Great Salt Lake. She is twenty-eight years old. The same age I was when I was seeking solace from this inland sea. We are on a pilgrimage to chart the changes of a capricious body of water.

From the corner of my eye, I see a flash of wings. Burrowing owl. I turn. The owl has just landed on a barbed-wire fence post. We stop. *Its yellow eyes could burn grasses with its stare.* We blink before the burrowing owl does. These small diurnal owls with long spindly legs are tricksters, ground dwellers. Once inside their mounds, their calls register as rattlesnakes, the dry shaking of their tails instilling a warning: "Do not enter." For me, they are the signature species of the sage flats of the Great

Basin. A second owl, hidden in the sage, flies. Both owls meet on top of their mound.

I am home.

It has been twenty-five years since *Refuge: An Unnatural History of Family and Place* was published, a quiet book about the rise of Great Salt Lake in the 1980s and the death of my mother and grandmother from cancers caused by, I believe, radiation fallout from nuclear bomb testing in the Nevada desert.

Much has changed since that moment in time. The record-high lake level of 4,211.85 feet above sea level reached in January 1987, the month of my mother's passing, is now countered by drought so severe that Great Salt Lake has reached a historic low of 4,189.00 feet in the North Arm near Promontory Point. The previous record low was set in 1963 at 4,191.35 feet.

We are witnessing a shrinking lake, one that has fallen from close to 3,300 square miles in 1988 to less than 950 square miles today. You might say this is the cyclic nature of Great Salt Lake. But that is only partially true. Researchers show that the lake has dropped an additional 11 feet from pre-settlement levels, due to the anthropogenic fact of our species using too much water. Consider that the harebrained Bear River Diversion Plan, tied to the construction of other regional water projects like the Lake Powell pipeline, promises Utah's water to China, and you begin to see the craziness of politics in Utah. Add to the mix climate change (two words that were not part of my vocabulary in 1983 when Great Salt Lake was rising), which is increasing drought conditions in the American West, and you begin to see an ongoing pattern in the state of Utah's refusal to take water conservation seriously, as they contribute to the rapid decline of a dying lake in a withered basin. Talking about the weather used to be small talk. No longer. Today, talking about the weather is a dialogue with survival. Making sure there is enough water to support Great Salt Lake and its natural systems is a prudent conversation.

The *Spiral Jetty* is before us. When I was writing *Refuge*, Robert Smithson's *Spiral Jetty* was underwater. I visited for the first time close to a decade ago, when it was newly exposed; it was glistening with salt crystals, a blinding glare on the flats. On this day with Alisha, it is a black spiral made of basalt stones, a study in contrast against the white lake bed baked, cracked, and folded from the heat.

Alisha has spent the past year walking the boundaries of a disappearing lake. She is a land artist in the same tradition as Robert Smithson and Nancy Holt, only instead of creating spirals and *Sun Tunnels* on the salt flats, she creates ephemeral art that belongs to the act of creation itself.

For a time, Alisha lived near Willard Bay on the edge of Great Salt Lake. Every morning and evening, she would walk the dike that held the water in. Her saunters were invocations and benedictions. And when she learned that the very dike she had found solace on was made from the remains of the Fremont Indians' village, even from their very bones, she turned her shock and outrage into art. On a winter day after a snowstorm, she made a pictograph out of sandstone that she had crushed into a powder with a mortar and pestle, a gesture to acknowledge the harm done and to honor the lives of the Fremont people, whose bones and shards had settled on the shores of Great Salt Lake. Carrying a bucket of red powder onto the snowy dike made of archaeological remains, she created a symbol and sign of her own, drawn with her own hand, as an homage to the ancient artists whose pictographs still remain in caves along the lake as a forgotten language.

"We are walking our choices," she says.

Alisha turns and points to what appear as islands on the horizon—Antelope, Fremont, Gunnison, and Dolphin. She tells me these are no longer islands at all, but rather bodies of land now exposed with no skirts of water surrounding them. In the case of Gunnison Island, the once protected nesting colony of white pelicans is now vulnerable to coyotes crossing the lake bed, where a plethora of eggs and young pelicans await them.

It is a changed landscape. We walk the *Spiral Jetty* together on Labor Day weekend, other pilgrims walk with us. I hear fragments of conversations with words like "entropy" and "apocalypse" and "drought" wafting on the hot, dry wind. And when we reach the center of the spiral, I hold the same question I held twenty-five years ago: "How do we find refuge in change?"

### Tears

Alisha tells me that water from Great Salt Lake is heavier than regular water, especially the water from the North Arm near Gunnison Island, where it is 27 to 28 percent salt.

"I know because I had to carry it," she says. Several gallons of lake water slosh in the back seat of her car as she dreams of another ritual through art—acts of peacemaking.

Gilbert Bay on the South Arm of the lake closest to Salt Lake City is 13 to 15 percent salt as the result of the split nature of Great Salt Lake; it's divided in half by the railroad causeway.

We, too, are vessels of salt water. Our tears when viewed under a microscope are crystallized salt mixed with water. When falling, tears are composed of proteins, enzymes, oils, and antibodies suspended in salt water. They both lubricate our eyes and protect them, in addition to shepherding our emotional releases that create chemicals to thwart pain and alleviate stress.

Rose-Lynn Fisher, in her work *The Topography of Tears*, has researched the chemistry of tears. While photographing them under a microscope, she discovered that tears of sorrow and tears of joy have a completely different chemical composition, as well as a different molecular structure. "Like a drop of ocean water each tiny tear drop carries a microcosm of human experience," she says.

I recall the years when I experienced Great Salt Lake as "my basin of tears." At times, I felt as though I were drowning in the salt water of both my tears and a rising inland sea. Close to three decades later, I see Great Salt Lake differently, not as a landscape of grief but a place of exposure, an amplification of our own state of mind. Henry David Thoreau called Walden Pond "Earth's eye," a mirror of our own nature. Great Salt Lake is a similar "lake of light," a storied landscape animated by our own experience. When Thoreau was asked how deep Walden Pond was, he responded, "As deep as we are . . . Some people say it is bottomless." The same holds true for this lake of salt and brine and floating islands.

What is a mirage in times of drought?

Three white pelicans are walking the lake bed. At first glance, I thought they were storks, which I knew do not exist here. I looked twice, and then recognized them as pelicans, gaunt and pale, their bills and gular sacs white and salt-encrusted. Gone were the vibrant orange bills that flash health during the mating season. Their potbellies padded with honeycomb spaces of air so they remain buoyant in the water were also gone, physical evidence of their state of hunger. These birds were suffering from starvation, thirst, and exposure. They were walking toward death.

Alisha and I wonder if the reason they stopped here is that they don't have enough energy to fly to Gunnison Island where they live. Why this weakened state? Pelicans typically lay two eggs in a nest in any given year. Only one in four chicks in the colony survives to adulthood. Coyotes walking onto the island create chaos among the young pelicans: some are killed by the predator; some are scared into the water with a fluttering of wings; and others take to the air prematurely and land at Promontory Point, where with no freshwater to be found they face death by starvation. The pelicans we watch are refugees of the drought, unable to fly back to Gunnison Island or fly east to reach freshwater where the parent birds are feeding.

The young pelicans seem conscious of their predicament, gathered together as wounded relics of Earth weary in a season of dying. Beyond them, dotting the salt flats from the *Spiral Jetty* to the water's edge, at least half a mile away, are scattered piles of feathers, dozens and dozens of dead pelicans, their juvenile wings splayed across the sand like crucifixes, their chests hollowed out by ravens.

*If I can learn to love death, then I can begin to find refuge in change.* I do not believe that by repeating this mantra I will learn to love death until, perhaps, it is my own and I become like the pelicans, searching for relief in a desert of pain.

The magnitude of life that flocks to Great Salt Lake is a winged testament to life. Millions of birds and hundreds of species have been returning to this remnant of Lake Bonneville for millennia. Alisha recounts going out last fall to count eared grebes on the lake with the biologist John Luft of the Great Salt Lake Ecosystem Program's Utah Division of Wildlife Resources. The result of their aerial survey: five million birds in migration. Once they arrive at Great Salt Lake, the elegant grebes with a swatch of gold on their cheeks give up their feathers in a grand molt. Their flight muscles atrophy and they can be found on this inland sea feasting on brine shrimp and flies until October or November. These multitudes of birds become a multitude of hope even in drought, especially in drought, because of their resilience. And then, in a flash of collective recognition and urgency, millions of eared grebes take flight in the night and continue on their journey south.

Tears of joy. Tears of sorrow. Great Salt Lake has always held contradictory emotions in balance. In the jubilee of returning birds, a band of white pelicans continue to walk their deaths like pale monks on a pilgrimage they may never complete.

## The Sea

The American West is on fire. Smoke obscures the edges of Great Salt Lake. Alisha and I separate, each of us seeking our own solitude. We walk. We walk away from the *Spiral Jetty* with space between us in the direction of the white pelicans. We walk the lake bed for what seems like hours in the bald heat of the afternoon. I feel my age, as a person who has weathered both flood and drought. Diaphanous clouds sweeping across the sky create a veil of shadows on the pastel landscape of mountain ranges and floating islands, pink water in a bloom of algae. My mind notes most of all the stillness of this place.

In 1987, it would have seemed perverse to follow pelicans on land; I had never witnessed them walking at all, only bobbing on the surface of the waters of the Bear River Bird Refuge in circles of cooperative fishing, scooping up the minnows in their great pouches and throwing back their heads to swallow them.

Now, I follow them, as though this is a normal occur-
rence, three pelicans on land who are skirting the lake, each
foot stoically placed in front of the other, creating tracks like
braids on the cracked salt beds. I take off my shoes as an act
of solidarity and walk behind them, these righteous novices of
the salt desert walking themselves toward death. The surface is hard, with quartz crystals that jut up like razors, and
it glints with reflected light. This is harsh country where one
must squint to see. I step around another pelican carcass, its
head, pulled apart from its body, a few feet away. A necklace
of salt crystals adorns the feathered chest; the bones of the
decaying wings are broken revelations. Someone has scratched
"S O S" in the lake bed.

I am desperate to get to the lake, but the beauty of the barrage of patterns and textures on the salt flats slows me down.
Salt deposits create the illusion of a brocade fabric. Puddles
of warm salt water spaced every three feet or so soothe my
bare feet. Up ahead the lake bed has peeled back like old
paint, brittle to the touch. Farther out still, the surface reveals squiggly lines that look like sutures on skulls, until the
sutures morph into cobwebs and the white network of salt
becomes lace.

Close to the lake's edge, I enter a conflict zone. Something equivalent to tectonic plates has reared up like mountain
ranges through the stress of expanding and contracting forces
on the ground; I see it as an electrical current running along
the salt flats.

Here, Great Salt Lake is a vast mirror of water. A shin-
high line of sea foam forms a gateway to the silky pink waters
so shallow that the salt reefs are visible like white coral. I shed
my clothes and enter the body of Great Salt Lake.

I walk in water knee-deep and warm until gradually, maybe half a mile out, the lake reaches my chin. I lean forward and surrender to the depths and allow myself to be held by Great Salt Lake, buoyed by this body of water that I have loved all my life. I float on my back, gazing up at the sky in the most joyous state, bliss married to awe. I am of this place. My body and the body of this lake are one. I have surpassed my mother's age when she died. I am approaching my grandmother's age when she mentored me in birds. Great Salt Lake continues to show me the cyclical nature of things. And yet always there is the paradox. Although much has changed in this octave of time between flood and drought, the essence of the land and my own essence remain the same.

Without thought, I baptize myself by the authority vested in me, not God, not the patriarchy, with only the lake as my witness. My immersion is complete. When I rise, I laugh out loud—I have violated the first rule of a swim in Great Salt Lake: keep your head above water. I am blinded by the burning salt. I cannot see. I cannot flush the salt out of my eyes with freshwater. I can only turn toward what I think is the direction of the shore and continue walking until the burning subsides and returns me to a renewed vision.

I see a blurred Alisha walking toward me. She bends down to touch the salt crystals. She is not my mother or my grandmother, but she offers me the refuge and courage of women who dare to live by their own authority, trusting their instincts, and follow their calling to create beauty in the midst of despair for another generation. She holds a vision of a retreating Great Salt Lake not as a vanishing presence, but as a guidepost for what is to come. She seeks both the isolation of and the connection to an enigmatic landscape. She courts the discomfort of heat waves and freezing temperatures as she makes art that few people will see. Ephemeral by design.

When I was writing my book about a rising Great Salt Lake and the deaths of the women closest to me, I didn't know then what I do know now: we can survive our own personal losses. This is what gives us our voice. But it is in the losses of the larger world—call it a grieving Earth—that our collective sanity and survival are threatened. The only way to proceed at this moment is to walk with the pelicans and not fear where they are leading us. Braided tracks in an exposed lake bed of salt will be our path. And a young woman who dares to scatter sandstone powder on snow in remembrance of and restitution to those who have not only been forgotten but violated, is herself a reimagining of our place in the world. She is my guide now, the artist, the alchemist, the maker of rituals calling forth an awakened state of seeing.

For a westerner, it felt like an abundance of water in a year of drought. We stood at the overlook of Great Falls watching the Potomac River funnel through the Mather Gorge—named after Stephen T. Mather, the first director of the National Park Service. The cascading rapids and dramatic pour-offs were mesmerizing and soul restoring in the extreme heat. High humidity and temperatures in the upper nineties were drawing larger crowds than usual at this eight-hundred-acre national park, only fifteen miles from our nation's capital.

At sunset, I stood on one of the viewing platforms with a dozen or more people: a friend from Rwanda, a family from Pakistan, another family from India, and three women from Saudi Arabia, all of us searching for words to express the awe we were sharing in the last light of day.

Later, a couple from Washington joined us. "We come here every week," they said. "D.C. would be intolerable in the summer without Great Falls. It is our refuge."

America's public lands—more than 640 million acres of forests, deserts, prairies, wetlands, and seashores, many protected through our national parks, monuments, wilderness areas, and wildlife refuges—are our inheritance. We the People are land-rich.

As a child growing up in Utah, I saw Zion, Bryce, Capital Reef, Arches, and Canyonlands National Parks simply as an extension of my own backyard. But even though I am a frequent visitor to Washington, I did not know until this summer that these eight hundred acres on the edge of the Potomac were part of the national park system, or that close to a million people come here annually.

Great Falls has been a gathering place of water and humans for ten thousand years, beginning with the indigenous people whose petroglyphs can still be seen on the cliff faces of the gorge. Starting in 1784, George Washington helped fund the locks and gates of the Patowmack Canal, engineered to skirt the turbulent waters of Great Falls, making it easier to shepherd goods from one side of the river to the other. Distinct stonemason's marks left on the nearby ruins of the canal match the "signature" on the foundation stones of the White House and the United States Capitol.

In the twentieth century, Great Falls was the end of a trolley line that originated in Georgetown and the site of an amusement park complete with a carousel. The park was destroyed by a flood, a reminder that nature rules, something we tend to forget.

A flurry of black vultures crossed the river at dusk to roost. Half a dozen kayakers circled in the currents below the falls, looking up at the rapids and wondering if they had enough light to make one last run. Bass fishermen, perched on the banks like herons, reeled in their lines one last time. Our national parks are sanctuaries, staying places.

I wonder why we hear so little about the fate of these wild, open spaces from our nationally elected officials when these lands mean so much to the soul of America, as well as its economy. I would like to hear the words "public lands" spoken in every election debate, with candidates holding both government and corporations accountable in their oversight and use. The fact of more than three hundred million visits to our national parks last year tells me I am not alone. I read headlines like this: "GOP Platform Endorses Disposing of Federal Lands," but find bipartisan outrage over the selling off of our public lands, be it to the states or the highest bidder at the Bureau of Land Management's quarterly oil and gas leasing auctions, beginning at two dollars an acre.

Remove our national parks and wildlands from the United States and what remains? An intolerable and lonely self-constructed world without the wisdom and beauty of a landscape much wiser than we are. We need human endeavor and intelligence, but we also need the intelligences of the wild—the millennial authority of redwood trees, the forbearance of bison, and the lyrical sermon of a wood thrush at dawn.

Can we extend freedom to all living things? And in so doing, save ourselves from the folly of our own ambitions?

Standing at Great Falls on a hot, humid day when the political temperature in Washington registered like a fever, an uncommon peace came over me. I allowed myself to believe that in another hundred years, there will be others standing on this same brink of beauty, grateful for all that remains wild and wholesome and free.

3

When we drop fear, we can draw nearer to people, we can draw nearer to the earth, we can draw nearer to all the heavenly creatures that surround us.

—bell hooks, *Where We Stand*

## ❖ THIS MOMENT: EROSION OF DEMOCRACY
*November 9, 2016*


It is morning. I am mourning.

And the river is before me.

I am a writer without words who is struggling to find them.

I am holding the balm of beauty, this river, this desert,
so vulnerable, all of us.

I am trying to shape my despair into some form of action,
but for now, I am standing on the cold edge of grief.

We are staring at a belligerent rejection of change
by our fellow Americans who believe
they have voted for change.

The seismic shock of a new political landscape is settling.

For now, I do not feel like unity is what is called for.

Resistance is our courage.
Love will become us.
The land holds us still.

Let us pause and listen and gather our strength with grace
and move forward like water in all its manifestations:
flat water, white water, rapids and eddies,
and flood this country with an integrity of
purpose and patience and persistence
capable of cracking stone.

I am a writer without words who continues
to believe in the vitality of the struggle.

Let us hold each other close and be kind.

Let us gather together and break bread.

Let us trust that what is required of us next
will become clear in time.

What has been hidden is now exposed.

This river, this mourning, this moment—

May we be brave enough to feel it deeply.

And then, act.

*Preparation* ❖ *One Encounter, One Chance*
*There is no beginning and no end to the preparation for a tea cer-*
*emony. For a student of tea, her life embodies and reflects her readi-*
*ness, and yet each gathering presents her with an opportunity to*
*be fully alive at this time, on this day, in the arc of the season. In*
*Japan, there is an expression:* ichigo ichie. *Roughly translated, it*
*means "one encounter, one chance." As she harvests water and lays*
*coals for the fire, she orients her whole focus toward the evanescence*
*and particularity of this one meeting.*

Castle Valley is a small desert hamlet in southeastern Utah
near the banks of the Colorado River to the north, the La
Sal Mountains to the south, Porcupine Rim to the west, and
Adobe Mesa catching first light in the east. It is a community
that values starlit nights and solitude, a town of self-described
recluses, renegades, and ruffians disguised in the respectable
form of teachers, architects, gardeners, environmentalists,
militiamen, peaceniks, winemakers, goatherds, artists, writers, photographers, potash workers, entrepreneurs, and retired

oilmen. What binds us together is the beauty of this red rock landscape and a stillness so uncommon that we count on the wing beats of ravens to remind us we have not become deaf to the noises of the outside world.

We are surrounded by hundreds of thousands of acres of public lands, lands that belong to all of us in this country we call America. These lands are a varied palette of color and geography from sagebrush seas ubiquitous in the West; to petrified sand dunes now monuments of stone; to buttes and mesas, hoodoos and spires; to arches and windows blown open by wind, water, and time. This is an erosional landscape where geology reveals the open history of Earth.

Sarah Hedden and I are neighbors. We have been friends since she was a child. She was born in Castle Valley, the second daughter to Eleanor Bliss and Bill Hedden, back-to-the-landers who sought a simpler life after graduating from Harvard. Her sister is an artist named Chloe. Sarah is a sophisticate in a rural setting.

I moved here with my husband, Brooke, in 1998. We left Salt Lake City because it felt crowded. Our need for wildness pulled us south. We are writers and have made our lives about watching shadows and light. In the desert, some call it a pastime. For those of us living in Castle Valley, it is our morning and evening occupation.

As westerners, we take our public lands seriously. We know they are our birthright as American citizens. They are the lands we graze, mine, drill, frack, log, wander in, and recreate on. They are also the lands we recognize as our national forests, seashores, wetlands, national parks, and wildlife refuges. Breathing spaces, I call them, in a society increasingly holding its breath. Our public lands are being exploited and compromised by the fossil fuel industry's last gasp of power in this era of climate change. They are also at risk of being trampled by what the writer and desert rat Edward Abbey called "industrial tourism." The undermining of our public commons is at a fever pitch, just as there is a growing national movement to sell our public lands into private hands, to the highest bidder.

### Bowl Tea ❖ Meditation
*November 8, 2016: Donald Trump wins the presidential election. He will become the forty-fifth president of the United States of America, defeating Hillary Clinton, who won the popular vote by more than three million people.*

### Opening ❖ Presence
*To open the ceremony, the host strikes the singing bowl three times. The first tone summons body; the second, mind; the third, spirit. She then bows to her guests.*

Sarah Hedden is an architect of sacred space. She is preparing a tea ceremony in Castle Valley, Utah, inspired by the teachings of Wu De, a tea monk ordained in the Soto Zen tradition, who studied the gongfu tea ceremony under Master Lin Ping Xiang. She is dressed in a long black robe, simple and sleek, and casts an elegant form against the white wall of the tea room as she engages with the ritualized gestures of tea making at the low wooden table made by her father. Schooled at Berkeley's School of Architecture, she left the traditional confines of her profession and returned to the red rock desert.

We gathered together inside the Hedden home, eight neighbors in need of solace.

We were mindful of the preparations required and being made for the tea ceremony.

### *Purification ❧ Consecration*

*Even though the tea ware is "clean," the host must purify each vessel in front of her guests as a show of respect and to consecrate their time together. For the duration of this ceremony, all are equal. With the nondominant hand, she pours hot water from the kettle into each of the tea bowls. Taking each bowl with the dominant hand, she decants the water into the wastewater vessel while spinning the bowl at a forty-five-degree angle. Moving counterclockwise, she purifies her own bowl last.*

We felt sickened even as we bathed ourselves in the red water of the Colorado River as a form of purification that morning after the election. The whole presidential outcome felt like a betrayal. Some of us saw it coming. Some of us didn't. We didn't understand the rancor among us, the invisibility of those around us, even members of our own family whom we had never bothered to ask how they were feeling in a country increasingly hostile and foreign to them. In a world more global than local, more fast-paced than focused, many of our fellow Americans had gotten lost. Now they felt seen. Their candidate outside the political system had won. We felt we had failed our own nation, not by voting against Donald Trump, but by watching others voting against themselves. We had been awoken and we were in pain.

### *Steeping ❧ Respect*

*Quieting the heart with her breath, the host picks up the kettle. Tea is prepared from this place of stillness and nowhere else. She showers the teapot with hot water to warm the vessel before adding the tea leaves and "rinsing." This first encounter between leaves and water is an invocation, inviting the spirit of tea to be present for the ceremony. In this way, the host shows the tea her utmost respect.*

We respect each other. We respect this moment of abrupt change. We respect the slow, conscious pace of ritual, of deep tradition that settles our souls in place, where we can find our own architecture of meaning even as everything around us feels like it is in a state of erosion. Falling rocks cascading down the mesa signal that the outer landscape is mirroring our inner landscape. Present tense. Sarah brings out the container of tea and opens it: an aged pu-erh from the 1960s. We respect the tea as we pass it around the table and smell the Earth.

### Serving ❖ Fluency

*Through the ceremony, the host balances the qualities of precision and fluency. Each movement is performed with her full attention, yet completed in one breath without hesitation. As each bowl is filled, a line is drawn, linking the vessels together as part of the whole.*

Awaiting our tea, each of us reflected on the lands that have determined who we have become. This had been our intention for the ceremony. I cannot know where others around this tea table traveled during this pause. Our eyes were cast down, the first time my eyes had rested in days. But what came into my focus was Bears Ears, two buttes adjacent to each other that from afar resemble their namesake. A full moon rose in my memory; we had been in Dark Canyon for seven days. I was leading a group of people. In truth, they were leading me. My father was one of those on the trip. Strange things happened. We witnessed a lightning bolt strike a juniper; the charred bark is charged bark to the Diné, worthy of being kept inside medicine bundles. We continued walking down the wash with burned bark in our pockets until tiny frogs took hold on our legs. We wondered why, until the smell of damp leaves and a thunderous roar reached us. We scrambled up the hillside for safety, energized by our fear of being whisked away, only minutes later to watch a flash flood hurling cottonwood trees uprooted and boulders the size of cars downcanyon. Nature's fury left us shaken. My father spoke the word: "lucky." After sunset, a rare rainbow at night followed. Not long ago, he told this story to his great-grandsons, with the import of a blessing, "May you go there, one day, too."

These lands, sacred lands newly part of the Bears Ears National Monument, were at risk of being rescinded or reduced by the nation's new president. The reverence this place inspires in some is what others, in revenge, seek to destroy. They call it a "federal land grab." Jonah Yellowman, a Navajo spiritual leader, says, "Bears Ears is special . . . very spiritual . . . It's a protector of this land through prayers and songs. Why do you want to undo your shield? That would be a mistake like opening a door for something bad to enter."

Preparing tea is a way for me to locate my patience.

### Infusing ❖ Reverence
*The same tea can be infused many times. The host and guests show their reverence and dedication to the tea by filling and emptying their bowls repeatedly until the tea steeps clear. Often, the most potent bowls of tea are the least "saturated."*

Sarah pours the pu-erh into the bowls with the sound of water falling from great heights, creating a small pool into our earthen cups, and gracefully hands each of us our tea, which we lovingly receive. We drink in a shared meditation that honors the paradox found in wilderness, where one feels alone yet part of the living community that surrounds us. Birdsong and the humming of insects initiate a calm heart, just as the flame of the candle before us soothes our souls. I see in the bowl of varied hues the ocean tides, high tide, low tide, and I try to steady my hands between sips to reach some kind of equilibrium where no waves create the slightest disturbance. I am disturbed by our present situation in which these public lands held in the public trust will be sold to the rich, the corporate, and the careless, who desire them for their own taking, with an eye for profit over beauty. I see the razed lands, the roads, the rigs, the frack lines and flares, the burning fractured desert—and in between sips my mind is contemplating violence. I drink the last tide pool of tea—close my eyes and swallow my rage. When I open my eyes, Sarah meets mine with hers, dark and penetrating. She leans toward me to receive my empty bowl. Our heads bow, acknowledging the exchange. I wonder if she sees my fire?

People tell me there are trade-offs involved in getting what we want. I see these as compromises, an action I try to avoid. I am holding my ground, we are holding our ground, with reverence that is public and private, like this tea ceremony.

We sip four more bowls of tea; each time the quality of the tea is refining itself as the Earth refines herself. We are complete in our silences.

### Connecting ❖ Openness
*Each time the tea is served, the host brings the bowl to her heart and offers the tea with an open and unobstructed gaze. In this way, both host and guest give and receive benediction.*

———

We are met in ritual and in community.

### Completion ❖ Harmony
*Even though the practice is never-ending, the host must bring the ceremony to a close. Rinsing the bowls, she serves each guest a last mouthful of clear water. She then strikes the singing bowl three times and bows.*

The tea ceremony is over. Sarah invites us to speak. In the aftermath of the seismic shift in American politics and all its ramifications for land, wildlife, borders, clean air, clean water, and all that is at stake with a warming planet, we tell stories. We tell stories that remind us we will resist and insist that our communities be built upon the faith we have in each other, as it has always been—and, most important, upon the faith we have in these lands that have shaped us. We anticipate, we plan, we caress our dreams, even as we fight for a civilized society in the midst of a violent overthrow of democracy and decency. We acknowledge and recommit ourselves to a different kind of power, the enduring power of Earth.

On our public lands, daily acts of respect must be practiced with the precision and attentive gestures of a tea ceremony. There, what the right hand does and what the left hand does is as mindful as an *unceasing* prayer rising upward like the slow swirling smoke from a fire circle burning in the desert.

## ❖ NAHODISHGISH: A PLACE TO BE LEFT ALONE
*December 31, 2016*

On Wednesday, December 28, 2016, President Barack Obama established the Bears Ears National Monument. Not only is this a beautiful gesture in the name of protecting 1.35 million acres of red rock desert through the Antiquities Act, but the opening paragraph of the proclamation is a beautiful description of the land itself: "Rising from the center of the southeastern Utah landscape and visible from every direction are twin buttes so distinctive that in each of the native languages of the region their name is the same: Bears Ears."

Within this historical document, the reader will find a language more akin to poetry than public policy, well worth reading out loud around a dinner table or campfire. Too often the politics of place obscures the spirit of a place. But the authors of this proclamation have created an evolving narrative of wonder, both human and wild.

Here are two of my favorite passages culled from the document:

> Ancestral Puebloans followed, beginning to occupy the area at least 2,500 years ago, leaving behind items from their

daily life such as baskets, pottery and weapons. These early farmers of Basketmaker II and III and builders of Pueblo I, II and III left their marks on the land. The remains of single-family dwellings, granaries, kivas, towers, and large villages and roads linking them together reveal a complex cultural history. "Moki steps," hand and toe holds carved into steep canyon walls by the Ancestral Puebloans, illustrate the early people's ingenuity and perseverance and are still used today to access dwellings along cliff walls.

From earth to sky, the region is unsurpassed in wonders. The star-filled nights and natural quiet of the Bears Ears area transport visitors to an earlier eon. Against an absolutely black night sky, our galaxy and others more distant leap into view. As one of the most intact and least roaded areas in the contiguous United States, Bears Ears has that rare and arresting quality of deafening silence.

What follows these evocative scenes of people in place is a stunning litany of plants and animals that inhabit the Bears Ears region. Call it a poetics of place, a natural history in which each tree, each plant, and each creature is named with reverence and respect.

Consider this liturgy of wildflowers:

The alcove columbine and cave primrose . . . grow in seeps and hanging gardens in the Bears Ears landscape. Wild-flowers such as beardtongue, evening primrose, aster, Indian paintbrush, yellow and purple beeflower, straight bladder-pod, Durango tumble mustard, scarlet gilia, globe mallow, sand verbena, sego lily, cliffrose, sacred datura, monkey flower, sunflower, prince's plume, hedgehog cactus and columbine bring bursts of color to the landscape.

I bring these details of language to the foreground because this kind of care on the page creates compassion for a living, breathing world that is often unnoticed or dismissed. The anonymous authors of this presidential declaration believed in the power of the word, just as President Obama has given us the word of law that these precious, vulnerable, enduring lands in southeastern Utah deserve our highest protection.

Nothing is forgotten in this proclamation. It reads as its own creation story.

At a time when politics is so rancorous, so partisan, so blatantly tied to special interests, especially in the American West, where what is valued is what can be sold, the designation of Bears Ears National Monument signifies a grace note in the centennial year of the National Park Service.

America's national parks and monuments are our inheritance, not what we own but what has been passed on to us by those who believed that through generosity and love, a committment to care would continue.

The U.S. government listened to the leadership of Native Peoples. They heard the voices of the Navajo, the Ute Nations, the Hopi, and the Zuni, members of the Bears Ears Inter-Tribal Coalition who asked for the protection of their ancestral lands to both honor the graves of the Ancient Ones and ensure the collection of medicinal plants, that they might continue the sacred nature of their ceremonies for future generations. Traditional knowledge in partnership with scientific knowledge allows us to work together with the richness of our diversity of views instead of being divided by them.

We can all celebrate this triumph with the tribes as fellow residents of the Colorado Plateau. We can honor the abundance of life beneath a night sky of stars that has arched over these erosional landscapes for eons. It is this eternal beauty, timeless and transcendent, that can temper the malfeasance of small-minded politicians who threaten to undo what has already been done. "In Beauty it is finished," says the Navajo Blessingway.

The evolutionary story of wonder has been written and revised as an ongoing narrative of change in a world much larger than ourselves. The eloquent proclamation of Bears Ears National Monument reminds us what Native People have never forgotten: we belong here with all other beings who are rooted in Earth.

## ◈ WILL BEARS EARS BECOME THE NEXT STANDING ROCK?

*May 6, 2017*

After seven years of organizing, the Bears Ears Inter-Tribal Coalition—made up of the Hopi, Navajo, Uintah and Ouray Ute, Ute Mountain Ute, and Zuni Nations—played a key role in securing the protection of 1.35 million acres surrounding Bears Ears from development and resource extraction just before President Obama left office.

But in our climate of political myopia, one of President Trump's first political acts was to order the Interior Department to review the size and scope of national monuments larger than one hundred thousand acres created since 1996. He complained that these designations "unilaterally put millions of acres of land and water under strict federal control," called them a "massive federal land grab," and directed Interior Secretary Ryan Zinke to review and reverse some of them.

There is a subtext here, as his order made clear. Monument designations, the document said, can "create barriers to achieving energy independence" and "otherwise curtail economic growth." Among the likely beneficiaries of any reversals are the oil and gas industries, mining and logging interests, and commercial development.

In issuing this order, President Trump—who has never visited Bears Ears—apparently chose to listen to the bellicose politicians of Utah and do the bidding of Senator Orrin Hatch and Representatives Rob Bishop and Jason Chaffetz, who complained that Utahns had been cut out of the process. Call that another alternative fact. The lawmakers claim it was an endgame move by the departing President Obama to create a "midnight monument."

The truth is, the establishment of Bears Ears National Monument was a healing moment of historic importance. A unique agreement was reached between Indian tribes and the United States government for a collaborative approach to the management of Bears Ears. It was a clasp of hands across history. It was also about America looking into the deep future rather than into the narrow exhaust pipe of today. It was about drilling for hope and dignity, rather than fossil fuels.

But now Bears Ears could very well become another kind of Standing Rock in both desecration and resistance—not in the sense of fighting back through an encampment that spurred violence from the police, but rather a quieter resistance, more spiritual than political. Bears Ears, like Standing Rock, is another example of a new colonialism, with the government bulldozing Indian sovereignty and privileging Big Oil. "If the Trump administration moves forward with their interests, they are taking us backward 100 years, rupturing trust once again between the federal government and Indian people," Regina Lopez-Whiteskunk, a former councilwoman from the Ute Mountain Ute Tribe, said.

No president has ever attempted to abolish a national monument, and it is unclear whether a president has the power to do so without Congress. And no president in the last half century has reduced the size of a monument. If President Trump rescinds or radically reduces Bears Ears, this will be a historic first and will inevitably be disputed in the federal courts.

Bears Ears is a cradle of Native American history. Far from creating a "midnight monument" willed into existence at the slash of a presidential pen, the Obama designation provides these sacred lands with the protection that has long been in the prayers and dreams of tribal leaders.

"Bears Ears is all about Indian sovereignty," said Russell Begaye, the president of the Navajo Nation. The removal of one square inch from Bears Ears National Monument will be seen as an assault on the home ground of Native Americans in the American Southwest, a disrespect for their ceremonial lives and the traditional knowledge of their ancestors. Hundreds of thousands of artifacts are buried in the serpentine canyons and shifting pink sands of Cedar Mesa, hidden, until exposed by rain or wind or theft. The desecration of Indian graves has prompted FBI raids and convictions.

But it's not just about local desecration. So much of the American West these days is under threat of development and fossil fuel extraction. Our very sense of wildness and wilderness is at stake, from Grand Staircase–Escalante National Monument in Utah to the Organ Mountains–Desert Peaks in New Mexico.

"This is a war on our public lands," said Senator Tom Udall, Democrat of New Mexico.

"We are not just protecting these lands for our people, but all people," Jonah Yellowman said.

As a Utahn, I have spent considerable time in the pinyon-juniper-laced mesas and sandstone canyons of Bears Ears. This is a landscape of immense power where ancient handprints left on red rock walls are a reminder of who came before us and who will follow.

If President Trump is successful in rescinding Bears Ears National Monument, it will be a breach of faith with our future and our past. One park or monument at risk means all are at risk. Pick yours: Yellowstone, Yosemite, Grand Canyon, Big Bend, Acadia. The federal Bureau of Land Management has proposed issuing oil and gas leases just outside Zion National Park, one of the nation's most visited parks. Forty national parks are vulnerable to oil and gas extraction.

A portrait of Andrew Jackson has been newly hung in the Oval Office over Donald Trump's shoulder at his request. The portrait might remind our forty-fifth president of how Jackson signed the 1830 Indian Removal Act, which lit the match to America's criminal treatment of Native People. The Trail of Tears is just part of Jackson's legacy. His face still remains on the twenty-dollar bill—fitting perhaps, since so much of the battle over land is the battle over the dollar.

No amount of money is a substitute for beauty. No amount of political power can match the power of the land and what the indigenous people who live here know. If we do not rise to the defense of these sacred lands, Bears Ears National Monument will be reduced to oil rigs and derricks, shining bright against an oiled sky of obliterated stars.

It is 2155; the Colorado River is now an ephemeral river that runs only in the spring due to the aridification of the American Southwest. "Drought" is too kind a word for where we are now.

Canyonlands National Park has been left alone and remains a geologic park, though it's accessible only by enclosed viewing stations at Island in the Sky and the Needles Overlook that are cooled by solar power. It is too hot to descend into the canyons below. Travel by car or bus is prohibited. The roads are closed, historical scars reminiscent of a time when the world was fueled by gasoline and people drove cars without thinking. The relentless heat has buckled and cracked the pavement. Entry by foot is rare, though some remaining Desert Mothers and Fathers make their yearly pilgrimages to Druid Arch at their own peril, driven by the force of their religious convictions.

Virtual reality goggles are provided at the lookout stations where hardy visitors, many of whom knew these erosional parks as children or from the cherished photographs of their ancestors, come to remember when these red rock landscapes were places of inspiration and a desert ecology blossomed each year. No longer; the land can't support much life at all. The goggles repopulate the barren landscape with the plants and animals that once lived in this high desert: sage, chamisa, blackbrush, brittlebush, globe mallow, primrose, yucca, prickly pear, and willows. Cottonwood trees redrawn along the mighty Colorado draw gasps. Ringtails, mountain lions, and mule deer also inspire awe.

The travelers leave the virtual and look out over the real: Ravens can still be seen (tricksters that they are) in the red rock chasms lifted up by afternoon thermals. A few reptiles remain, eating scattered insects—among them collared lizards, whiptails, and rattlesnakes, which are adapting to a more meager diet and whose dry desert rattles can now be heard more as a haunting than a warning.

Canyonlands National Park is staffed by robots who have been programmed to tell the geologic story of Canyonlands and the story of the life that once flourished here. They look like their human counterparts of past decades, in the gray-and-green uniforms and stiff brimmed hats. The difference is they can withstand the extreme temperatures of well above 120 degrees Fahrenheit and do not need water, now rationed among the few residents who manage to live nearby.

"There have been two great exoduses in the Colorado Plateau," the robot says. "One in the Holocene, led by the pre-Puebloan people, and the other in the Anthropocene, which is occurring now. Climate refugees are retreating not only from the rising seas on the East and West Coasts of the United States of America, but from the rising heat in the Desert Southwest. America's National Relocation Parks scattered throughout the Midwest and Great Lakes region are sites for internal migration as the Great Escape continues. In this new era of climate conformation, we are learning to adapt to the conditions we once denied."

The national park robot turns to the visitors: "I invite you to step outside briefly and feel the burning beauty uninhabitable now to most species."

## *I. Yunnan Province, China*

The temple keeper stepped out of the small room into the opening where a fountain rose from the middle of the terrace. He was dressed in saffron robes and his name was Daniel. It had been his voice we heard chanting above the river.

He walked to us. Brooke stood. I barely looked up from the bench where I was sitting. The temple keeper put his hands on mine. He spoke slowly, deliberately. Aaron, our guide, native to this area, translated, "He says this happens sometimes, women lose the excess of all they are carrying. He said this place has powers that can overtake people, but that you will be fine."

At this point, I was so sick—having shit my guts out and thrown up everything I had eaten for days—I didn't care about explanations, I just wanted relief. Empty and aching on the verge of delirium, the outback of China was not where I wanted to be.

Daniel spoke again.

"He said that he is going to get a vial of medicine for you to drink."

The temple keeper turned and disappeared back into his

quarters. I was lying on Brooke's lap, looking up at the precipice required to climb up in order to get out. Whatever I had been carrying from the rim of the canyon, I had lost: especially, the illusory mind that believes we are more than our biology.

Earlier that morning, Aaron had prepared ti kuan yin tea for the three of us beneath the pavilion that overlooked the Shaxi Village located on the Tea Horse Road. Ti kuan yin is one of the most elegant of Chinese oolong teas, known for its floral quality akin to the scent of orchids. It is associated with Kwan Yin, the Tibetan goddess of mercy, who stands on the edge of Erhai Lake in the town of Dali in China's Yunnan Province.

Our journey from Dali had become a vertical dreamscape into remote mountainous terrain reminiscent of the Kaibab Plateau near the Grand Canyon in Arizona, thick with ponderosa pines anchored in red soil. I felt at home until we saw monkeys.

Our descent into this canyon promised to take us to seventeen stone grottoes devoted to the goddess of mercy built in the Tang and Song dynasties, from the eighth century to the eleventh century. I think about mercy, a word I seldom use, a word I would do well to embody, *a disposition to be kind and forgiving; compassion or forbearance, especially shown to an offender.*

This place was made known to me by a whisper from a young woman I met in Shanghai. She told me I must see the shrine of Ayang Bai devoted to the Divine Feminine, a holy pilgrimage made by women for thousands of years, where they made their prayers known to the goddess.

After tea, we set out on foot, crossing the threshold marked by a three-tiered sandstone arch—I stopped and had to remind myself where we were. Aaron and Brooke had hurried down the trail.

I was walking slowly, deliberately, noticing small details:

the slight drop in temperature, the music of wind between the pines, the offerings of bundled sticks placed on eroding hillsides by those also making this pilgrimage. I had begun to feel queasy, light-headed, unstable on my feet, but kept walking, trying to breathe in the freshness. My stomach was being ambushed. I ignored my body until it had doubled over in a knife-blade-sharp pain followed by a violent release; there is no denying the flesh. I would walk a few feet then heave—walk down another switch-back and squat in the trees. Brooke was far ahead. I just kept trying to take in where I was, the red rocks, the pines, the jays, the familiarity of the land, until the hand wrapping of sticks placed purposefully at bridges, or at the base of selected trees, turned sinister. Becoming weaker and weaker, I feared the territory I was in and its insistence that I pay attention, as its gravitational force kept drawing me down to my knees.

The temple keeper returned with the potion. I sat up. He talked to Aaron. Aaron nodded his head and spoke to Brooke: "She needs to drink this. She will become unconscious and sleep for some time. When she wakes up, she will be fine."

I looked at Daniel and said, "Thank you." He gave me the drink. The vial felt like a mercy as I held it and thought of my father's anger should I die far from home, doubting if sorrow would ever reach him from this distance. I didn't care. I drank whatever was in the vial—horribly bitter—and that is all I remember.

The steep stairs carved into the side of the mountain were no longer an obstacle, but a rising toward fate. I could feel the footsteps of women before me and behind me through the millennia urging me upward. Whatever the temple keeper had given me reached me as an elixir. Miracle or medicine, it didn't matter. I was back in my body upright and walking. We bypassed dozens of small grottoes, stone niches dripping with ferns that framed the intricately carved deities shadowed inside. They captured my peripheral vision as we climbed quickly to the top of the mountain—Brooke worried that my energy would wane. Close to the large horizontal grotto we paused, caught our breath, and prepared ourselves to enter the shrine of the goddess.

Aaron, Brooke, and I looked over our shoulders across the vast ravine to the other side of the canyon. My western eyes saw wilderness, but that was another illusion.

The afternoon light intensified. We ducked inside the cave. There she was—Avalokiteshvara—illuminated in the female form. The goddess of mercy was meticulously carved into the sandstone wall with a turquoise aura painted around her. I judged her to be twelve feet tall, but that could have been the measure of my awe. The Buddhist text the Lotus Sutra describes Avalokiteshvara as "a bodhisattva who can take any form. She can be male, female, adult, child, elderly, human, non-human, in order to teach the Dharma." A shape-shifter, she is also known as Kwan Yin, and she emerged before us as a flaming vision of both disruption and compassion. I wished my mother and grandmothers were here with me to witness the heat of her presence. A small rectangular niche appeared in the center of her chest where her heart should reside. Brooke and Aaron speculated over why the empty space. I could not listen to their chatter. My eyes flashed a simmering impatience and they left.

Kwan Yin's right hand was raised upward with palm closed at shoulder height; her left hand protected a bowl resting on her lap. I raised my heels to look inside the bowl—it held her heart. I wept over what every woman knows. We give away our hearts daily. What remains is emptiness.

Stone-carved curtains (like those often seen in theaters) scalloped above the goddess, then hung down on either side of her, giving the appearance that Kwan Yin's secrets had just been revealed. The goddess sat on her throne against the blackened wall of the grotto. She was flanked by two attendants: one held a box, the other a water vessel. Her eyes looked beyond me, nothing personal, to the view across the valley. She cast her gaze toward the sandstone cliffs where a large stone stood erect in the presence of towering pines rooted in pink sand. Birdsong became her voice.

I stared at Kwan Yin until I was too weak to stand, and sat on the cold floor of the grotto feeling the longing and desires, the pain and the power of all the women who had walked here. I felt the power of my own ancestors who had walked the path of heartlessness.

I paid my respects to the goddess—lowered my head—then climbed the necessary steps and exited the cave.

The rock wall on my immediate right caught my attention. Inside a large hollowed niche was a vagina, approximately three feet tall, carved out of black stone poised on a pedestal. It appeared as a smooth oblong mountain standing upright with a slit running down the center. Here were the lips of the Divine Feminine, from which all things are born—the site of our emergence—set apart, exposed, swollen, and wet, consciously oiled by the hands of pilgrims so it remains perpetually moist. What my friend from Dali had whispered in my ear weeks ago, I was now witnessing. Pure feminine power. I knelt on the carved lotus pillow at its base and prayed.

I prayed for strength to remain open and receptive.

I prayed to love and be loved in all its manifestations.

I prayed to be generous, to give and receive.

I prayed for the forgiveness of those I have harmed.

I prayed that I might survive my griefs and express my gratitude.

I prayed to honor differences, while seeking unity.

I prayed for discernment, to praise what is beautiful and to sanctify what is not.

I prayed for the poor and I prayed for the lonely.

I prayed for the health and wholeness of all beings, human and wild.

I prayed for my body and the body of Earth, believing we are One.

I prayed for arousal that leads us to birth.

I prayed for rain in times of drought.

I prayed for mothers in their times of need as they meet the needs of others.

I prayed for each woman, whose heart has been ripped from her chest through sorrow and love, through violence and abuse, through forgiveness and grace.

I prayed for the wisdom that rises within us when we no longer bleed.

I prayed to the Divine Feminine upon which our consciousness depends.

I prayed for courage that we might face what is coming.

Two guardian deities stood outside on either side of the yoni, both of them in the act of charming snakes, one with her mouth open, one with her mouth closed. This was not Eve being seduced by Satan. This was knowing how to handle skillfully that which threatens to kill us.

What has threatened to kill me is the patriarchy, not because there are men in power, but because patriarchy is an institution. Institutions have no heart. They have agendas, self-serving mythologies delivered through religion, politics, business, and every other hierarchical bastion of influence that subjugates the poor, the marginalized, the disenfranchised—largely, women and children.

The patriarchy replicates itself in order to protect its interests: power in the form of control and commerce. Hoarding power is hoarding fear. Scarcity rules. Sharing power is a belief in what the next generation knows and that it will benefit a sustaining view of the future. This is an evolving consciousness that transcends the individual, and fosters the many. Perhaps this is the subversive stance Kwan Yin is demonstrating in the Shibaoshan grotto. In Japan, Kwan Yin is male. In China, he is transformed into female. The space of compassion remains open and infinite as she shares her love with others. In this clarity and paradox, her power is her emptiness. She offers her heart, which she alone placed inside her bowl, realizing what feeds her. She gives others a chance to replicate not the withholding of power but the regeneration of power through love.

These stone statues have survived thousands of years. They know something through the visitations of women who have emptied themselves in order to stand before them and be filled again by all they have lost. My friend from Dali told me that the Bai women, indigenous to this part of China, make their annual pilgrimages by bringing not only their dreams and aspirations, but their griefs and transgressions. They lay their blessings and burdens at the feet of the goddess and make offerings to the yoni. They bring oils and lubricate the stone lips in a gesture of assurance that life will continue even in the presence of death. The women run their oiled fingers and hands down the slit that has pleasured them, hurt them, ruined them, and seen them split open again and again by those they loved; they smother the widening crack with oil, acknowledging that this is the treacherous threshold each of us has had to cross in order to live and breathe our way, and the future of humanity, into being.

And I can imagine that as each woman touches the yoni, she feels the river of her own desires swell—leaving her in a state of wanting.

Our origin stories begin here.

No wonder I'd had to purge myself, trust a male gatekeeper, risk death, and awaken in order to come to this place of beginnings sculpted in stone. I walked back up the canyon past the stick offerings, mindful of the pink sand at home and the pink sand here in this remote part of China. The bridge between these two landscapes is sensation, what my body holds, what my body feels, and what my body remembers. I picked up my pace to meet Brooke and Aaron on top of Shibaoshan Mountain, where they were experiencing a different view of where we had been.

## II. The True and the Real
JUNE 20, 2014
*The Salt Lake Tribune*
Opinion Piece

I stand in solidarity with Kate Kelly and her plea to grant women equal standing in the rights, responsibilities, and privileges of the Church of Jesus Christ of Latter-day Saints, including the right to hold the priesthood.

Revelations occur. Whereas polygamy was once sanctioned through revelation, now it is not. Whereas African Americans were told they could not hold the priesthood, now they do. Doctrines that denied dignity or defied the rights of law to individuals within the LDS Church have changed through modern-day revelation.

The time has come to shift the religious inequality toward women and allow sisters to lead alongside their brothers in prayer and power and purpose.

For the Mormon Church to continue to preserve this spiritual patrimony is to affirm its organizational misogyny. Why is it apostasy to ask for half of its membership to have equal power under God? Why is a vision to ordain women worthy of disciplinary action and excommunication, when twelve-year-old boys are "given" the priesthood? Why are men and women not equal under God's eyes?

This kind of governance should not be tolerated. And it should not be tolerated by those of us who are members of the Church of Jesus Christ of Latter-day Saints.

The question must be asked: What are you afraid of?

In 1977, I watched the Mormon church undermine the passage of the Equal Rights Amendment in Salt Lake City. It is a well-known and documented story. And in 1979, I watched Sonia Johnson similarly demonized and disciplined, ironically, by her local congregation in Virginia, as well, for speaking out for the rights of women, which led to her excommunication. And in 1993, I witnessed Professor Cecilia Konchar Farr exercise her voice concerning violence against women at Brigham Young University, and when she spoke out on behalf of a woman's right to choose to have an abortion, I watched her charged with "violating her responsibilities as a university citizen" and accused of "undermining the faith of her students." She did not pass her three-year review and was denied her teaching contract.

At this same time, the historian Laurel Thatcher Ulrich,

Pulitzer Prize–winning author and MacArthur Fellow, was rejected by BYU's Board of Trustees as a keynote speaker at BYU's Women's Conference. Was it because Ulrich was a founding member of *Exponent II*, a feminist journal for Mormon women? The year 1993 was also the year of "The September Six" excommunications. Six Mormon scholars, half of them feminists, were excommunicated for raising questions of sexism, homophobia, and intellectual inconsistencies within LDS religious doctrine.

This is our history. I thought the era of retribution was behind us. Apparently not. Kate Kelly speaks for all of us within the LDS Church who care about an equality of power for women—active members and dissident members like me—men and women, both—who believe there is no difference in the spiritual aspirations between men and women, gay, straight, or transgender. Each of us are the creators of the world we wish to live in, with equal power, equal voice, and equal opportunities beyond the womb.

At a time when sexual assault, rape, and repeated acts of violence against women are under public scrutiny and part of the public conversation that is happening around the world, the Mormon church's ongoing policy to withhold ordination from women is its own act of violence.

Before my mother died, she faced her young granddaughters and said, "I pray that one day you, too, will hold the priesthood."

I believe my mother's voice was prophetic, delivered with love and wise intention. Kate Kelly is delivering this intention now and it is not without the labor pains of a movement with momentum. I do not believe Kate Kelly should be disciplined for her vision of women ordained. Nor do I believe she should be excommunicated for exercising her voice in public. Her disciplinary hearing, set in Virginia, where she no longer resides, is another attempt to silence women by a world religion run by men.

Behind Kate Kelly and Ordain Women, there is a long lineage of women, old and young and in between, not interested in asking for permission or hoping for a revelation from above, but rather, ready and willing to carry this vision forward in prayer and in action, for the simple reason that it is time. This is not an act of apostasy, but an act of self-respect, and a belief that the Church of Jesus Christ of Latter-day Saints will honor its sisters of faith, not punish them.

TERRY TEMPEST WILLIAMS
*Castle Valley, Utah*

## III. Transformation

NOVEMBER 23, 2018
Castle Valley, Utah

We are eroding and evolving, at once. Let this be my mantra to be repeated daily. What if beauty dwells in the margins of our undoing and remaking? Why do men continue to be the gatekeepers of our bodies and spiritual life, even those who stand with us? What will happen if the patriarchy and the Divine Feminine continue to be in conflict with one another, as we witnessed in the hearings of Judge Brett Kavanaugh and the testimony of Professor Christine Blasey Ford as she shared her story of being sexually assaulted by him? What if confirmation in today's world simply means the patriarchy wins? What if the #MeToo movement is the beginning of redefining love, energy, and power? Can self-love and self-respect become love and respect for the planet?

Kwan Yin, the goddess of mercy, sits in a grotto in China

holding her heart inside a bowl ready to give it away; Kate Kelly in Utah calls for women to have parity with men, so that the power of the priesthood within the Mormon Church becomes a power shared in co-creation; and the priest and scientist Teilhard de Chardin sees the evolution of the Earth in partnership with the evolution of consciousness. This he names "Christogenesis," where Jesus becomes the catalyst for a spiritual evolution tied to the act of becoming. We begin to see a changing paradigm based on the regeneration of love, not power—but still I question our human exceptionalism.

*Is Earth not enough?*

I need these words tattooed between my shoulders so heaven can read them burned into my skin when I lie on the ground breathing in sage and listening to the ravens flying over me.

Jesus Christ is my brother, not a god, this is the heart of the matter.

In the desert, I inhale the dust of the cosmos and try to exhale my ego. I am not the center of the universe; I am part of an expanding consciousness becoming conscious of itself in relationship to everything else. I do not fear excommunication from anything save the pink sand beneath my feet and a night sky of stars penetrating darkness.

There is a different way of knowing the world and I believe it begins with the Encounter. The thirteenth-century Japanese Buddhist monk Shinran, who founded the Pure Land School of Buddhism, speaks of a practice as not something we do, but rather something we become—a practice allows us to become more of who we are.

What is my practice? I believe in the practice of Encounter.

I encountered Kwan Yin and in that meeting encountered myself. The empty space where her heart once was became my own emptiness. A beautiful rupture. A rupture not only acknowledged but seen and felt as a severance from my true nature. I was born into a religion foreign to my soul. It cut out my heart. Kwan Yin handed my heart back to me. Something happened. The stone bowl held in Kwan Yin's hands became a sound bowl struck by my own desire and longing in one clear reverberating note: Love.

Whatever I know as a woman about spirituality I have learned from my body encountering Earth. Soul and soil are not separate. Neither are wind and spirit, nor water and tears. We are eroding and evolving, at once, like the red rock landscape before me. Our grief is our love. Our love will be our undoing as we quietly disengage from the collective madness of the patriarchal mind that says aggression is the way forward.

One night, I watched the full moon rise over Adobe Mesa with friends from the vantage point of our home. The moon slowly rose higher and brighter until its light created shadows on the stone patio. We turned and faced our shadows, inviting them to dance with us, while the willow's shadows also swayed, as we swung our arms above our heads, our bodies moving joyously together.

The Divine Feminine is not a mystical presence outside us, but an embodied presence within us made of flesh and bones, xylem and phloem, fur and scales, inhabiting every inch of this planet we call home. Humility is the way. Evolution is the path. Revolution is coming as our wellspring of desires finally meets Earth on its own geologic terms. We are eroding. We are evolving. This is my mantra. The time has come to stop seeing ourselves as saviors and instead see ourselves as human beings on a burning globe capable of acknowledging the harm we have caused. Do we dare to hold our severed hearts in our hands as both an offering and a sacrifice in the name of all that is now required?

October 3, 2017
My Dear Father:

I am sitting in my office at the Harvard Divinity School, listening to the tolling of bells, sixty bells ringing in remembrance of the fifty-nine individuals slain in Las Vegas and the one gunman who killed them and himself in a singular act of violence.

Why? How? And what are we to make of this, one man in two hotel rooms with an arsenal of guns, perched on the thirty-second floor like a sniper, with an automatic weapon, picking off random individuals in a mass slaughtering. And then he turned the violence on himself. We will never know his story, his motive, his focus and fury.

What I think we do know, Dad, is the context and contrast in our own family. I think of Rich, your brother, my uncle, and all the gun shows in Vegas and beyond that he has attended. He is a collector of guns who values their craftsmanship, and he appreciates their stories. He makes a distinction between "brown" guns and "black" guns, the latter being another name for assault weapons. He is a serious hobbyist and a hunter who both loves animals and turns his rifle, his sharp eye looking through the crosshairs in his scope, on elk, deer, bison, prong-horn, prairie dogs, rabbits, and coyotes.

I think of him on the border of Mexico as a Minuteman securing America's border. I think of the material passed out at these gun shows rooted in a distrust of our government, the belief not only in the Second Amendment but in the religion of violence.

I love Rich. Deeply. He is a man of integrity and intelligence and is tender to those he loves. He believes in God and honors his Mormon. He is an adamant supporter of Donald Trump. How? Why? This I do not understand, and yet we have always gotten along. You were raised in the same home, by the same mother and father. You served our country. You have been a hunter. You gave me a pearl-handled pistol after I wrote *Refuge*, to protect myself. You have since laid down your guns. You have left your home-ground religion, as I have. You do not follow Trump. Your spiritual beliefs are your own. I want to know what you believe, dear Father, so I may better know my own beliefs and how a change of mind occurs.

Simone Weil writes, "It is not my fault if I believe I owe it to you to keep you informed of what I am thinking." I am thinking that the gunman, and every shooter who has entered a school, a shopping mall, a church, is not someone other than ourselves. I believe that whatever one human being is capable of doing, I am capable of doing also. I am asking myself: What kind of violence am I perpetrating on this planet? What kind of shadowed self am I harboring as I project my goodness on the world? This is what terrifies me. We are ultimately animals belonging to the same species. And it feels as if we may be going mad.

Every day, I feel the barrage of bullets I am trying to duck—the hate speech coming out of the White House; the injustices perpetrated repeatedly against black people, brown people, and

Native People; and the war being waged against wildlife and our public lands. These bullets are made of words that are wounding all of us; I feel them wounding me, killing my concentration, murdering my sensibilities as a writer trying to use the same letters to make words that might create beauty, not ugliness. How can the same language bear such different intentions? Or does it? Maybe my words and the words of our president are both trying to convince the other that our way is right.

We each are the authors of our own certitude.

Again, I turn to the words of Simone Weil: "I thought that the life leading to this good is not only defined by a code of morals common to all, but that for each one it consists of a succession of acts and events strictly personal to him." I am asking myself, Father, what is my "code of morals"? And in the end, can it be considered as an embrace of manners—how we treat one another—how we listen and respect one another, even acknowledging the dignity and rights of other species?

"There are two languages that are quite distinct although made up of the same words; there is the collective language and there is the individual language," Weil writes. What is the language of God? What is the language of Earth? What were the last words spoken by the gunman in Vegas? What is the individual language of our president when he flies back to the White House from witnessing the suffering of Puerto Ricans? What is my language to my own brother, who is suffering his own emotional and mental hurricane? How are we all connected?

This is what I am thinking, Dad, here in my office, having just finished reading *Waiting for God*. Simone Weil is writing my mind, my wounded mind, and addresses "a certain time of oscillation." These words move me and I want to share them with you:

*It is in affliction itself that the splendor of God's mercy shines, from its very depths, in the heart of its inconsolable bitterness. If still persevering in our love, we fall to the point where the soul cannot keep back the cry "My God, why hast thou forsaken me?" If we remain at this point without ceasing to love, we end by touching something that is not affliction, not joy, something that is the central essence, necessary and pure, something not of the sense, common to joy and sorrow: the very love of God.*

*We know then that joy is the sweetness of contact with the love of God, that affliction is the wound of this same contact when it is painful, and that only the contact matters, not the manner of it.*

I love you, Dad. I miss our contact, seeing your eyes and feeling your arms around me. Settled in Cambridge, Massachusetts, far from the Rocky Mountain spine of the American West that holds the Wasatch, the Tetons, and Castleton Tower upright, I feel I am in exile from all that gives me standing: the land, the mountains, the desert, our family. And yet, I am drinking more deeply from the fountain of knowledge and inspiration than I have ever known, and so I look at my two hands—the hand of being uprooted and the hand that is touching light—and I am learning to bring them together in prayer.

My attention to the world is increasing. My humility is shattering my former self. I know nothing, Father, except what I love. I love you. Please write me your heart.

Your seeking daughter,

Terry

◆

October 8, 2017

Dearest Father:

Here is the truth: I miss the American West terribly, so much so that the other day as I sat down to make a grocery list it somehow morphed into an accounting of all the things I long for at home in the desert.

Here is my list:

1. Sage
2. Meadowlark
3. Collard Lizard
4. Sandstone
5. A Night Sky of Stars
6. Wind
7. Rain
8. Heat Waves
9. Lightning
10. Clouds
11. Coyote
12. Water
13. Moon
14. Jackrabbit
15. Antelope Squirrel
16. Mule Deer
17. Turkey Vulture
18. Arrowhead
19. Handprints on Slickrock Walls
20. Ringtails
21. Great Horned Owl
22. Raven
23. Cottontail
24. Globe Mallow

25. Mountain Lion
26. Sand
27. Bone
28. Stones
29. Juniper
30. Pinyon
31. Rainbows
32. Turquoise
33. Bluebirds
34. Black Widow Spiders
35. The Smell of Rain in the Desert
36. The Colorado River Running Red
37. Milk

"Love has made me the gift of affliction," writes Simone Weil. I am an affliction of my love for the desert, Dad, not any desert but the red rock desert of southern Utah, the same desert that is now under siege as Zinke sets his intention on paper to reduce Bears Ears by half. As you well know, Governor Herbert and the Utah Congressional Delegation advocate for a 90 percent reduction of Bears Ears, with Grand Staircase–Escalante National Monument becoming three small postage stamp–size monuments.

As much as I am loving being in Cambridge and studying at the Divinity School, I also feel estranged from my Mother Country that nurtures me. Here is one truth: I have never felt more alive intellectually, and spiritually engaged. Here is another: My soul feels diminished by not smelling the sweetness of sage after a rainstorm. And there is a third thing: I am enlivened by both communities. These are not complaints, only the awareness, dear Father, that I am braiding these truths together into a life I understand is very privileged.

To be rooted is perhaps the most important and least recognized need of the human soul.

—SIMONE WEIL

Uprooted. This is my spiritual reckoning. I know in our last phone conversation you said you were worried about me, that I was thinking too much. But this feels like the right time to interrogate and explore my loyalties, ask myself what my responsibilities and obligations are, and to whom. All I understand now is the power of change. Perhaps one day I will find my personal prayer that will call me home to become a true contemplative in the desert.

Simone Weil found a prayer and a path to God through George Herbert's poem "Love." Here it is—perhaps you can share this with Jan and read it together:

Love
Love bade me welcome; yet my soul drew back,
    Guilty of dust and sin.
But quick-eyed Love, observing me grow slack
    From my first entrance in,
Drew nearer to me, sweetly questioning
    If I lack'd anything.

"A guest," I answer'd, "worthy to be here":
    Love said, "You shall be he."
"I, the unkind, ungrateful? Ah, my dear,
    I cannot look on Thee."
Love took my hand and smiling did reply,
    "Who made the eyes but I?"

"Truth, Lord; but I have marr'd them: let my shame
    Go where it doth deserve."

"And know you not," says Love, "who bore the blame?"
"My dear, then I will serve."
"You must sit down," says Love, "and taste my meat."
So I did sit and eat.

What I believe in, Dad, is Love. For me, wherever I feel and find Love and Beauty, there I find "God." If I am honest, this is what I am in the service of. These have been my markers that have led me to action. If we follow our heart's path of unconditional love and service in the name of Beauty, we will be on a path toward God on Earth, with no need for heaven. It is right here, right now.

I know you would add work. I hope you are smiling.

Thank you for reading my wanderings in each of these letters. It feels good to be in conversation with you. I miss you and cherish the relationship that is ours. When we are in close proximity, there is no need to discuss these ideas—Love and Beauty is felt in the chaos, heartbreak, and intimacy of family; or in the dazzling moment of the solar eclipse we shared in August. Away, here in Cambridge, I want you to know what I am thinking, because this is the mental landscape I am inhabiting now.

Arms around you. I hope you and Jan can make it up to the Tetons before the aspens lose their gilded leaves. The last bull elk must be rounding up his harem for the season. If I close my eyes, I can hear them bugling against a crisp star-struck night in Lupine Meadows.

I love you, Dad. I am so happy to hear that you and Hank, Brooke and Rex, all had dinner last night. Please give Dan my love when you see him.

Always,
Terry

❖

October 15, 2017

Dearest Father:

The weekends have become our time for retreat. Because the distances in the Northeast are small in comparison to where we come from, five hours north, south, or west feel like nothing but a welcome stretch for the eyes. Each Saturday and Sunday, we find ourselves in wild nature, be it Maine or Cape Cod or the Catskills, which is where I find myself today. (As you know, Brooke is in Castle Valley, so he did not go with me.)

Doug Peacock's son, Colin, married his longtime sweetheart, Dena Adler. Her family is from New York. Her father is a financial wizard, the polar opposite of our beloved Douglas Arapahoe Peacock, with his embrace of bears.

A four-hour drive from Cambridge delivered me in a glory of autumn foliage in the midst of a landscape that feels more remote than it actually is. Although the mountains are not sharp-edged granite crags so familiar to us in the Tetons or the Wasatch or the Sierras, the mountains in New England carry their own impressive weight as massive wooded fortresses like Katahdin rising from Baxter State Park in Maine or the Green and White Mountains that create the backbones of Vermont and New Hampshire, or in this case, the Catskills that provide a dramatic backdrop to the largely progressive hamlet of Woodstock, New York.

Joy is the sweetness of contrast. I am seeing it now.

Simone Weil is my reading companion once again, as I continue to underline her words. In her beautiful essay "Reflections on the Right Use of School Studies with a View to the Love of God," she writes, "Our deep purpose should aim solely at increasing the power of attention with a view to prayer." And then goes on to say, "Above all it is thus that we can acquire the virtue of humility, and that is a far more precious treasure than all academic progress . . . No knowledge is more to be desired. If we can arrive at knowing this truth with all our souls we shall be well established with the right foundation."

Dad, you have given me this "right foundation," call it a Theology of Mountains. You have walked your prayers up and down western summits, always with a hunger for the long view. This morning, looking up at these red, yellow, and orange draped hills, it gave me a much-needed perspective as to what will survive us in these dark political times. And then, there is always the tenderness of deep friendships like the one Doug and I have shared for more than three decades.

Colin and Dena asked if I would co-officiate their wedding ceremony with a rabbi who was close with Dena's family. It was a beautiful blending of two spiritual views represented by two families. One Jewish, one (shall we say) Earthist.

The rabbi Marsha welcomed everyone beneath the canopy of burnished roses and dahlias. She gave a traditional wedding prayer in Hebrew. I then presented Colin and Dena with a white buckskin pouch that they had filled earlier with the sands and soils from seven sites significant to them, both individually and together: Tucson, Arizona; Central Park, New York; Emigrant, Montana; Amagansett, New York; Moab, Utah; Jackson Hole, Wyoming; Juneau, Alaska. Both the rabbi and I blessed the couple with our guidance and spoke of the gifts we have received from knowing them. I shared my belief that marriage is a spiritual practice that evolves over time. And then the rabbi delivered the "Seven Blessings" in Hebrew, after which I offered my own interpretations. These were mine:

**Blessings**

1. LOVE—May you be blessed with a love that is
   wild, tender, and enduring, honoring each other's
   solitude as well as touching bone.
2. HOME—May your door always be open to
   others—may your table be set with gratitude.
   May you feed your children as you have been
   fed, lovingly, from Earth itself. With candles lit,
   may your home be a source of light.
3. FRIENDSHIP—May the spirit of Coyote continue
   to tease, amuse, and surprise you. May the spirit
   of Raven continue to show you the way, when you
   are together and apart. And may the spirit of Bear
   keep you strong and remind you to respect each
   other always. May Rabbit keep you kind.
4. CURIOSITY, KNOWLEDGE, WISDOM,
   AND GROWTH—May you never forget hunger
   and thirst. May you remain humble in your
   privilege and powers. May you be generous. May
   you stay curious and open.
5. HEALTH—May you cherish the vitality that is
   yours. May you keep your bodies strong even in
   times of illness and pain. May you heal the wounds
   of each other by remembering to listen to what is
   not being said and what is. May your mind, body,
   and spirit be One.
6. COMMUNITY—In community, anything is
   possible. Find it. Build it. Belong.

The rabbi then invited Colin to break a glass (wrapped in
cloth) with his foot, the fragility of life acknowledged.

This ceremony brought me into a circle of hope, Dad, as

I witnessed the integration of beliefs into a beautiful whole. Judaism intermingled with American environmentalism as its own spiritual orientation. I thought of Mimi, who always said "1 + 1 = 3."

Doug offered a "Father's Blessing" by saying, "My children have a heavy workload ahead of them as they work to ameliorate the suffering of climate change around the world. We must carry with us a newfound empathy alongside our love."

And then, we danced.

In *Waiting for God*, Simone Weil says, "It is only necessary to know that love is a direction and not a state of the soul. If one is unaware of this, one falls into despair at the first onslaught of affliction."

You have always taught us, Father, to serve others, to cherish the gift of honorable work, and to recognize this is where our dignity is found. Our work, if we are lucky, sends us in the direction of our destiny. Call it soul work. Doug Peacock is a powerful example of soul work. To think we all met on the trail in Glacier in 1982, as we were hiking hut to hut, what an ongoing blessing.

Weil writes, "He whose soul remains ever turned toward God though the nail pierces it, finds himself nailed to the very center of the universe. It is the true center, it is not the middle; it is beyond space and time, it is God."

Simone Weil inspires me because she belongs to no one and everyone. By that I mean she refused to be baptized in the Catholic Church, even though she considered herself Catholic. She refused to join the Communist Party, even though she believed in protecting the rights of the working class and joined them in their factory work and suffering. She was committed to both piety and revolution, embraced God and the God beyond god, engaged in both contemplative prayer and action—

all the while interrogating justice with her body—well, as you can see, she has become a true heroine of mine. I identify with her because I feel I do not belong to any orthodoxy, nor wish to, and yet, I feel a profound tie and commitment to the life of the Spirit and paying attention to patterns, signs, and synchronicity like cairns in the desert to help us find our way.

I do not know who or what God is, dearest Father. I do not see God as a human-shaped being in white robes and beard as Mormonism promised us. It is far too limiting and restrictive, not to mention bound to the patriarchy. But I do believe in a higher power illustrated in the creativity of the Universe. I believe we are made of stardust.

I believe in a cosmology of care and the sanctity and adaptive intelligence of evolution. I believe in the marriage of our divine nature with all of life and the mysteries that sustain us. If the "Creator" is in fact responsible for the "Creation," is Earth not enough?

Know of my love as I await your response,

Terry

October 20, 2017

Dearest Father:

Greetings from the Lassen Volcanic National Park, seventy-five miles from Redding, California. It is a glory among our public lands, a stark landscape akin to Yellowstone, a ring of volcanic peaks that rivals anything I have ever seen. Mountain passes rising 8,500 feet from sea level and vents of steam rising from hillsides, alongside mud pots. Alpine lakes mirror the sky and I can only imagine the stars that must feel close enough to touch beneath a night sky.

Today I bought my "Senior-Lifetime Pass" for entrance to all national parks and federal recreational lands. Under the current administration it cost me eighty dollars. It only cost you ten dollars when you turned sixty-two under the Clinton administration in 1995. No doubt, the higher costs for all visitors now entering our national parks will prohibit some U.S. citizens from entering these national shrines, which means fewer people to fall in love with these lands that the Trump people are hell-bent on destroying. Forgive my political commentary, but there it is.

A humble and elegant man named Felis Ruis, whom I met recently, agreed to go with me to see Lassen en route to Petaluma. He is from Mexico, and crossed the border twenty-five years ago. He is now an American citizen. We knew driving through the park would be a three-to-four-hour diversion, but worth it.

Still reading and rereading Simone Weil's collection of letters and essays, "Waiting for God," where she talks about how the whole of Christianity is in looking—"a truth that goes almost unrecognized today, is that looking is what saves us"—and she speaks of the "abode of God." Surely, it is here. Felis had never been to a national park before. This was his first. When we stood at the south summit lookout awestruck by the 360-degree view encircling us above the smoke of the Santa Rosa fires where extinct volcanoes pierce the sky, he turned to me and said, "This is the best day of my life." And I knew he meant it.

When we stopped to view Lassen Peak, 10,463 feet above sea level, barren and reverential in its austerity, with its history of fire, the two of us stood alone in the chill of this autumn morning, humbled beyond words. Felis finally said, "It's just Mother Nature, you and me and God." As we drove down the summit, I noticed tears streaming down his cheeks. He said, "Sixteen years ago, I was in a coma unable to move, very close to death, my gallbladder having burst—I am alive today to pay my thanks to God that I am alive to witness his Creation." Then, I began weeping.

"When a soul has attained a love filling the whole universe, indiscriminately, this bird becomes the bird with golden wings that pierces an opening in the egg of the world." I witnessed Felis Ruis with his "golden wings" soar in beauty, Dad. And an opening was created in both of our souls. "Humility is attentive patience," Simone Weil writes. "We are living in times that have no precedent, and in our present situation universality, which could formerly be implicit, has to be fully explicit. It has to permeate our language and the whole of our way of life."

How to love this world? And share it? We must make time, take the time to allow for natural diversions in our day. We have made a cult of busyness and in so doing we have forgotten the simple truth of paying attention to the view before us, between us, in a word, a cultivation of intimacy. "The love of the order and beauty of the world is thus the complement of the love of our neighbor," Simone Weil says. In nature, our intimacy with the land becomes our intimacy with each other. An elemental impulse rises to say, "Isn't this beautiful?" Or as Simone Weil says, "The love of our neighbor in all its fullness simply means being able to say, 'What are you going through?'"

This is what Felis and I shared today, Dad. For the rest of our road trip after we left Lassen Volcanic National Park, we talked about the truths of our lives, including what it means for him to be an immigrant at this moment in time, even though he is an American citizen. He knew every grove of trees that we passed along Route 5: pistachios, walnuts, almonds, peaches, plums, and the burned ground ready for another crop of tomatoes. "This is the work of my people, my family," he said. "I have to know these things." I shared stories of our family and our Mormon background, how Mother's kin fled Utah for Mexico so they could practice polygamy in peace, in Colonia Dublan. I gave him a copy of *The Hour of Land*. And he gave me a window into my heart's greatest conflict: how shall I serve?

Do I continue to teach at Ivy League schools like Dartmouth and Harvard, teaching the privileged and already proven brilliant ones, the ones who will govern, lead, and influence the world—or return home, Dad, and teach at the Salt Lake Community College, where the need is great and so is the potential? Look what it did for Louis. He had never read a book until he walked through their doors as a Rwandan student. Whatever you have given to SLCC, my dearest father, has been more than worth your investment, it has changed lives and I am so grateful for your example to serve where you are rooted, in the ways that you are needed. You knew the value of education and you knew the impact of a practical vocation, not abstract, but real, work done with your hands: shovel, dirt, and pipe. The working man and woman are the backbone of our society.

I was so moved by the students at the Shasta Community College. They were not privileged, they were not entitled, they were soldiers, men and women who had served in Afghanistan and Iraq, they were children of addicts, who ran away from home at fourteen. One woman told a group of us that after she ran away, her uncle found her walking on the highway and brought her home to live with their family. She refused to go to school. For one year, every day, she sat in the corner of a particular coffee shop and listened to conversations. She listened to people talking about the books they had read, the art they had seen, their concern for the health of the seas and the environment. She saw how people listened to one another and paid attention to their questions. After a year, she decided she wanted a life of the mind that could lead her to these kinds of intimate conversations and found her way to Shasta Community College. Before she left, the barista said to her, "I have watched you for a year, you are not the girl who walked in 360 days ago." She said it was the first time anyone had ever seen her, let alone acknowledged her growth. These students I worked with were single moms with kids with health issues, they were the poor and unsupported, working three jobs and attending school—and they all had powerful stories to tell. They all want to write and they are willing to do the hard soul-stirring work to do it. Whom do I serve, my beautiful father? That is my question for you. And what is serving me?

Please write me back with your wisdom.

Your loving and questioning daughter,

Terry

4

"You have to carry the fire."
"I don't know how to."
"Yes, you do."
"Is the fire real? The fire?"
"Yes it is."
"Where is it? I don't know where it is."
"Yes you do. It's inside you. It always was there. I can see it."

—CORMAC MCCARTHY, *The Road*

## ◈ BOOM! EROSION OF BELIEF
*December 2, 2017*

—

What is beauty if not stillness?
What is stillness if not sight?
What is sight if not an awakening?
What is an awakening if not now?

The American landscape is under assault by an administration that cares only about themselves. Working behind closed doors, they are strategically undermining environmental protections that have been in place for decades and getting away with it, in practices of secrecy, in deeds of greed, in acts of violence that are causing pain.

Like many, I have compartmentalized my state of mind in order to survive. Like most, I have also compartmentalized my state of Utah. It is a hidden violence that we all share. This is the fallout that has entered our bodies; nuclear bombs tested in the desert—Boom! These are uranium tailings left on the edges of our towns where children play—Boom! The war games played and nerve gas stored in the West Desert— Boom! These are the oil and gas lines, frack lines from Vernal to Bonanza in the Uintah Basin—Boom! This is Aneth and

Montezuma Creek—the oil patches on Indian lands—Boom! Gut Bears Ears—Boom! Cut Grand Staircase–Escalante in half—Boom! And every other wild place that is easier for me to defend than my own people and species—Boom! The coal and copper mines I watched expand as a child—Huntington and Kennecott—Boom! The oil refineries that foul the air and blacken our lungs in Salt Lake City—Boom! And the latest scar on the landscape, the tar sands mine in the Book Cliffs, closed, now hidden simply by its remoteness—Boom! Add the Cisco Desert, where trains stop to settle the radioactive waste they carry on to Blanding—Boom! Move the uranium tailings from Moab to Crescent Junction, then bury it still hot in the alkaline desert, out of sight, out of mind—Boom! See the traces of human indignities on the sands near Topaz Mountain left by the Japanese internment camps—Boom!

President Donald J. Trump will try to eviscerate Bears Ears and Grand Staircase–Escalante Monuments with his pen and poisonous policies. He will stand tall with other white men who for generations have exhumed, looted, and profited from the graves of Ancient Ones. They will tell you, Bears Ears belongs to them—Boom!

This is a story, a patronizing story, also a condescending one. I see politicians and Mormons discounting the tribes once again, calling them "Lamanites," the rebellious ones against God, dark-skinned and cursed. That is their story. Racism is a story. The Book of Mormon is a story—Boom!

Perhaps our greatest trauma living in the state of Utah is the religiosity of the Mormon patriarchy that says, as I was told growing up, that we had no authority—women, Indians, black people, brown people, gay people, trans people—it was only those who were white and male who could hold the priesthood over us, telling us the way to heaven is through them. All my life I was told I could not speak, that I had no voice, no power except through my father or husband or bishop, and then there was the prophet—Boom! I refused to perpetuate this lie, this myth, this abuse called silence. If birds had a voice, so did I.

Environmental racism is the outcome of bad stories. A by-product of poverty. In Utah, yellow cake has dusted the lips of Navajo uranium workers for decades, who are now sick or dead—Boom! There is no running water in Westwater, a reservation town adjacent to Blanding. Local municipalities refuse to provide Navajo families with a basic right—Boom! But we are not prejudiced—Boom! If you speak of these oversights, call them cruelties, we as Mormons are seen as having betrayed our roots and our people. These are my people. Boom! This is who I am—Boom! A white woman of privilege born of the Covenant—I am not on the outside, but inside. Boom! It is time to look in the mirror and reflect on the histories that are ours.

We are being told a treacherous story that says it is an individual's right, our hallowed state's right, to destroy what is common to us all: the land beneath our feet, the water we drink, and the air we breathe. Our bodies and the body of the state of Utah are being violated. Our eyes are closed. Our mouths are sealed. We refuse to see or say what we know to be true: Utah is a beautiful violence.

Do we dare to see Utah for what it is: an elegant toxic landscape where the power of oppression rules by repression; our proving grounds of fear? What are we afraid of? Exposure. Boom! Our denial is our collusion. Our silence is our death. The climate is changing. *We have a right and responsibility to protect each other*—resistance and insistence before the law. We are slowly dying. We are ignoring the evidence. Awareness is our prayer. Beauty will prevail. Native People are showing us the way. It is time to heal these lands and each other by calling them what they are—sacred.

May a congress of Raven greet us in ceremony. May we recognize our need of a collective blessing by Earth. May we ask forgiveness for our wounding of land and spirit. And may our right relationship to life be restored as we work together toward a survival shared. A story is awakening. We are part of something much larger than ourselves, an interconnected whole that stretches upward to the stars.

Coyote in the desert is howling in the darkness, calling forth the pack, lifting up the moon.

*On December 4, 2017: President Donald J. Trump, with Utah senator Orrin Hatch by his side, reduced Bears Ears National Monument by 87 percent and Grand Staircase–Escalante National Park by 50 percent. Lawsuits have been filed by several environmental groups, the NRDC and the Center for Biological Diversity among them; other plaintiffs include the Native American Rights Fund, Utah Diné Bikéyah, Grand Canyon Trust, Friends of Cedar Mesa, Patagonia, and Earth Justice.*

◈ **BLUEBIRDS**

Monument Valley is a hallucination without drugs. It is a kaleidoscope of colors that turns by the sun's wrist. Red sandstone bleeds into pink and deepens into lavender fading into blue until sunset offers a surprise encore of golden light and we watch the desert glow.

We spent the night here after a full day of storytelling shared inside the Diné Welcome Center. We were in Indian Country. From dawn until dusk, people told stories—Hopi, Tewa, Ute Mountain Ute, and Diné or Navajo, Native and non-Native alike. Everyone was invited. Stories wrapped around us like Pendleton blankets. Time expanded; what we imagined in the telling became truth.

I was with Fazal Sheikh, an American photographer who lives in Switzerland. We were guests of Utah Diné Bikéyah, a nonprofit organization committed to protecting Bears Ears National Monument.

We had been traveling together in a spirit of collaboration, experimenting with image and text, visiting friends along the way. After President Trump's evisceration of Bears Ears and Grand Staircase–Escalante National Monuments, these desert lands seemed much more vulnerable.

———

The spring winds had come and with them, dust devils whipping up the sands like banshees. It's a volatile time in the red rock desert. The Bureau of Land Management had just held an online oil and gas lease sale in Utah, successfully securing bids from fossil fuel companies for 45 parcels of land, 51,400 acres, the majority of them in southeastern Utah. Many of them are near the ancestral Puebloan villages of Hovenweep, home to 2,500 people between 1200 and 1300 A.D. who left a rich and distinctive record of habitation, from towers built on boulders to intricate mosaiclike stone-constructed dwellings and ceremonial kivas.

The United States government is continuing the destabilization of other national monuments with its insatiable appetite for fossil fuel development, as if gutting Bears Ears and Grand Staircase–Escalante National Monuments was not enough. Add Hovenweep National Monument and Canyon of the Ancients National Monument to the Department of the Interior's list of desecration sites, yet another violent assault on Native People and ancestral burial grounds.

The National Park Service asked the BLM to hold off thirteen of their leases in close proximity to these archaeologically rich monuments. The BLM refused.

What does it mean to refuse?

REFUSE rɪˈfjuːz/ *verb*
verb: refuse; 3rd person present: refuses; past tense: refused; past participle: refused; gerund or present participle: refusing
1. to say or show that you are not willing to do something.
2. indicate that one is not willing to accept or grant (something offered or requested). "she refused a cigarette"

*synonyms*: decline, turn down, say no to;

reject, spurn, scorn, rebuff, disdain, repudiate, dismiss, repulse;

shake one's head, send one's regrets;

baulk at, demur at, protest at, jib at, draw the line at;

*informal* pass up;

*informal* knock back

"he refused their invitation to lunch"

withhold, not grant, disapprove, deny, discountenance;

*informal* give the thumbs down to

"the Council refused planning permission"

antonyms: accept, grant


informal: (of a thing) fail to perform a required action.


And what are other ways to say "I refuse"?


*verb* deny; say no

- decline
- ignore
- protest
- rebuff
- reject
- turn down
- withdraw
- withhold
- demur
- desist
- disaccord
- disallow
- disapprove
- dissent
- dodge

- evade
- nix
- regret
- repel
- reprobate
- repudiate
- shun
- spurn
- beg off
- brush off
- dispense with
- give thumbs down to
- hold back
- hold off
- hold out
- make excuses
- not budge
- not budget
- not buy
- not care to
- pass up
- refuse to receive
- send off
- send regrets
- set aside
- turn away
- turn a deaf ear to
- turn from
- turn one's back on

It is the last synonym that feels the most accurate to me: *to turn one's back on.*

Donald Trump's Bureau of Land Management is turning their back on beauty.

My belief in an American ethic of place being led by the United States' federal government is eroding. We must decouple environmental protection and the health of our public lands and the communities adjacent to them from both the political right and left. Neither side is to be trusted. And those we can trust may not be able to go far enough.

We must look to each other to find enduring ways to honor, respect, and protect the life that surrounds us.

I refuse to comply with the rules and ruthlessness of this administration's actions. I believe as Abbey said, "We will outlive the bastards."

Belief is tricky. One day I do. One day I don't. Believe. But there are things I believe that have never wavered. My belief in God is not one of those.

Not long ago, I made a list, my attempt to address this question: "Do I believe in God?"

It went like this:

God as an old white man with a beard—*No*
God as a human—*No*
God as a being—*No*
God as energy—*Yes*
God as consequential—*Don't know*
God without definition—*Yes*
God as a creative force in the Universe—*Yes*
God as natural processes in motion—*Yes*
God as evolution—*Yes*
God as gravity—*Yes*
God as love—*Yes*
God as forgiveness—*Yes*

God as beauty—*Yes*
God as a no and a yes—*Maybe*
God as wrathful and merciful—*Perhaps*—*This one scares me.*
God as Mystery—*Most certainly*

I realized through my Q & A exercise that my problem is with the word "God," for all the limitations it has placed on my imagination, such as "God the Father." This was the beginning of my erosion with Mormonism in particular and religion in general. It happened early. I watched birds and studied them. If I dreamed of a great horned owl and saw one the next day, that was normal, to be expected. If a yellow warbler came into my mind, it was not unusual for me to hear one. As a child, I came to understand my relationship to nature was reciprocal and that nature had a relationship with me. We called to one another. We called one another into being. What I mean by that is we have evolved together. I still have a tailbone. I trust what I see and I believe what I feel. Trusting direct experience is the open door to revelation. This was my foundation for faith. It still is.

We had been brought into a waking dream where hundreds of people gathered in the desert somewhere between Utah and Arizona. State lines mean little in Indian Country. We climbed up a hill with our vehicle and abruptly dropped down into a sizable clearing of sage where dozens of pickups were parked. We parked next to them, and walked to where eight bonfires burned, four on each side of an open space reserved for what was to come. Families and friends gathered around the fires in silence. Some stood. Some sat on folding chairs. Waiting. Watching. We were the guests of Jonah Yellowman. Tonight was the last of the Yeibichai dances. Jonah had spoken of the Blue Bird People. The explanation our host gave us in his pickup truck before we entered the community in firelight was this: Ceremony moves us from sadness to joy, from feeling numb to feeling alive, to being part of a community instead of being isolated, as one often feels on long winter nights in the red rock amphitheater of wildness. We drove the rest of the washboard road with the constellations as our maps. Orion was rising above the southern horizon.

We were touching the outer circumference of something that was not ours, but something we could feel in our shared desire for balance and renewal on the eve of the spring equinox.

What is the reach of ceremony?

Pinyon smoke rose from two structures where the dancers would begin and where they would end. The smell of burning cedar permeated the grounds. And then, the sound of rattles began. Before our eyes, faces the color of midnight blue became birds became dancers whose high-pitched voices called forth the spring as winter surrendered. The repetitive chants wrapped us into a trance and I forgot the cold and closed my eyes, remembering the sweet songs of bluebirds that greet us each April. Those in need of healing were met by the winged ones who restored their spirits by calling out the wounds of grief and discord housed in the body as disease. We watched sparks from the fires rise as exclamation points.

It was just as we had been told, but could not have imagined. The Blue Bird People arrived through a haze of wafting smoke, dancing and singing through the corridors of fire, realigning the world with each deliberate gesture. Hands raised, rattles held, shimmering apparitions born of the stars. These night dwellers have a name that will not be named. Those who called for a healing will remain unknown. Those who stood in the ripples of their power were stirred. We were folded into the tightly woven cloth of community, even as guests.

We left the gathering in the wee hours of the morning and Jonah drove us back to where we were staying. He got out of his truck and walked us to our rooms. With the Pleiades above us, he turned to me and said, "Now, you have a story to tell."

"But this is not mine to tell." I said.

"You will find it—the story that is yours."

Back home in Castle Valley, Fazal and I got out of the car. Two bluebirds, male and female, flew over our house. They landed in the cottonwood not yet clothed in leaves. We looked up. The bluebird pair lingered. Brooke met us at the front door and noted they were the first bluebirds he had seen this year.

We set the table and cooked dinner. We talked. We slept. We dreamed.

In the morning when I awoke, I saw the shadows of birds, wings hovering outside, silhouettes appearing inside on the blinds. Bluebirds. Through the wooden slats I watched a female bluebird treading air with her wings, her blue-feathered body suspended. She was staring in my direction with her small black eyes and black beak slightly opened. I believed she was seeing her own reflection in the window.

Another bluebird, turquoise in sunlight, came up behind her. She rose, he rose, in a fluttering of wings, and then both disappeared into a circular opening in the overhang of the roof that once housed a light—a perfect place for a nest. The courting birds flew out, each one in a different direction. The female returned to the window—hovering—and our gaze met once again—I held my breath so I wouldn't scare her as she kept flying in place, our eyes never leaving the other. I left the window and moved to the window seat, where she followed me— still hovering—still focused. It was as though she wanted to come inside. He, too, followed her and pulled his turquoise wings forward and backward with an intensity that bordered on urgency or panic or both.

Brooke was my witness. Together, we opened all the doors in the house and then, he left for the day.

Fazal rose and we prepared breakfast. The table was re-set. The coffee was made and poured. Scrambled eggs, mixed with onions and green chilies, were steaming on the plate. We were about to sit down together. Instead, as if called by something unheard, I walked out of the kitchen to the far window in the bedroom where I had last seen the bluebirds' flurry of wings. In the corner, the male bluebird sat between the blinds and the window. To my astonishment, he was not anxious, but calm. I slowly raised the blinds and knelt beside him. He let me slide my right hand beneath his breast and cup my left hand around his back. I felt his beating heart through his feathered chest. I stood up with the bluebird in hand, and as I walked into the living room, he cocked his head and I saw my own reflection in his small black eyes. I quietly called to Fazal. He met me in the living room, smiled, and gently stroked the bluebird's head as we carried him outside where a flock of bluebirds were flying near the house. I opened my hands; the bluebird flew, joining the others, and then, disappeared.

Just like that.

Can we ever know the reach of ceremony?

My brother Hank works with his hands day in and day out, digging trenches, laying pipe that natural gas or water or sewage might flow through. At night, he makes art, creating sculptures from the cut and remaindered steel pipe he puts in the ground. He also uses the discarded detritus of machinery he finds to make his pieces. I cannot name the parts, but when Hank welds them together, he creates objects of wholeness and beauty: a dancer in an arabesque made out of twisted metal. A woman in prayer. Lovers entwined.

For Christmas, Hank made me a Bird Man—his arms outstretched like wings, now rusted and mottled. His eyes look straight ahead. The beak is pronounced. The Bird Man's right knee is bent, his left foot is about to be raised in dance. I did not see the full measure of my brother's creation, nor how prescient the Bird Man would be, until now as the flock of bluebirds encircled him.

My belief in nature is the nature of my faith as a human being humbled before the gods we live among. The god made in my own image that I was introduced to as a child now circles the fire with all the other gods—those with feathers, fins, and fur, scales and tails and multiple legs that crawl among the flowers, plants, and trees. Stories can be understood in a myriad of languages. Translation becomes a matter of listening to what one feels as well as what one hears. I do not view this communion with other species as acts of idolatry or witchcraft or momentary madness, but rather the practice of good manners among neighbors, where peace is maintained through mutual respect and consideration. We learn from one another. Without manners, violence enters the room. Without the decency of imagination, narcissism leads.

For many of us raised in various Christian traditions, a personalization of God in human form is eroding. Human exceptionalism is destroying the living world. For me, a providential faith rooted in religion has evolved into a cosmic faith that supports a conscious unity within all Creation. When I held the bluebird in my hands, I was also holding my own liberation. This is not a metaphor but "an ecology of mind," where we can change the nature of reality through our focused attention, which is another form of prayer.

Earth has always been a sphere of geologic forces capable of rupturing the surface of things, but now we, too, are force fields of consciousness capable of shifting fixed patterns of thinking. This is the enlightened Anthropocene, not just the destructive one.

If we are to flourish as a species, an erosion of belief will be necessary, that says we are not the center of the universe but a dynamic part of an expanding and contracting future that celebrates and collaborates with uncertainty. The perpetuation of biblical self-identification is harming us and everything else on this planet we call home. Recognizing the dignity of each living thing, mobile or fixed, insect, animal, tree, or mushroom, has broadened my love for this world and diminished my need for a god in heaven. We have multitudes of gods on Earth.

What is ceremony but a reminder of the power we can summon together? A sense of harmony is remembered and comes to us in the way of dreams that present themselves outside the normal parameters of time and space. It is also sacred teachings passed on through time. A guide appears with an invitation to participate in something mysterious where we yield to that which cannot be named. We can say yes or no, but sooner or later we can no longer deny that if we continue to stand on the front lines of pain without a deeper understanding of what we intend for our children and those who will follow them, we are a species devoted to death. The future is created through actions—good and evil. We are called to serve the beauty that hovers just beyond our reach, outside, because we intuit what we lack inside, enthusiasm—which comes from the Greek word *entheos*, which means "the god within." Our task is to open the doors for this reunion.

Birds know flight—when to leave and when to return—and where to stay to flourish. They orient themselves to the stars on late-night sojourns where mixed flocks of many species migrate in spring and fall. Many a night I have overhead their sweet murmurings as a lullaby for slumbering lives below. I return to the firelight illuminating the Blue Bird People dancing themselves back home with the spirits of their ancestors, healing the illness that comes from losing our balance.

We are a species known as *Homo sapiens*, often paralyzed by despair, having forgotten who we are together in our adamant claims of difference. Fortunately, we live among other species, many unknown to us, who show us how to enter the home of another and offer the gift of attention and presence, which is an exercise in vulnerability. We learn to listen. Night after night, when all is dark and quiet, the shock and recognition of coyotes' voices rising unexpectedly—howling, singing, yipping—remind me I am not alone. It is not without its fear. We can get hurt.

In circumstances too strange and private to recount, I found myself standing in a room trying to get to sleep with an enor-

mous bat (easily registering a two-foot wingspan) and a wasp
the size of my index finger, both flying aggressively around
me. I kept ducking, running around the room corner to corner, trying to dodge their attacks. It would have been funny if I
hadn't been so scared. The bat could have been carrying rabies,
and the wasp is known for a venomous sting that can send
one into shock. It was a game of hide-and-seek. They would
hide and I would seek cover, until they would emerge, flapping
terror into the room, and I would bolt once again to a safer
corner. When the bat finally perched itself upside down on the
mother-of-pearl frame of *The Last Supper* hanging on the wall,
I took that as my exit. I fled into another room to sleep. The
only problem was there was no bed, only a chaise with a musty
woven throw that I put over me. Nevertheless, I quickly fell
asleep with all doors and windows closed.

The next morning, I went on my way.

During the day, I felt strange, not quite queasy, but not
steady in mind, either. And I noticed I had something like a
mosquito bite on my thigh, nothing significant. It just itched.
Later that night, as Brooke and I were getting into bed, he
asked how I got the bruise on my leg.

"What bruise?" I said.

The bruise on my thigh was a red-brown circle three inches
across. I had no idea how I got it. I looked at the bruise more
closely; there was a bite mark in the center. As if all that was
needed was my examination, the bruise started blistering
before our eyes. I thought of the night before—the bat, the
wasp—and then it came to me.

Both Brooke and I had the same thought: brown recluse.

Who knows when that throw on the chaise in the strange
house I found myself in had last been thrown or wrapped
around anyone's body? I believed this was where the reclusive

spider with the brown violin marking on his back bit me. I had disturbed his peace.

I would later learn that brown recluse spiders (*Loxosceles reclusa*), ranging from a quarter to a half inch in size, are secretive and shy, finding refuge in dark, undisturbed places. They tend to hunt at night, stalking their prey rather than waiting for insects to be caught inside a web. Their bite releases a necrotic venom that liquifies flesh, causing the dead tissue to eventually slough off and creating an open wound, an ulcer so corrosive it can eventually expose bone.

Depending on the location of the bite, plastic surgery may be required, and secondary infections are common.

The bruise in humans is caused by the spider clipping the blood vessels with its bite, leaving the blood to pool into the skin tissue. It usually takes six to eight hours for the bruise to appear and up to ten to twelve days for the ulceration to occur. Blistering, swelling, and the eating away of skin follows; not always, but that is the pattern.

There is nothing you can do but wait—which is what I did, as I watched the skin on my inner thigh begin to blister and boil before my eyes.

Not all bites from brown recluses become necrotic. Mine did not. It cooled down and stopped bubbling after a week. (Our son from Rwanda recommended rubbing the inside of a banana peel on the bite; it helped). I was lucky; even so, the brown recluse left its mark and a slight indentation on my leg. A friend of mine calls it "Earth acupuncture." Personally, it felt like a warning and an inoculation—from what, I cannot say. At the very least, it was an encounter. Brown recluse venom will stay in a person's body for up to a year and affect the immune system. The smallest of creatures can take us down with their secret powers when we least expect it. We live among highly focused, formidable gods.

> The energy of life becomes available when the conditions of single-mindedness are met. It is important to hold in mind that this is the way of life.
>
> —HOWARD THURMAN, *Disciplines of the Spirit*

If courage is sustained focus, then belief is energy that fuels our spirit. We keep going. Belief evolves over time. If we are curious, and committed to growing, adapting, and responding to changing conditions, we must interrogate our maps. My erosion of belief is asking me to let go of what is comfortable, the familiar, and be open to possibilities that I haven't dared to consider, even the acceptance and devotion to other gods outside of my own image, no matter how dangerous. I, now, refuse to see Earth as anything less than our common place of divine habitation. We can begin to tell our own stories of crucifixion and resurrection.

"What this country needs is a businessman for president," says Gatewood, the banker in John Ford's classic western *Stagecoach*, set in Monument Valley. He briskly leaves town with a satchel full of money stolen from his clients. Ford's film was made in 1939. Some eighty years later, we indeed have a businessman for president, and he, too, is stealing from his constituents, only it's more than money. Donald J. Trump and one of his chief henchmen, Interior Secretary Ryan Zinke, are robbing the American people of incomparable protected landscapes like Grand Staircase–Escalante and Bears Ears National Monuments in Utah.

Conservation groups have denounced President Trump's use of the Antiquities Act of 1906 to strip protections from these lands as not only unprecedented, but illegal. The Bears Ears Inter-Tribal Coalition has called it "an assault on Indian Sovereignty."

For almost a decade, the Hopi, Navajo, Ute Mountain Ute, Ute Indian Tribe, and the Pueblo of Zuni had been calling for the protection of the Bears Ears area—1.9 million acres of red rock canyons and mesas in the southeast corner of Utah—

as a national monument. Maps were drawn from traditional knowledge, honoring the sacred nature of Bears Ears, two pinyon-juniper fringed mesas revered by Native People. These hallowed lands are where the bones of their ancestors are buried, where their medicine is found and collected from native plants, where their ceremonies are held. Local and national environmental groups became allies, as a majority of Utahns and American citizens supported this campaign to create a new national monument in the remote red rock desert of southern Utah.

Their efforts paid off. On December 28, 2016, President Barack Obama signed a proclamation establishing the 1.35-million-acre Bears Ears National Monument. It was the first time in American history that Western science agreed to join traditional knowledge in a cooperative management agreement between federal agencies and Native Peoples.

The agreement was short-lived.

Four months later, President Trump signed an executive order charging Interior Secretary Zinke to review all national monuments of more than one hundred thousand acres that had been established between 1996 and 2016. Out of the twenty-seven monuments that met that criteria, six were seen as "too big" and recommended for dramatic reductions. Two of the six monuments were located in my home state of Utah.

On December 4, 2017, in the rotunda of the Utah State Capitol, flanked by Utah's top Republican politicians, President Trump signed a new proclamation to gut Bears Ears National Monument by 85 percent, leaving two disconnected parcels and changing the monument's name to "Shash Jaa," privileging the Navajo language over those of the other tribes, and to slice Grand Staircase–Escalante National Monument in half.

The president said he was returning these lands to the American people. That was a lie—these lands were already under our stewardship. Our public lands are our public commons.

Two million acres of now unprotected wild lands, where it is estimated that some one hundred thousand archaeological sites belonging to pre-Puebloan people exist, are now open for business. Oil and gas leases within the released lands of the former monument can now be auctioned off in online sales; coal and uranium mining claims can be activated; and industrial tourism without the proper checks and balances can begin its assault on this fragile desert landscape.

As Natalie Landreth, staff attorney for the Native American Rights Fund, points out, President Trump's order opens these lands to "entry, location, selection, sale" and "disposition under all laws relating to mineral and geothermal leasing" and "location, entry and patent under mining laws." What had been an honoring of Native People's claims as sovereign nations has been turned into an open market for corporate claims for fossil fuel development. The long view of protection has been swapped for the short view of extraction. Open lands for the many are now open markets for the few.

"This is taking public lands that belong to the American people and selling to the highest bidder," Landreth said. "There is just no other way to understand it." The five tribes have filed a lawsuit against President Trump and federal agencies, as have national and local environmental groups and Patagonia, the outdoor clothing company.

The Utah congressman John Curtis, a Republican, has introduced a bill that would provide protections for archaeological sites in the areas President Trump stripped from Bears Ears. It also promises no new leasing for mineral development in those areas. But tribal leaders who oppose Trump's action say the Curtis legislation is largely smoke and mirrors, providing little real protection; and because Congress indisputably retains authority to create national monuments, the bill, if passed, would nullify the tribes' right to sue the federal government and render moot the other lawsuits defending Bears Ears.

The rights of Indian sovereignty must be defended. The integrity of the Antiquities Act of 1906 must be upheld. No U.S. president has ever undertaken this kind of review of our national monuments. No U.S. president has ever reduced a national monument by this size, let alone two in the same state; four other national monuments are still at risk of reduction. A dangerous legal precedent could be set. If the courts rule that a president can shrink already designated monuments by proclamation, no national monument—from Katahdin Woods and Waters in Maine to Muir Woods in California—is safe.

The story of Bears Ears National Monument is a story of power. The power of the land, the power of the federal government, the power of the Mormon Church (which dominates Utah politics), the power of the fossil fuel industry, and the power of Native People who have inhabited these lands for millennia.

When Senator Orrin Hatch held a news conference about Bears Ears shortly after Trump's executive order last spring, he said, "The Indians, they don't fully understand that a lot of the things that they currently take for granted on those lands, they won't be able to do if it's made clearly into a monument or a wilderness." Pressed by a journalist for an example, he replied, "Just take my word for it." In that moment, the Mormon Church was in full view.

The Native American author Vine Deloria, Jr., came to the University of Utah to speak in 1974; his topic: cultural geno-cide. He called out the Mormon Church's Indian Placement Program as racist. It was a common practice among Mormon families to raise a Navajo or Ute child in their homes and "ed-ucate" the child in the ways of "the Spirit." The program was encouraged and supported by the Church of Jesus Christ of Latter-day Saints to "benefit their salvation."

Deloria's message was a knife slicing into my conscience: Shame on all of you within the LDS Church who think our people are better off in your homes than in their own homes with their own families. He said something about not needing our charity, but our respect; not needing our culture, but their own. I heard him. His ire entered my bloodstream and trav-eled straight to my heart. I felt the pain of the oppressor, as one who had been taught to believe we were "a chosen people" and that I was right, and then, suddenly, in that moment, I came into an abrupt understanding that I was wrong.

It was only a matter of time until I left my home religion. But I have never left my home ground, or stopped loving the place and the people I come from.

Recently, I visited with Jonah Yellowman, who has become a close friend. I respect and trust him, relying on his kindness, his humor, and his generous wisdom for insight. In the blood-red shadows of Monument Valley that stretch across sage and sand, what endures is what is standing—the iconic right and left mittens of Monument Valley. We spoke about what it means to heal and how it is not good for sadness and depression to invade a community.

Struck by our insignificance in this vast expanse of layered time, I find myself on the edge of an unknowable spiritual power emanating from Jonah and the land itself. I asked Jonah how he was doing after Trump's decision to rescind much of the monument.

"Bears Ears is a sacred place for us," Jonah reiterated. "Now, it is threatened. We have to go deeper."

I keep thinking about what he might mean to go deeper and how this might set us on a very different course as a people rooted in a place called Utah, and for that matter all of us who live in America. Jonah has consistently said, "We are not just protecting Bears Ears for our people, but all people."

I am tired of being told I am on the far side of left-leaning politics, that I am an environmental extremist, an ecoterrorist, an activist. I am tired of my own anger, which is easily triggered and accessed by a Trump tweet or another act of aggression laid out by the Department of the Interior, such as opening up the Arctic National Wildlife Refuge to oil drilling just because they can, even as fossil fuels are headed the way of the dinosaurs.

I don't want to live in a binary world of either/or, rural or urban, politically correct or incorrect, or, most damaging of all, segregated into a world of black or brown or white. We have all been diminished by this ongoing fight over wildlands in Utah. And in the case of Bears Ears, the people I know and love on both sides of this issue, those who are in favor of the monument and those who are not—when we sit down and break bread together, what we can all agree on is that we love these lands and share a desire for a future that includes wild and reverent spaces where the wing beats of ravens register as prayers and the sweet smell of sage brings us back home.

We need to find a common language alongside what binds

us together rather than what tears us apart. We need to have the hard conversations between neighbors and family and really listen to one another.

Perhaps Jonah's call to go deeper is a call to acknowledge the power that resides in the Earth itself, the organic intelligence inherent in deserts and forests, in rivers and oceans, and in all manner of species beyond our own. We cannot create wild nature, we can only destroy it—and in the end, in breathtaking acts of repentance, try to restore what we have thoughtlessly removed at our own expense, be it wolves or willows or cutthroat trout or these precious desert lands.

Bears Ears is a place of power. Anyone who has walked this mysterious landscape of buttes and mesas, and experienced the embrace of red rock canyons animated by the handprints of the Ancient Ones carefully placed on sandstone walls, cannot stand by and be witness to its demise at the hands of those who care only for what the land can produce, the real estate that can be sold, or the commodity land can become.

Utah's red rock wilderness, as vulnerable as it now is, will survive us with or without presidential proclamations. But we may not survive without it.

### ❖ A BEAUTIFUL, RUGGED PLACE: EROSION OF THE BODY

"We are only lightly covered with buttoned cloth; and beneath these pavements are shells, bones and silence."
—VIRGINIA WOOLF, *The Waves*

We had just celebrated my father's eighty-fifth birthday. Louis Gakumba and I were driving back up to Jackson Hole. Brooke texted me, "I love you. Pull over to the side of the road. Call me." I knew it was Dan. I had been thinking of him as I was mesmerized by the immense cumulus clouds building in the west.

"Is Dan dead?"

"Yes."

"How?" But I already knew.

Dan had told me in April that he purchased the rope, that he was exhausted, that he couldn't bear it anymore, "it" being life, that he saw no end or purpose to his suffering.

"I'm done, Ter."

And I believed he was telling the truth.

"I am proud of him," I said. Brooke was not prepared for my response; neither was I.

————

Dan Dixon Tempest hung himself on July 27, 2018, in the stairwell of his apartment building. He was found on his knees. The police never notified our family.

A close family friend, Darol Wagstaff, Dan's landlord and mentor, called my father.

"John, I'm so sorry about Dan," he said.

"What's wrong with Dan?" my father asked.

"He's gone."

"Gone where?"

"He hung himself this morning."

My father had left his card on Dan's door: "We are gathering at Callie's house. You are welcome. Love, John."

Dan never came.

"What is the alternative?" Dan wrote in a notebook I found after his death.

He was a philosopher who wrote his master's thesis on Wittgenstein and the eloquence of logic and language. He also laid pipe for the family business for decades, until he moved to California with his wife, took a job in logistics, and then was laid off after the economic downturn in 2008. He had a long history of depression, which led to isolation, which led to drinking to numb the pain, which led to opioids, which led to several runs of rehab. He took a job at HawkWatch International, banding and releasing raptors in the wildlands of Utah, Wyoming, and New Mexico. He loved the hawks and eagles, especially the red-tails. One day in the desert, we sat on our front porch and he told me it took three men to bring in a golden eagle, how magnificent they were, the range and reach of their vision, but the red-tailed hawks were his favorite because they yielded. They seemed to understand what was happening to them, that their lives were not in danger. The birds became his passion and his metaphor, but they weren't enough.

Not long before his death, he texted me: *"I'm at my limit, sis— haven't slept in 3 weeks . . . no sleep . . . no sleep . . . I am eroding."*

A few days passed.

*". . . to understand something is to be liberated from it"*

*". . . and I can't get pass'd bein' liberated . . . where did I go wrong sister . . ."*

My reply was this: *"You haven't gone wrong, Dan. You are a brilliant man. You just need to keep going and find your creative groove that will pull you to your destiny—This I believe."*

He sent me an image of a bound mummy on a bound horse.

Later, Dan sent me the talk by Malcolm Gladwell on David and Goliath. He texted this quote: *"As the playwright George Bernard Shaw once put it: 'The reasonable man adapts himself to the world: the unreasonable one persists in trying to adapt the world to himself. Therefore all progress depends on the unreasonable man.'"*

And then this: *"You can't concentrate on doing anything if you are thinking, 'What's gonna happen if it doesn't go right.'"*

*"I'm winding down on the whole existence thing . . . I want to be free . . . stardust . . ."*

I responded, *"These are hard and lonely times. I don't have much hope and then . . . There are these moments of beauty, a million people marching for justice, Dan. Stars in the night sky in the desert, your caring voice. I love you."*

*". . . just make sure you get me in the air . . . been buried too long . . . xoxo"*

*"Dan, I want to know what you know, please write. This is what I listened to this morning in my own Dark Side of the Moon: On Being—The Soul in Depression."*

"I have 2day . . . no point anymore . . . pretty much need to see things in these last days."

"I love you."

". . . just put me in the air . . . all I ask . . ."

"I hope you will bury me first, Dear Heart. In the desert."

". . . won't be around then Sis . . ."

"I need you to be, Dan."

"We all do—you, me, Hank."

". . . Ter . . . I'm not fuckin' around . . . mental illness is taking me out."

"I believe you can get help, Dan. I hear you—and I am listening to what you are saying. There are medications that really can help, but you need a doctor and to take them on a schedule. You know this—"

". . . evolve . . . I can deal with that."

"I know you suffer—God knows, you are one of the strongest people I know, and most tender and smart. You are a beautiful soul, Dan."

". . . my brother said the same thing this afternoon . . ."

"Do you believe us?"

". . . si . . ."

"I believe the three of us are evolving together—each in our own ways. Did you listen to that podcast I sent you? It's powerful."

". . . agree . . . I just need a back door . . ."

"What do you mean?"

". . . w/u and hank to deal w/it"

"Deal with what? Forgive me, I just need to understand what you are saying—a back door?"

". . . come on . . . i'm not spelling it out."

". . . i don't want to be here anymore . . . pretty simple . . . you understand that . . . i hope anyway."

"Dan, I trust you and honor who you are and where you are. And I will forever believe in your greatness of spirit, as you con-

*tinue to face and embody the vitality and courage of staying with the struggle. I understand. But it breaks my heart. I think there are roads not yet taken for you, Dan. And medication could help you return to yourself. I will just be honest, but you have to want that—and I know you are tired. But life is life. And creativity is in you to express. This I believe."*

"... my legacy was being addicted ... I could never beat it ... but I was a sensitive/intelligent soul ..."

*"You still could beat it. That is not your legacy. Your illness has been part of your addiction, but that is not your legacy. You ARE a sensitive/intelligent soul. I love you, Dan."*

"... ditto ... just need to find some air for a spell ... xxx"

*"Dan, would you want to see Jonah Yellowman, a Navajo healer, this summer? He lives in Monument Valley, he's the spiritual adviser for Bears Ears."*

"... sure ..."

A few weeks pass. He sends me the song "Simple Man."

"... so much right and wrong in my life ... bipolar"

*"Thank you for the music, Dan. How are you today?"*

"... i'm ok. ..."

"... good day 2day ..."

Weeks pass, no word, and then, this:

*"For the Love of God—Listen to this song, Ter"*

*"I love you. How are you?"*

"... I think I have victory over dirt ... finally ..."

*"What do you mean?"*

"... i've done it all ... nothing else to prove ... open a new chapter ... xxx"

*"Beautiful."*

He sends me a link of Kim Kardashian addressing Congress and meeting with Trump.

"... *is this really where we're at* ... *?* ... *time to exit* ... *i'm cracking the sky right now* ... *luv ya* ..."

"*I love you, my beautiful brother. Paint. Write. Dream. For me. Xxx T*"

"... *can you call me* ... *it's real important.*"

I called Dan. He told me he had bought a rope. That he was going to go out "gently."

*Please write that addicts are good people, sis.* And then he said something that haunts me still: "*Why can't you see it, Ter. We're fucked. You keep hoping things will change. I'm fucked. The planet is fucked. It's time to exit. Face it, sis. It's time to let me go, time to let it all go.*"

There was a long pause. Neither of us spoke.

*Let me go.*

I said I would never let him go, nor would I ever give up on the Earth.

After our call, he texted me: "*Let go. Repeat: I bought the rope, Ter. I'm going out gently. No guns. I would not do that to my brain. I will not disappear in the desert. You will not have to worry.*"

I texted him again:

"*Please. I will never give up on you or your joy, Dan. You are alive, a testament to your strength and will for Beauty even in suffering. I love you.*"

"... *I'm goin' offline tomorrow for my sanity* ... *knock if need be.*"

A month later, May 9, 2018:

"... *Ter* ... *I'm suffering big time right now from deep loneliness* ... *my question* ... *?* ... *Do I reach outward to institutions or go inward to art* ..."

*"Both, my dear heart, each supports the other . . . Paint, write, photograph. Seek the insight and help of an institution to steady your mind and then create out of what you are seeing, feeling, and learning once again. Please believe in your own creation born out of suffering and live. I love you, my beautiful brave brother."*

No response.

June 7, 2018:

*"Tempest Family Name Meaning . . . English (Yorkshire): nickname for someone with a blustery temperament, from Middle English, Old French tempest(e) 'storm' (Latin tempestas 'weather,' 'season,' a derivative of tempus 'time')."*

*"It's in our name, Sis . . . the weather is changing . . ."*

The last text I received from my brother was on June 8, the same day Anthony Bourdain hung himself.

*". . . r u okay?"*

I was out of range, traveling. I had been bitten a few days before by a brown recluse spider. Dad had told him. What I should have asked was "R u okay?" But I didn't. Instead, I wrote this:

*"I am okay. Skin didn't go necrotic. Lucky. But it was scary. I see you have tried to call several times. We are in a remote place where phone service is slight. Thank you. I love you. T"*

No one heard from Dan after June 8. He hung himself forty-nine days later. Who did he talk to? Where was he during those long summer days? Alone—holed up in his apartment? Downtown, mingling with the homeless? In the end, this was where he found his community, these were his peers with whom he found comfort and was comfortable. Were there moments of insight and peace, having made a decision to end his life, or was it only darkness? What do you do with all that darkness? Hank asked, "Where does darkness go?" Why that day? That moment? Where were we? He had a family. We were not there. My brother died of isolation—*knock if need be.*

I never did.

"Doesn't the blood of every suicide splash back on our faces?" David Sedaris wrote about his sister's death by suicide.

My brother hung himself.
They found him on his knees.
I am on my knees.
I cannot breathe.

When you lose a sibling, you lose yourself.

We were a tribe of four: three boys and a girl. Steve, Dan, and Hank. I was the oldest. Steve died from lymphoma in 2005. He was forty-seven years old. Dan died by his own hand. He was fifty-six years old. Hank and I are survivors. We know our DNA is a perfect match after being tested to see if we were a match for our brother Steve, who needed a bone marrow transplant in 2004. We were not a match for our brother and could not give him our cells. We struggled then. We are struggling now. But this death is different from the others. Death by suicide has teeth, and when it bites, it will not let you loose.

A noose. My brother's suicide is a noose around my neck and it is tightening. The questions left will never be answered.

Grief is a physical landscape where no place feels safe. It is a state of being where sorrow holds the eyes steady. I stare. I stare out the window. Hours pass without moving. I stare at people who talk to me and hear nothing they say. I stare at burning candles. I stare at the sea. I stare into darkness unable to sleep. And when I do sleep, it offers the comfort of forgetting until I wake up and pain is there to greet me. The next day, flares of anger erupt unexpectedly. When I am able to function out of necessity, showing up to work, going to the grocery store, I get ambushed: a piece of music, a sentence, a memory, a person. The tears stream down my cheeks. No one can help me. Grief is my brother, my sibling. When I embrace grief, I am embracing him. This is how I feel him near. I ache. My heart hurts. We loved each other. Grief is my companion now. Everyone and everything else is a distraction. Sometimes appreciated. Sometimes resented. People don't know what to say. I want them to say something. Alone in an empty parking lot, I scribbled a note on a piece of paper and pinned it on my jacket that said, "My brother committed suicide—Please talk to me." I walked in circles for more than an hour, but there was nobody there. I didn't really want to talk. I needed someone to notice what couldn't be seen; I wanted another chance at loving Dan better.

In my private moments I believed I could help save a piece of land or save a species, a prairie dog or grizzly bear, but now I know I couldn't even save my brother. Grief burns through the bullshit. Death by suicide. Dan warned me. I chose not to see it, I chose denial instead of action. I heard his words, but I failed to hear the pain. In the end, it's rarely the large gestures that count, it's the small ones. I knew my brother was suffering. I knew he was in pain. I knew he was alone. I could have knocked on his door and held him.

But I didn't. I just kept living my life as though everything was fine.

That's one side of the story. Here's the other side. Dan was an alcoholic, an addict. He lied. He lied for decades. He told me stories in which, against all odds, he was always the hero, the strong one, the one who fought for justice, the one who watched, the one who outsmarted everyone and survived. He told me these stories so many times, I believed him. A mythology grew around him, part cowboy with two-toned boots worn out through hard living, part Seneca the wise, brilliant one, steeped in philosophical puzzles and truths. The six-foot-three armed outlaw and sage. On a good day, he could outwork anyone in the trenches with his strength and stamina. He read and understood the texts of Nietzsche and Husserl and Heidegger and Wittgenstein as thoughtfully as any scholar I knew, because he had lived the questions of what it means to be human and embody existential angst. I loved our conversations for all he saw that I missed. He painted wild nature and his own inner nature in bold colors and strokes. He lived in a ruthless duality like the black-and-white pastel that hangs in my study. And in moments of levity, we laughed, we laughed and gossiped and teased each other. He told me whatever story he knew would lure me in, and it did. I believed he was sober. I believed he was no longer using. I believed the red rash on his body was bed bugs, not scabies. When he asked for money, I gave it to him. And when things got bad, when he was barely bones from not eating, when he was on the streets of Salt Lake City or passed out in a motel room drunk from apricot brandy or beer, I was there to rescue him. I was always there by his side, both of us with our cowboy boots kicking up the dirt in the big moments between life and death, but rarely was I there in the small ones, the everyday moments of darkness and depression that he bore alone.

As a member of our family, he was our visual reminder of pain (or was it disturbance?), especially our own; sometimes we tolerated him, often we feared him, and when he was not present, we missed him because he could be so charming and beautiful. His smile would break my will to be tough. His perceptions were acute. He was my shadow, my secret suffering, my loving brother who as an adult was never truly known by anyone but his addictions.

My father, my brother Hank and I, uncles, aunts, and cousins were there, friends, too, until we weren't. Until we were tired of being used, abused, played, and manipulated, until we knew in our gut, especially through love and anguish, that nothing would change until Dan decided to take the next step. There were so many next steps and so many steps backward. *Please write that addicts are good people.* Alcoholism is a disease. Mental illness is exactly that, an illness. But often we don't see it that way. We see only our loved one's bad behavior, their actions that wounded and betrayed us. Failing to acknowledge the severity of their afflictions, we see what appears as a lack of discipline and resolve as flaws and weaknesses. It is a violent cycle, where the rats win and scurry through what little belongings they have left, save the skulls and Milagros and crucifixes that hang on their white walls. Rehab started looking like an institutional scam to milk codependent families of their savings. On bad days, it is easy to think this. But through it all, my beloved brother Dan suffered valiantly, privately, for decades, believing there must be a reason he was still alive in the midst of his demons; he was among those too sensitive for the world, until he started losing his mind. We were not so different. When we looked at each other, we both would smile, saying we had the same eyes, gray-blue, sometimes green, and we do or we did—my fingers stop on the keyboard—Dan's eyes turned inward. My eyes turn outward. Perhaps my addiction is optimism instead of seeing what is true and real, that just like us, the Earth is engaged in its own evolutionary fate.

We have to let go of what we desire. I don't want to let go. I wanted my brother alive, even if he was suffering. My brother is dead. They found him on his knees. *I am so proud of him.* He finally did what he said he would do—my beautiful brother chose to end his suffering by one of the options available to him. I could have knocked on his door. He could have opened it and we could have cried together.

Stay with me.

On the night my brother Hank and I drove to the office of the medical examiner to identify Dan's body, the blood moon of the lunar eclipse was hanging low on the eastern horizon, red-orange slowly rising with the high-pitched barking of dogs. We rang the doorbell in the back of the building. A technician who worked the night shift opened the door. We told him we wanted to see our brother. It wasn't possible, he said. We pleaded. We told him the police never notified our family, that we found out from a friend who was Dan's landlord. We needed to see him. We needed to see that he was dead.

The technician said he was so sorry, but he could not do that. He said we could talk to the medical examiner. He called him and handed us his phone as we stood outside.

The medical examiner said, "Yes, we have a body with the name Dan Tempest. Yes, he committed suicide in the morning around nine o'clock, and yes, he died from asphyxiation." For the next fifteen minutes, the doctor took us through the process, how he would have passed out after two minutes, how the oxygen supply would have been shut off to the brain and he would have died. Our brother's brain, his brilliant brain, his gift and his nemesis.

"It's a relatively painless death," the doctor said. "I am sorry about your brother. By law, we cannot let you see him

until his body has been released and accepted by a mortuary."
He paused. "That should be tomorrow."

❖

*I am eroding*—Dan said to me.

I am eroding—I say to him now.

Fire. I see the mountain burning. I see the preternatural glow at sunset and sunrise. In the American West, summer is now the season of smoke and flames. Smoke is choking us, clouding our vision. Nothing is sharp-edged anymore or clearly defined. The world is a haze, out of focus, blurred.

My heart is burning. A person commits suicide in America every thirteen minutes.

Most don't leave notes. The act itself is the message. What is happening to us? My brother told me I was in denial. We are committing suicide on this planet. But isn't hope a moral obligation? What are we hoping for? What do I refuse to see? To sorrow in the suffering of the world together may be what we need to embrace now, something beyond hope, deeper than hope, which is to honor our grief of a changing world. I refused not only to see the pain behind my brother's words, but to feel it. I was there with the big gestures, but I failed with the small ones. Repeating images. A knock on his door. A cup of coffee shared. I could have cleaned his apartment.

Rather than anchoring our hope beyond the struggle, always projecting ahead, perhaps locating joy within the struggle through our full presence can be our essential gesture at this moment in time. To feel the pain of now and not look away. To act not with the hope of moving forward, always forward, but to see the wisdom of stepping sideways as we create a different space, a more conscious space in the direction of pause, where we can breathe and gather ourselves so we can gather others around us and create a community of care, even within our own families, especially our own families.

In my home state of Utah, grief is a state of mind. Our public health and the health of the planet are being undermined. There is no more room for denial. Denial erodes truth. Our actions and inactions are killing the Earth's natural systems, of which we are a part. Suicide. We are creating unnatural histories, and they all have a similar plot. My brother took his life and left us behind, death by his own hand. I stare at my hands.

What does it mean to pray?

My brother is dead. Say it again. He hung himself. Say it again. He killed himself. Say it again, finally, my brother committed suicide, no, that is politically incorrect, we now say "death by suicide." I understand. That word: suicide. A beloved bequeaths their pain to you. Dan left no suicide note, but his stone-cold, emaciated body was its own narrative, with the signature of red abrasions written around his neck. There is no stigma, only sorrow for what is lost.

On July 18, 1992, Dan left me a note after staying at our home. It was a simple letter with two questions:

Terry,

Who is going to ride your wild horses after you are gone?
Who is going to drown in your deep blue sea?
I love you,

DDT

I have kept this note above my desk ever since.

After Dan's death, I found a photograph he sent me of a three-story redbrick building with a white horse looking outside the middle window, closed. Beneath the photograph he typed "William Cooper." I thought that was the name of the photographer, but in further research I found Cooper to be an American conspiracy theorist and the author of the book *Behold a Pale Horse*, published in 1991. I am certain Dan read it. Some call it "a militia manifesto." Dan's uniform was desert fatigues, knee-high gaiters, and combat boots, wearing a black sweater complete with a Blackwater insignia. With his black Ray-Ban aviator glasses, he could look formidable. He was well armed, as is most of my family. The book is about how the United States government has betrayed its people, how the American Dream is a lie, and why the "Shadow Government" must be taken down. William Cooper, who served in the navy, was said to have had military intelligence clearance, and had a large following. He also believed in extraterrestrial aliens as a malevolent force on the planet, that John F. Kennedy was assassinated because he was about to reveal what the American military knew, and that aliens were among us. Dan felt alien. In 1998, there was an arrest warrant on William Cooper for tax evasion. On November, 5, 2001, Cooper was "murdered" in a shooting exchange with Arizona state troopers, only enhancing his cult status.

There is so much about my brother I did not know. He had allegiances to the militia.

Sometimes, I worried what Dan might do. Sometimes, we were afraid of him.

◈

My brother the philosopher, the hawk whisperer who caught and banded birds of prey and released them to the winds; my brother who hung steel and dug ditches as a workingman paid hourly wages; my brother, "too sensitive among wolves," chose to take his own life. What he didn't realize is that he took mine with him. He took our father's life, too. And our youngest brother, Hank, the strongest of us all, the one who never fell for Dan's manipulations as I did. He only kept asking Dan what he loved.

Our family knows death. All families do. But suicide buries one beneath an avalanche of questions. The morning we were about to have a small family memorial, my father said to me over breakfast, "After Diane died, I read every book I could find to answer why, I must have read a dozen or more, *Why Bad Things Happen to Good People*, Elisabeth Kübler-Ross's *Stages of Grief*, all of those. And then, one day, I stopped reading them. I realized for myself the answer is—there is no answer. You just have to deal with it."

The bouquet of sunflowers fell off the mantel onto the floor. I awoke to sunflower petals strewn across the carpet. I picked them up, one by one, and placed them in a pouch with two grouse feathers from Brooke and an owl feather that fell from the sky, snatched before it touched the ground. A gift from Louis. I took the red-tailed hawk feather resting on our bookshelf, given to me by Dan.

I arrived in Salt Lake City from Jackson, Wyoming, in a daze. Hank would meet me at the mortuary at 8:30 a.m. On my way, I called my father. He was not doing well.

Hank greets me at Sunset Lawn. We hold each other

tight, and then walk into the funeral home that we know too well. We sit in the lobby and say little. The funeral director welcomes us and tells us the cremation will begin at nine o'clock and will take roughly six hours to completion. You are welcome to leave and come back when we call you to pick up the remains.

"We will stay," Hank says. I look at him. He is resolute.

We ask to see Dan's body. We tell the funeral director we would like to spend some private time with Dan. He tells us that would be difficult as he is covered in plastic. We ask to have the plastic removed. There is a long pause. We say we want to touch his body before he enters the crematorium. The funeral director says he will see what he can do. He returns and says it will take some time to remove the plastic. We say we have time. The funeral director disappears.

After twenty minutes, we are taken into the back of the mortuary, where cremations occur. It is clear to us that this area is not meant for the public or for families. The door is opened for us and we see Dan's body draped in a white sheet. His shoulders are bare and his hands are folded one over the other above the sheet. We stand on either side of Dan's body, his beautiful long body. We are left alone with our brother.

Dan's face is beautiful. I expect his eyes to open. His skin is translucent and a deep peace has settled over his body. There is the slightest smile on his face, not forced or fixed by morticians. His body has been washed, that is all. We see him clean and pure.

I pull out my pouch. Hank and I each take a grouse feather and place one east and one west beneath his hands, his beautiful hands that we could finally touch and hold—surprisingly feminine hands in spite of a lifetime of digging. I hear him say, "*I have finally mastered dirt.*"

Other phrases return to me:

"*Give me the sky, I've been buried too long.*"

"*I have the rope, Ter. I am done.*"

He is done. We are undone. Into his resting hands we place feathers: the owl feather in his left hand, the red-tailed hawk feather in his right, *the one bird of prey that yields.*

Hank and I, without words, intuitively place the sunflower petals on his heart laid bare . . . a pile of many petals to draw out the darkness from his troubled heart into light; Hank places one petal on his throat, where a wide red line circling around his neck reveals his choice, and I place two yellow petals on his forehead, one vertical and one horizontal, making a sunflower cross. In that moment, I heard Dan's voice as clear as the day, "Sunflowers, Ter, do you get it? Don't you get it?" I paused, and then burst out laughing. Yes, I got it—the Sunflower Clan! I had forgotten. I had forgotten the beauty of a late summer walk we made together through a radiant field of sunflowers, the last time Dan was at our home. Brooke and Dan and I were on an afternoon stroll, Dan noting how all the sunflowers were facing the light. We made vows as self-appointed members of the Sunflower Clan to take care of one another and remind each other to follow the light in times of despair.

"Can I love myself enough to change?" Dan asked as we walked waist high in the yellow-petaled field. "Can I, sis?"

I saw Dan's choice as an act of self-love, a quick change of form from body to spirit.

Could his suicide have been an act of courage, carried out by his own hands? His beautiful hands. His desire, finally, for a quick transformation of his burdened soul after decades of suffering. Maybe that's why the first thought out of my mouth on hearing he was dead was one of support.

I return to his body, cold. There is no romance here, only the brutality of truth. My brothers are before me. Count them. Hank is alive, Dan is dead. Steve is dead. I am the eldest, why was it not me?

Hank and I stood on either side of Dan's body, now placed inside the blue cardboard box he would be burned in. We said our prayers to each other on Dan's behalf. And then, if I am honest, I felt Dan's impatience, eagerness, "Let's go—"

A man in a black suit from the mortuary entered and asked if we wanted more time. We said we were ready. The man thought we meant that we were ready to go.

Hank told him, no, that we would be staying through the entire process.

"Are you sure?" he asked.

Hank said yes. By his side, I was following Hank's lead.

And so the man in the black suit pulled the two doors open that revealed the cremation chamber.

The chamber was computerized. He set the dials to heat the furnace. Hank and I watched the neon numbers rise from 400 degrees Fahrenheit to 1100 degrees. It was hot enough; he then pushed a button and the chamber door opened. Inside, we witnessed the flames, fueled by natural gas and sounding like rocket boosters. The man nodded that now was the time. Hank and I lifted the box holding our brother's body into the flames.

The chamber door came down.

The man in the black suit closed the two white doors and left. The roar of the furnace audible.

Hank and I sat on a love seat against the wall. It was covered in red fabric with gold dragonflies. Nothing else in the room was comforting. It was a room of discard and storage:

filing cabinets, vases, plastic flowers, cardboard boxes, urns decorated with flags or doves or sunsets. A small desk with a computer on it. A few stray chairs with overhead lights.

Clearly this was not a space intended for the contemplation of loved ones.

I got up and turned the lights off. It suddenly became very dark. Hank, forever the wry one, said, "Nice atmosphere, Ter."

Another man in a black suit, an acquaintance from high school, came to check on us and asked if we might not be more comfortable sitting in the lobby. Hank and I said we were fine, that we would wait.

"It may take up to six hours," he said.

"We're cool," Hank said.

I smiled.

"Is there anything you need?"

"May we light a candle?" I asked.

His mouth moved sideways. "Let me check," and then he left.

Hank and I looked around the room. We spotted two candles on the shelves. And remarked at how uninspiring the art was, including a print of a misshapen girl in a pinafore holding a disgruntled cat. Then there was the one with a garish sunrise whose bright orange rays appeared to be spiking through a forest of lime-green trees. Our favorite, we concluded, was the tipped-over milk can in a garden of gladiolas.

My friend from high school returned with his practiced solemn demeanor and said, "I'm sorry, Terry, no candles can be lit as it is against the fire code."

"Of course," I said. And then we all burst out laughing.

◈

Time passed, two hours, then three; Lyn Dalebont, a dear friend close to Dan, came to see us and the three of us shared stories as we sat on the floor together. An astrologer, she read Dan's death chart for us. He was born on a lunar eclipse and he went out on a lunar eclipse.

"One for the record books," she said, "with all of Mars's energy behind it."

On the night Hank and I went to the medical examiner's office to identify Dan's body, I recalled once again how we held each other's hands as the blood moon rose above the Wasatch Mountains with caged dogs howling behind us.

"He was a warrior," she said.

I flashed back to seeing Dan's body for the first time after his death and thinking to myself how noble he looked. That was the word that came to me. Hank and I could not believe this was our brother. Dan was dead. This was true. The disbelief began to evaporate as I stroked his forehead. In life, he looked like our father. In death, he resembled our mother. Hank and I sat down on the brocade couch in silence. Dan's peace helped us gather our composure, and we believed seeing Dan's body would help soothe our father's heart. We left the room, closed the door behind us, and found Dad in one of the mortuary waiting rooms, having finished signing the last documents, including Dan's death certificate.

We told him we thought it would be good for him to see Dan's body, that he looked peaceful, and it would make it real. He hesitantly agreed. We descended the steep steps with Hank and me on either side of him, and then we entered the dimly lit room.

With our father between us, we put our arms around him as he faced Dan's still body. "I can't see him," he said. Shattered, he mourned his son, another son he had now outlived. And then, his eyes were finally able to focus. "He looks like a noble warrior who could have belonged to any time."

His hair was combed back, long curls touched his shoulder. His beard was brown with gray streaks. He was thin, too thin, his high cheekbones accentuated his chiseled face.

"He looks like Diane," our father said. "Everyone always said he looked like me."

We sat on the couch across from Dan for some time. And then, Dad stood up abruptly.

As we left, he put his hand on Dan's shoulder. "Thank you, Dan."

The door opened. I jumped, startled. The man in the black suit entered again. "You may want to leave now—I am about to shift the bones."

"We are staying," Hank said. "I made a vow to my brother."

The man in the black suit then introduced himself. His name was Brian Raabe. We shook hands. He pulled the white doors open. The heat from the retort seared our faces. Mr. Raabe took off his jacket and folded it neatly and placed it on the back of a chair. He then put on a pair of long gray welding gloves. We stood behind him as the chamber door to the crematorium was drawn up.

Dan's body was burning. Our brother's rib cage had become white paper prayer flags flapping inside the flames. His arms looked like wings, and in that moment Dan was Icarus, kin to the eagles he loved and released in Utah's wilderness.

We watched Mr. Raabe rake Dan's bones with the grace of a Zen master, in meditative motion like a dance with the dead. His body was being disassembled, spread across the floor of the gray brick chamber. Hank and I were mesmerized witnessing the beauty Dan was becoming, how the process was vaporizing a human body from flesh to spirit.

And then, after the final rearrangement of bones, Mr. Raabe stepped back with his rake, assessed the situation, and pushed the button once again as the door to the chamber closed. Mr. Raabe took off his gloves and placed his rake to the side. We walked back into the low-lit room as he shut the white doors. We thanked him. He nodded his head as we resumed our place on the love seat of dragonflies.

Our friend who stood with us said she felt blessed to have witnessed what we had, as she had not been present at her father's cremation, unaware it was an option. She used the word "healing," although I am not sure what I heard, as the moment had transcended anything I could rationally comprehend.

Hank and I sat in silence for another stretch of time; another hour or two passed and Mr. Raabe returned, this time inviting us to watch him gather the bones before he ground them into ash.

The doors opened, the chamber door rose, and Dan was gone. The chamber was empty. I was shocked by the void that only hours before had held his physical body. Mr. Raabe put the welding gloves back on and began raking Dan's remains rhythmically into stainless steel trays. Hank and I watched as our brother's bones were swept into view, now recognizable as parts of the human anatomy: the ball of a broken femur, finger bones, ulna, radius, rib fragments, a shard here and there, a glimpse of skull, his jaw, and many vertebrae, all being lovingly raked into the trays through the deliberateness and artistry of Mr. Raabe's care. With the larger fragments now gathered in two trays, he took out a fine brush and swept the dust and smaller particles of Dan into another smaller tray with such tenderness, we stood in awe of the reverence and respect this stranger was showing our brother. This was a holy act, a ritual performed with great dignity, usually unseen and unacknowledged by anyone.

We followed Mr. Raabe into a stark room where he would separate the bones further before they would be ground into ash. He excused himself and left Hank and me alone with our brother's cremains.

Hank and I stood before trays of white bone fragments.

"What are you thinking?" I asked.

"Probably the same thing you are thinking," Hank replied. "Are they coyote, rabbit, or raven?" he said, smiling.

"How many times have we come across similar piles of sun-bleached bones in the desert?" I asked.

We wanted to touch them, but instead placed our hands just close enough to feel the heat emanating from them. The remaining energy of our brother's life was being transferred into the palms of our hands.

There is no hierarchy in death.

*. . . no hierarchy of lives. It is this hierarchy that allows them to be inferiorized, stigmatized, and brutalized while other lives are privileged . . .*

*We are prisoners of an ideology that prevents us from seeing the world as it is.*

*We are captives of a view of things that gives them a false appearance of self-evidence.*

*Our task is to change the world—no—our task is to change our view of the world.*

There is no hierarchy in death, there are only bones.

◈

Mr. Raabe returned. We did not speak. We simply watched him meticulously separate the bones with long narrow tweezers. He looked for metal and found some in Dan's teeth. With special pliers, he pulled out fillings and placed them in a box with other fillings from the dead to be recycled, with proceeds going to the local children's hospital. Bone fragments were then separated into what looked like pieces of coral; smaller pieces resembled shells; then Mr. Raabe took an even finer paintbrush and swept the last particles of Dan into what looked like a small ripple of sand found on the periphery of Pacific Coast beaches. He brushed the bone dust into a metal container, followed by the sorted bone fragments.

He turned to us and quietly asked if we were comfortable watching him grind the bones. It would take roughly fifty seconds. We said yes. He turned on the switch like a morning blender, and we listened to the bass notes of our brother become the melody of ash.

And then, it was silent.

"Would you like to feel the last heat from your brother's life?" Mr. Raabe asked.

Hank and I held Dan in our hands for the final time.

Dan's ashes would be placed into a simple black container that Hank could put in his backpack and carry into Utah's West Desert, where Dan banded and released golden eagles to their vast terrain of sky. Mr. Raabe took the container, opened it, and poured the warm ashes inside. We inhaled our brother. The box was closed. Mr. Raabe handed Dan's cremains to Hank.

We thanked Mr. Raabe for the grace of his work and for taking care of our brother. We experienced it as a sacred rite.

"It is my privilege and my calling," he said. "I know that I am the last person to touch the body of an individual who was loved. I take that very seriously." He paused. "Thank you for witnessing what I do."

Mr. Raabe walked Hank and me out to the foyer of the mortuary. Everyone had gone home.

We shook hands again.

"One more thing," he said. "It's been my experience that when you scatter Dan's ashes, there is usually a sign that lets you know when you have found the right place—the shape of a cloud, the call of a bird, some sign in nature."

Hank told him that he planned on taking Dan's ashes into the Cedar Mountains west of Salt Lake City.

"A beautiful, rugged place," Hank said.

Mr. Raabe smiled. "My family name is German. When translated into English, Raabe means 'raven.' I want you both to know I felt your brother's essence. I had a strong feeling we would have liked each other."

We carried Dan's remains to our father's house. We walked inside and found John (as Hank calls him) sitting at his desk waiting for us. We sat down and told him this story.

Dan's ashes weighed eight pounds seven ounces, the same weight as when he was born.

It is also the weight of a gallon of water one carries in the desert.

❖

Two days later, Hank put Dan's ashes into his backpack and headed toward the Cedar Mountain Wilderness Area, several mountain ranges west of Salt Lake City in Utah's Great Basin. Hank hiked for four hours straight up a particular peak that both he and our father knew, and that Dan inhabited during the winter months when his work entailed taking deer carcasses out to the West Desert to lure golden eagles down to the foothills for yearly population counts.

Hank did, in fact, recognize a sign, a stone pinnacle in the shape of an eagle head very near the summit. He knelt down on the pale steep ground where a flat spot emerged next to a bare-boned tree sculpted by the wind into the shape of a cross. Hank released the white ashes of Dan's body to the earth and sky, acknowledged by a circling hawk above that he could hear but not see—one body yielding to another.

"To dwell is to see things as they are," Evangeline Gray said. "And then, you stay and fight for those things you see for your community." This she has been doing for her community of Westwater for close to forty years. Since 1980, she has been advocating for the twenty-nine Native families who live there—Navajo, Paiute, and Ute Mountain Ute households— to have running water. To turn on a tap inside their homes and be able to fill a glass and drink it.

The town of Blanding, Utah (a stone's throw across the ravine that separates the two communities), and San Juan County have refused to make that happen. What would it take to bring water to Westwater? I asked my father, who spent a lifetime in the business of bringing water and natural gas to rural communities in the American West. "I know that country well," he said. "It wouldn't take long, maybe a week, digging a trench across a draw from one neighborhood to the other; laying the pipe; welding the pipe together and putting in a routine tie-in to the primary water system and turning it on. That's it. That goes for electricity, too." He paused. "Don't let them tell you it's about money. It isn't."

The town of Blanding passes the buck and says it's up to San Juan County; San Juan County says it is not their jurisdiction and turns it over to the Navajo Nation; the Navajo Nation passes the request back to San Juan County and argues that the responsibility falls to the state of Utah, and round and round they go with a bureaucratic boondoggle of excuses that leaves the town of eighty-nine individuals in the same situation: a community without water. Across the ravine, there are green lawns in the front and swimming pools in the backyards of white people.

Racism comes in many forms and disguises. Some of them are subtle and some of them are blatant; all of them are cruel.

"I stopped crying years ago," Evangeline said. "So many promises broken, too many excuses to name—now, we are trying to figure out what our next move will be."

Evangeline Gray is a tall woman, stately, with dark eyes that often squint when she smiles. She is a descendant of the medicine women of her people. I am struck by the strength of her hands. She wears a large turquoise ring on her left hand with a wide silver bracelet encircling her wrist; two large silver bracelets inch up her right arm. She parts her long brown hair on the side. We met a few years ago through the nonprofit organization Utah Diné Bikéyah, an advocacy group supporting Bears Ears National Monument and sacred land protection, along with indigenous rights and traditional ways of knowing.

When Evangeline was growing up in Mexican Hat near the San Juan River, her father and brothers worked in the uranium mines nearby, active from 1955 to 1968. Today, the Mexican Hat Uranium Disposal Cell in Halchita, Utah, just outside Monument Valley, is where 1.3 million tons of uranium tailings and waste were trucked in from the mill sites in the 1990s. The radioactive material has left a legacy in the bodies not only of those who worked in the mines, but of those who drank the water contaminated by the tailings that leached into their communities. Most of Evangeline's family are dead from cancer. It's a story shared by many Navajo families in the American Southwest. Many Utah families, my own among them, lived downwind from the nuclear bombs, made from the same uranium, that were being tested in the Nevada desert.

When I first heard Evangeline speak about the situation at Westwater and how long she had been advocating for her community, I was stunned.

"Don't be stunned," she said. "Be aware that this is what is happening in Utah."

Evangeline looked at me. "Ask yourself why." She looked over her shoulder in the direction of her community. "We are invisible to this town . . . No, it's worse—we don't exist."

Willie Grayeyes lives at Navajo Mountain, about four hours south of Blanding in one of the most remote locations in the United States. He has been the chairman of Utah Diné Bikéyah for the past five years, and his leadership has provided a consequential voice on behalf of Bears Ears National Monument. A respected Diné elder in his seventies, he casts a striking presence with his long gray hair pulled back in a traditional *tsiiyéé*, a sign of power among his people. His brown eyes do not waver and neither does his sense of justice.

Friends call him "The Hawk" because he misses nothing as he circles each issue, from voter registration to gerrymandering to income inequality. The traditional knowledge he carries with him keeps him five steps ahead of most everyone else. And then, after discussing hard-core policy issues, he will surprise the room by interjecting the word "love" when referring to the very people who want to undermine the 51 percent Navajo majority in San Juan County, the largest and poorest county in the state of Utah.

Willie has spent his entire adult life advocating for Utah Navajo communities, making sure children have a proper education, with schools built close to where they live so they don't have to travel four to five hours each way to and from school. He has been a proponent of decent health care, seeing to it that small clinics dot the reservation from one town to the next. Grayeyes is on the road constantly, traveling from Navajo Mountain to Shonto to Mexican Hat and Mexican Water over to Oljeto in Monument Valley to Monument Creek and Aneth, Utah, driving tens of thousands of miles each year across Navajoland.

For more than a decade, Willie Grayeyes served as a delegate from the Navajo Mountain Chapter House to the Navajo Nation, speaking out as a leader on behalf of the communities he represented. Last I heard, he'd clocked more than eight hundred thousand miles on the odometer of his blue Nissan Altima. Willie's car is well-known in southeastern Utah.

On November 6, 2018, Willie Grayeyes and Kenneth Maryboy won their elections as commissioners of San Juan County. It was a historic election, as it was the first time a Navajo majority carried the commission of three elected officials. This victory came after Grayeyes had long pushed for election reform and equity in reaction to the Republican gerrymandering scheme that intentionally split up the Navajo community into three different districts, denying them any majority.

Two months later, the headline in the *San Juan Record* read: "Date Set for Willie Grayeyes, Kelly Laws Hearing in Seventh District Court." The local paper announced January 22, 2019, as the trial date whereon the victory of the newly elected county commissioner, Willie Grayeyes, would be contested, and his residency in the state of Utah challenged by his Republican opponent, Kelly Laws. Grayeyes had defeated Laws 900 to 805 votes.

The case was to be heard by Judge Don M. Torgerson in the Seventh District Court in Monticello, Utah.

The *San Juan Record* reported:

The amended subpoena decus tecum, filed on Jan. 10, orders Grayeyes to the courthouse for testimony at a trial or hearing to produce the following documents or tangible things:

A: A copy of Grayeyes federal tax returns for the years 2015–2018.

B: A copy of Grayeyes Utah tax returns for the years 2015–2018.

C: A copy of Grayeyes Arizona tax returns for 2015–2018.

D: A copy of Grayeyes title and registration for any vehicles he owns.

E: A copy of the title and registration for any vehicles he has owned within the past five years, to the extent that such documents are in his possession, custody, or control.

F: Copies of any and all documents showing ownership of any property interests, or real property or land in Utah, Arizona, or anywhere in the Navajo Nation, including, without limitation, deeds leases, Homesite Leases, or allotments.

G: A copy of his current driver's license; as well as any other identification cards in his possession, custody or control, regardless of whether they are valid or expired, including, without limitation, state identification cards and tribal identification cards.

The documents also state that, "given the expedited nature of this proceeding, the minimum 14-day period for the production of documents does not apply."

This was round two in questioning Willie Grayeyes's residency and whether or not he had the legal right to hold the public office he had won in the 2018 election. Grayeyes had already succeeded in winning his own lawsuit against San Juan County in April 2018 after his name had been removed from the ballot by the county clerk John David Nielson, who declared that the candidate did not live in Utah. The U.S. district judge David Nuffer restored Grayeyes's voting rights and ordered his name be put back onto the November ballot after determining the county clerk had illegally backdated documents and falsified records.

It should be noted, as reported in *The Salt Lake Tribune*, that "the same judge ordered San Juan County to redraw its district boundaries in 2017 after determining that they amounted to racial gerrymandering. San Juan County is just under two-thirds Native American, but representation on the commission was skewed because of the district lines. New maps were also ordered for the school board districts."

On the morning of January 22, 2019, the courthouse in Monticello, Utah, was filled to capacity with dozens of citizens turned away. I was among the last to be seated. It was a largely white, Mormon audience from Blanding, Utah. Most of the Navajo citizens present that day, a dozen or more, were witnesses or potential witnesses and were asked to stay in the lobby outside of the courtroom.

Judge Don M. Torgerson entered the Seventh District Court. We all rose and were then seated. The trial of Willie Grayeyes began. The legitimacy of Willie Grayeyes's residency in the state of Utah was in dispute. It didn't matter that he and his family had inhabited Navajo Mountain for generations. It didn't matter that Mr. Grayeyes had said publicly that his residency is his birthright—residency defined for the Diné as where one's umbilical cord is buried. Willie Grayeyes's umbilical cord is buried on Paiute Mesa near Navajo Mountain.

The geographic coordinates that Mr. Grayeyes provided as his home address on Paiute Mesa (37 degrees 4 minutes 16.7 seconds North / 10 degrees 36 minutes West) in Navajo Mountain when he filed the official paperwork to run for office were placed under suspicion. Witnesses for Mr. Laws's case stated that there were no structures there to be found, and that the closest one to the latitude and longitude Willie Grayeyes provided did not belong to him.

The San Juan County sheriff dispatched Deputy Colby Turk to Navajo Mountain to investigate. Deputy Turk was the prosecution's first witness. With notebook in hand, I proceeded to take notes (and would later check them against the court transcript).

On March 27, 2018, Colby Turk made a field investigation out at Navajo Mountain. His task was simple: find out if Willie Grayeyes was a resident of Utah and lived at Navajo Mountain. The deputy went to Paiute Mesa, which Grayeyes cited as his home. He set his odometer at zero, so he could drive the seventeen miles beyond the Navajo Mountain Chapter House to Grayeyes's house.

"It put me in the middle of nowhere," Deputy Turk said.

Objections were made by the defense that the sheriff and deputy were operating beyond their jurisdiction on tribal lands. Objections were both overruled and sustained by the judge at various junctures as tensions mounted. State law kept colliding with Indian law. Who has jurisdiction over Indian lands? Was their investigation legal? Or was it a violation of Indian sovereignty? The word "probity" kept being bandied back and forth among the attorneys and the judge.

Fazal Sheikh, sitting on my right, is a photographer who travels around the world, often between Africa and America. "I feel like I am in Pretoria," he said.

The prosecution asked to show a video in the courtroom taken from the officer's body cam of the deputy interviewing Willie Grayeyes in Bluff, Utah, about his residency. The deputy said to the court once again, "My role was to confirm whether or not Mr. Grayeyes was a resident and lived in Navajo Mountain." We watched the footage of the two men talking in Bluff with Twin Rocks rising in the background like sentinels, but because of the wind, it was hard to hear what was actually being said. What we could hear was Willie saying to the deputy as he pointed to the ground with his finger, "My birthright is there—my structure is the land."

The prosecution continued building its case to prove that Willie Grayeyes was not a Utah resident. They said Willie Grayeyes had a girlfriend in Tuba City, Arizona, and that he spent many nights there; that his children went to school in Arizona. The defense had their rebuttal: the Grayeyes children went to school in Arizona because it was easier, the difference between an hour-and-a-half drive on dirt roads, difficult in winter, and attending schools in Blanding, four hours from where the family lived on Paiute Mesa in Navajo Mountain.

The prosecution made the argument that Willie Grayeyes owned no house in Utah, but did own a trailer in Page, Arizona, adding further doubts about his Utah residency. Mr. Grayeyes's counsel asked the court how many homes Senator-elect Mitt Romney had outside the state of Utah and if his legitimacy as a Utah citizen was being questioned.

A surprise witness was then called to the stand, sparking an objection by the defense team, which was overruled by the judge. Delton Pugh, a social worker employed by Family and Protective Child Services, who made monthly calls out to Navajo Mountain, was allowed to testify. Pugh gave a compelling case that he had never seen nor met Willie Grayeyes in the small community on Paiute Mesa; that the house closest to the coordinates Willie had given actually belonged to a man named Harrison Ross. The witness drew a map with all the houses on the mesa, giving a detailed account of the families who live there, the names and ages of their children, noting physical landmarks by each structure, and then he reiterated that he had never seen Willie Grayeyes on Paiute Mesa, nor did he know where he lived.

The trial went back and forth like a Ping-Pong game played between two different cultures. At times, it was hard to follow. Not only did different rules apply, but a different logic and cosmology belonged to the different sides.

The differences were highlighted most dramatically when Kelly Laws took the stand.

As he was sworn in, Laws gave his exact physical address in Blanding, Utah, stating proudly that he had lived in San Juan County for sixty-four years, which was his age. He said he had graduated from San Juan High School and had been married to the same woman and lived in the same house for forty years with three children. He identified himself as a field mechanic who worked for Wheeler for twenty-one years.

When his attorney asked why he had filed this suit against Willie Grayeyes, Laws said defiantly, "It's nothing personal . . . I am just trying to uphold and obey the laws of the state of Utah by which we live."

During the cross-examination period, the defense attorney

asked Mr. Laws how he came to believe Willie Grayeyes was not a resident of San Juan County.

"Everybody I talk to says he doesn't live at Navajo Mountain."

"Did you read it in the paper?"

"I don't read the paper [people in the courtroom laugh]—too biased!"

"And so your source was . . ."

"The talk of the town, the community is more reliable."

There was more talk between the witness and the attorneys, and then Kelly Laws said, "On September 5, I visited every home on Navajo Mountain when I was running for county commissioner."

He told of going to the house where the geographic coordinates Grayeyes wrote down had directed him, how he knocked on the door when he was campaigning and asked if Willie Grayeyes lived there. The man who answered the door said no. It was the same man described by the social worker: Harrison Ross.

"I went out to that house twice . . . Mr. Grayeyes does not live at Navajo Mountain at all. Look, I took this course of action so justice will be served!" Kelly Laws said emphatically.

The atmosphere in the courtroom was tense, with people in the wooden pews whispering to one another throughout. Reading the audience was easy; the majority of those in attendance passionately agreed with Laws's point of view, and believed he was doing the right thing. Clearly, Kelly Laws believed he was doing the right thing. Belief creates its own reality. Willie Grayeyes had won a state election illegally. He did not live here.

I was sitting next to Willie's grandson, Tristan Wilkerson, who was there throughout the trial listening, knowing exactly where his grandfather lived and where his mother was raised.

"Residency is where your influence is, where you place all your authority," Tristan said. "And Willie's work has been for and around Navajo Mountain."

The court was adjourned for lunch after several more witnesses all corroborated the prosecution's testimony. We took an hour break. It felt good to be able to breathe. Monticello had just received close to fourteen inches of snow. The roads had been treacherous from Moab, with sheets of black ice sending our car into a terrifying spin that threw us into the oncoming lane of traffic, out of control, until we stopped inches before slamming into a large juniper tree several feet off the road past the embankment. Miraculously, we were able to drive out of the snow. But the Abajo Mountains remained still and glistened white like ghosts who were settling into the high desert valley. It was bitter cold, well below zero, yet invigorating until it cut into one's lungs.

I was worried. Navajo friends from San Juan County wanted to know what had been said. The prosecution had spent the morning basically arguing that Willie Grayeyes was a liar. He didn't live where he said he lived. He had no house in Navajo Mountain that belonged to him, but he did own a trailer in Page, Arizona, where he also had a post office box. And he had no Utah driver's license, only an Arizona one. It was clear as stated by the prosecution that Willie Grayeyes was not a resident of Utah, and therefore his candidacy was a fraud. He should not be a commissioner in San Juan County.

When we returned to the courtroom, it was the defense's turn. Back in our seats, I teased Tristan about the book he was reading, *The Communist Manifesto*. "I bet you didn't buy that here in San Juan County," I said.

He smiled.

Willie was seated up front to the side, relaxed. Throughout the trial, I could see his stoic profile.

The first witness to take the stand was Avery Dennison, a Navajo medicine man from Tsaile, Arizona. "The Navajo sense of residency is very different from a white person's sense of residency," he said. "We believe that one resides where one's umbilical cord is buried."

Jeers could be heard from the largely white male Mormon audience.

Lena Fowler, a Diné woman of the Bitterwater clan who has served for ten years as a supervisor of Coconino County, Arizona, was the next witness. She gave a formal account of the Navajo Mountain community, which is in her jurisdiction, how there are 179 registered voters there, with 83 voting in the most recent election. She verified Willie Grayeyes's solid Utah voting record in San Juan County, unquestioned since 1984. She spoke of what the community is like, rural and remote. "No school, no store, no library, no laundromat on the Utah side of Navajo Mountain, just a senior center, a health clinic, and a Chapter House." She stated that the schools are in Arizona. She also stated that at this particular moment, a state of emergency had been declared based on the muddy road conditions and frozen water.

Lena Fowler discussed how much Willie does for the community regarding health care and education, how he is always on the road going to meetings and advocating for the well-being and rights of Utah Navajos. And how his leadership as former Chapter House president improved the conditions on Navajo Mountain.

Russell Smallcanyon took the stand next. He is a grazing officer for Navajo Mountain. Once a year, seventy-five grazing permits are given out at Navajo Mountain. You have to have a tally every year of how many sheep are on your permit. He authorized Willie Grayeyes's grazing permit on June 24, 2018, on Paiute Mesa. He was in compliance of that permit with his twelve sheep.

Peterson Zah, a former president of the Navajo Nation, took the stand next. The defense asked him if he was familiar with Navajo customs and traditions.

"Yes," he said. "My father was a medicine man."

"What can you tell me about a child's umbilical cord?"

Peterson Zah, who also has a background in law, said, "It is really interesting. We live in different worlds, our white brothers and sisters live differently, and we have different values. When a woman has a baby, the umbilical connects the mother and the baby and after the baby is born the umbilical cord dries and falls off. When that happens, you bury it in the earth, the Mother Earth, and it grows, it continues to grow like you. That cord places you in place. When the time comes, it provides you with a space, a place where you do other things. When you have a daughter and she goes through Kinaaldá' [her first period], you have that ceremony there, all your ceremonies take place there." He paused. "Everything you need is there, within this place. You are walking on it. Everything you need is here. You don't need to look anyplace else. Responsibility is expected."

He told the story of how he met Willie Grayeyes. "We went to boarding school together." He then said, "One day, four or five years ago, the president of Arizona State University asked who might give an important person a tour of Navajo Country. I thought of my schoolmate Willie Grayeyes. Willie met us at the entrance to Navajo Mountain. He drove us to the place where his umbilical cord is buried on Paiute

Mesa. We met several dogs and sheep. You know when you see him, the place is alive. You know he lives there. My guests said that they were interested in Navajo wedding baskets and Willie said, 'Oh yeah, my niece knows how to do that.' You can tell when someone lives there. He introduced us to all his nieces and nephews, sisters and relatives." Zah faced the attorney, paused, then said, "Residence to you is different than residence to me."

The last two witnesses were Willie Grayeyes's daughters: Navarina Boshane and April Wilkerson. April, the eldest daughter, took the stand.

"I am from Navajo Mountain. I am here for my father. I live in Phoenix. My mother was Sue Ann Little Grayeyes. When I was a little girl, I lived in Navajo Mountain. We moved with the animals. Then, when it was time to go to school, we went to the boarding school in Tuba City, Arizona, and came home to Navajo Mountain every weekend. My father cared about education. Page, Arizona, was closer and it had better schools than those in Utah. My father bought a trailer so we could go to school there, which we did from fifth grade through high school. My mother lived there with us, while my father worked and lived at Navajo Mountain. He was always on the road working for the Chapter House and the Utah Navajo community. We would visit him on the weekends.

"In 1987, my mother passed away from cancer. It was very difficult. My father lived with us for two years in the mobile home, helping us to get on our feet. When we were able to take care of ourselves, he returned to Navajo Mountain. I finished high school and took care of my younger sisters and brothers. Willie has not lived in Page since 1989. Today, the trailer is uninhabitable. Not condemned, but boarded up. My sister and I have plans to restore it."

The prosecuting attorney faced April Wilkerson and demanded to know where Willie Grayeyes lives and sleeps.

"You want to know where my father lives? He lives in his car. He sometimes lives with me at my cabin at Navajo Mountain. He sometimes lives with his sister Rose and sleeps under a shade hut on Paiute Mesa. But you ask where my father really sleeps? He has a horse, he puts out his bedroll, and he sleeps on the land where his umbilical cord is buried."

April Wilkerson looked at the judge. "My father's home is the land."

On Tuesday, January 29, 2019, Judge Don M. Torgerson gave his ruling from Utah's Seventh District Court: Willie Grayeyes is indeed a resident of San Juan County who lives on the Utah side of Navajo Mountain. The ruling says, "He is also from Paiute Mesa in the traditional sense—he was raised there, his umbilical cord is buried there, and his family counts the area as their place of origin." Judge Torgerson wrote, "He is connected to San Juan County as deeply as any resident of the County. In practice, he has always participated in the voting process in San Juan County. And his rich cultural history adds to his connection—he has always returned to the area and will always intend to return to the area when he has traveled away."

The controversy led by Kelly Laws and other white residents of Blanding, Utah, as to whether or not Willie Grayeyes had the legal right to be a county commissioner, ended. He was now free with fellow commissioners and engaged citizens to lead San Juan County in a new direction.

When I asked Willie how he deals with anger, he said, "It can no longer be about anger. It has to be about healing."

"We are turning heads," Willie said after the trial, "and those heads are turning outward and helping us. Bruce Adams called me the other day after the big snow"—he is the non-Indian San Juan county commissioner that Grayeyes and Maryboy serve with—"and said, 'How are your road conditions out there, Willie? What's happening? How can we help?' This was the first time anyone cared to ask about the muddy road to Navajo Mountain. I told him it was an emergency situation, in some instances a matter of life and death for some of our older people with food and medicines. We had given up. Together we mobilized."

On February 5, 2019, at the San Juan County Commission Meeting, County Commissioner Kenneth Maryboy introduced and read out loud a resolution "rescinding all prior resolutions of the San Juan County Commission opposing the establishment of the Bears Ears National Monument or calling for the dis-establishment or reduction of the Bears Ears National Monument." The resolution also opposed any legislation that negates presidential proclamations to establish national monuments under the 1906 Antiquities Act.

The snake
stops hissing
but the sound
keeps coming
out of the rocks.

—SHERYL NAKAI, FIRST GRADER AT MONTEZUMA CREEK
ELEMENTARY SCHOOL

Two days after Kenneth Maryboy introduced the Navajo majority commission's resolution in support of Bears Ears

National Monument, the San Juan County state representative Phil Lyman introduced a bill in the Utah State Legislature that allows the possibility for a county to split in two. *The Canyon Echo* reported the response by the mayor of Blanding, Joe Lyman: "If splitting the county would alleviate some of the political difficulties of overlapping a sovereign nation, it should be discussed as an option." The local paper went on to report, "The upshot of splitting the county along the lines of the Navajo Nation would ensure a solid white majority in the north, prompting some critics to call HB 93 a 'segregation bill.'"

Dwelling has different meanings to different people. We are eroding and evolving, at once.

Martin Heidegger states that dwelling has lost its original meaning. It has moved from a way of "being" in the world to "building," emphasizing structures. Being, building. Very different words with very different meanings. I find it becomes a matter of depth: where one belongs versus where one lives. It's the difference between the geographic coordinates of where one's umbilical cord is buried and where one's address is filed with the county registrar.

Charles Hallisey, professor of Buddhist studies at the Harvard Divinity School, introduced dwelling according to Heidegger as remaining in place, being "situated in a certain relationship with existence, a relationship which is characterized by nurturing, enabling the world to be as it is." And in Heidegger's own words: "The basic character of dwelling is to spare, to preserve . . . dwelling itself is always a staying with things," exactly how Evangeline Gray defines dwelling for herself and her community in Westwater.

For me, dwelling in place is like focusing a kaleidoscope on a particular point in a landscape and with a continual turning of the wrist finding infinite configurations that confound, compel, and comprise the complexities of one's community, including love, grief, and joy. If I keep writing about the Colorado Plateau that is my home among the red rock desert, it is only because it is what Hokusai showed us in his *Thirty-Six Views of Mount Fuji*.

"At 110, everything I create—a dot, a line—will jump to life as never before." At his death, eighty-eight years old, short of his dream of a century-plus of living, he is reported to have said, "If only Heaven will give me just another ten years . . . Just another five more years, then I could become a real painter."

I can never encompass the totality of my place of residence as a writer or as a citizen, but I can come to a deeper understanding of where I dwell through the diversity of stories of the people, the plants, and the animals who live here.

To know one place is to recognize every place as familiar.

I am now working away from the place I call home. The urban landscape of Cambridge, Massachusetts, has temporarily replaced the desert. But from a different vantage point, I am learning to see home from other angles while noticing shapes and patterns I may have missed upon living in such close proximity. For example, I am being contacted by trees, big trees, venerable trees, trees I have never known before: red oaks, white oaks, white pines and birches, alongside sugar maples. There are gifts in the shadows of exile.

I hear Willie Grayeyes, "The structure of where your home is doesn't matter—but where you think your home is, does."

If we were to take these ideas outside of the local to the "Terrestrial," as Bruno Latour suggests, and remove the term "human being" from our sense of identity and instead see ourselves as co-inhabitants with all other species on this planet we call home—could we dwell in place differently with one another? Willie Grayeyes understands that he belongs on

Paiute Mesa not because he has a house there but because this is the place where his attachment to his mother is his attachment to Mother Earth. Can residency be found in what we are connected to, rather than in what we exploit, ensnare, and exchange for our own gain by way of property, possessions, and prestige?

Not until we begin to understand the true costs of what we have lost and the pain we have inflicted on people and nature through the destruction of fragile landscapes and communities in the commodification and extraction of the Earth, can a healing between us take place. Our collective crisis of conscience and consciousness in this era of climate change is based on self-delusion, privilege, and our sense of entitlement, all of which continue to fuel the power and rapaciousness of our appetites. It is killing us.

There is justice to be fought for and found in listening to the integrity of knowledge and stories of those who still hold fast to a power beyond themselves, rooted in the Earth community.

If what divides us has us looking in opposite directions, as Evangeline Gray shows us in her fight for Westwater, where we cannot even see one another clearly enough to grant a neighboring community the right and necessity of water—how do we begin to see through our differences, with love and justice for all? Surely, this must become an epoch for We, not I.

During this same time frame of the trial of Willie Grayeyes and the historic shift from white leadership to Native leadership in the corner of southeastern Utah, the Mormon Church has also seen a historic shift. The Brethren quietly changed the language in the Church of Jesus Christ of Latter-day Saints' Temple Ceremony.

Headline: "On January 1, 2019, Women Are Given Equal

Power As Men in Mormon Temple Endowment." Mormon women no longer must promise to "harken to their husbands," as their husbands promise to "harken directly to God." Women's access to God is no longer mediated through men in this ceremony. Women can "now" speak directly to God.

As a woman who was born into these ceremonial vows through my mother and her mother and her mother's mother, I am relieved of this verbal bondage, heartened that these words of exclusion are now history. Women across the globe are slowly finding parity with men and exposing abuses of power within the deepest creases, now cracks inside the patriarchy.

Erosion.

Early in our evolution, we discovered as *Homo sapiens* through need and necessity that our imaginations can summon power. Fire became a dream ignited that enabled us to feed ourselves and gather round to share stories. Stories are power. Power resides in community. When power is denied and oppresses others, we can resist, and when we resist together, something else can occur, something new emerges. This is the essence of erosion and evolution in human time. In geologic time, transformation can be slow and corrosive, or catastrophic and quick. It may be a cataclysmic moment or it may happen incrementally over time. Deep change requires both. And it is not without its ruptures. It can be associated with devastation or determination. It can also be beautiful. Weathering agents are among us.

This is a time of exposure.

I dwell in Utah.
I am witnessing change.
Wind does wear down stone.

# Coda

I am light
I keep saying living in dark luminosity

—ETEL ADNAN, *Night*

## ❖ THE LITURGY OF HOME

"The plain fact is that the planet does not need more success-ful people," David Orr writes. "But it does desperately need more peacemakers, healers, restorers, storytellers, and lovers of every kind. It needs people who live well in their places. It needs people of moral courage willing to join the fight to make the world habitable and humane. And these qualities have little to do with success as we have defined it."

What are the qualities most needed in this epoch of the Anthropocene?

One of the qualities we might seek to cultivate is our capacity to listen.

Sue Beatty, a lead biologist at Yosemite National Park, now retired, offers an example. We met in 2016 inside the Mari-posa Grove, where she told me this story:

To remember why she does her job, two or three times a week Sue would walk through the Mariposa Grove, where the Giant Sequoias are known to be between two thousand and three thousand years old. She would imagine what they have lived through and witnessed. But one day when she was walk-ing through, her normal pattern of thought was disrupted.

I imagined the Big Trees speaking to her: "We are suffering. We are dying. Can you hear us?"

What she saw in the grove were roots trampled and soil erosion in the extreme. She looked up and saw how the Giant Sequoias were continuing to grow larger in spite of the road being only a foot away. People were parking their cars on the roots of the big trees. She noticed how the surface water was being diverted through roadside ditches away from the trees. And she wondered what actions she and her team could take to help alleviate their suffering.

Sue would tell you I am giving her too much credit, that this was a collaborative effort with her project management staff. Perhaps that is true, but I would tell you she is a modest human being whose sensitivity to the sequoias made all the difference. Sue Beatty had a vision of restoration.

"As a group we discussed what was needed to start planning for a restoration of the grove," she said. "I proposed along with Kimball Koch, the project manager, that we needed a comprehensive analysis of the Mariposa Grove: a complete inventory of the Giant Sequoias, wetland mapping, a hydrologic look at water diversions of roadside ditches, wildlife surveys of rare species, an anthropological study, and an evaluation of how visitors were currently using the grove."

Which is what they did. They gathered this information on the sequoias' behalf, which helped provide the basis for the planning effort to improve the habitat for the Giant Sequoias, in the belief that it would also improve visitors' experience.

What was wrong? Since the Mariposa Grove's protection by President Abraham Lincoln as part of the Yosemite Land Grant Act of 1864, millions of people's feet had been tamping down the sequoias' roots. Roads and buildings had been encroaching on their root systems.

The Big Trees were suffocating; they could not breathe. The xylem and phloem were not flowing properly. Neither were the natural waterways and wetlands.

What did Sue and her team recommend? Removing all the pavement in the grove so that the fragile root systems could heal; restoring some semblance of stillness to the chaos of park visitation. Roads would be realigned. A different vision would be sought. The Mariposa Grove would no longer be a place of entertainment and recreation, but a place of reverence and restoration. No more trams, no more vans, no more cars, but rather seekers who could hold the quiet with the sequoias.

The planning team took this data and their recommendations to the superintendent and management team of Yosemite National Park, who listened. Together they discussed with the leadership within the National Park Service the most ambitious restoration project in the history of Yosemite. The proposal for the restoration of the Mariposa Grove was approved. Forty million dollars was raised, much of it from citizen donations.

And for three years the big trees rested: the trams stopped; the parking lot was removed and relocated two miles away; visitors were redirected to other places in the park; and miles of asphalt were removed, roads taken out that impinged on the trees' root systems and replaced with gentle walking paths and trails designed for the ecological well-being of the trees; wetlands and waterways were restored; all commercial activities, from the gift shop to tram rides, ceased and were relocated elsewhere in the park.

Sue Beatty and her team listened to the land and responded not only from what they knew as scientists, but from what they imagined as individuals who cared. The status quo was no longer acceptable. The possible became the necessary. The Giant Sequoias were not objects to be studied, but sentient beings recognized as venerable members of the Yosemite community. Beatty and her colleagues acted by using the gifts that were theirs and changed the landscape on behalf of the Big Trees. The entire forest community benefited.

In the summer of 2018, the public was invited back to pay their respects to the Ancient Ones. Peace and stillness have been restored. Now, when you walk into the Mariposa Grove and stand before these great beings, you are met with an invitation: *Can you hear the trees speaking?*

Are we listening?

This is the Liturgy of Home.

> There is only one moment in time
> When it is essential to awaken
> That moment is now.
> —BUDDHA

This does not require belief, it requires engagement.

How serious are we?

◆ ACKNOWLEDGMENTS

The poet Mark Doty once said to me, "Anything, if loved enough and obsessed over enough, can become a way to talk about everything else." America's public lands have been my love and obsession. Here is my central acknowledgment: Whatever words I have written in *Erosion* have been born of my relationships: family, friends, colleagues, students, and experiences shared in place. I am not a lone writer.

Each essay in this collection represents a community of activists: laborers of love and landscape. Here are some of the organizations to which my particular debts are owed: Southern Utah Wilderness Alliance, Grand Canyon Trust, Round River Conservation Studies, Utah Open Lands, Elders Rising, Canyon Country Rising, Torrey House Press, Hell's Backbone Grill, Hawkwatch International, Friends of Great Salt Lake, Friends of Cedar Mesa, and the Bears Ears Inter-Tribal Coalition.

The following NGOs are central to the protection of wildlands and wildlife in the American West: Center for Biological Diversity, WildEarth Guardians, Earth Justice, The Nature Conservancy, Southern Plains Land Trust, Prairie Dog Coalition, Greater Yellowstone Coalition, Save the Yellowstone Grizzly, Yaak Valley Forest Council, Jackson Hole Alliance, and Earthfire Institute.

And these national organizations, with their political muscle, matter in Congress and the courts: Sierra Club, Natural Resources Defense Council, the Wilderness Society, National Parks & Conservation Association, Defenders of Wildlife, Waterkeeper Alliance, Alaska Wildlands Coalition, Patagonia, Inc., and the League of Conservation Voters. I would also include Planned Parenthood.

Brooke and I are indebted to the Western Environmental Law Center for representing us legally in our case regarding the purchase of oil and gas leases on BLM lands in Utah. Pro bono cannot be translated into words, only gratitude. Karin Sheldon, Jim Thurber, the wondrous Laura King, Erik Schlenker-Goodrich, and their entire staff have kept us buoyant in less than buoyant times.

Without the community associated with Utah Diné Bikéyah and the visionary leadership and moral imagination of Gavin Noyes as director, the essays exploring Bears Ears National Monument could never have been written. Jonah

Yellowman has changed my life. His quiet power is a wise and healing grace. Willie Grayeyes is a force of inspiration with his courageous leadership. Mark Maryboy has been a bridge builder between the Diné community and the Anglo community for decades. Angelo Baca is a leader in his generation. Eric Descheenie, brother in arms.

The women of Utah Diné Bikéyah humble me: Evangeline Gray, the medicine she carries; Mary R. Benally, her honest voice, alongside the activism of her daughters, Tara and Meredith Benally; Ida Yellowman, her sacred rage; Ahjani Yepa, her fearlessness; Cynthia Wilson, her commitment to indigenous foods as hospitality and resistance; Elouise Wilson and her sisters, Frances Sheppard and Evelyn Nelson, knowledge, strength, and laughter; Prestene Garnenez, her vision of indigenous education; Betty Lehi, her love of home; Loretta Posey, one who smells floods; and my highest respect to Honor Keeler, from the Cherokee Nation, a formidable leader on all fronts of Indian sovereignty and sacred land protection; Cora Neumann, her visionary leadership and righteous energy on behalf of women; Rachael Cassells, for sensing what is needed. Whitney Clapper for bringing us together.

My co-conspirator in the project "Exposure" is the artist Fazal Sheikh. He is singular in his capacity to listen, study, and create depths of beauty in his work. After months of photographing uranium mines, oil and gas developments, and toxic sites around the state, he said, "Utah is the most violent place I have ever encountered." This from a man who has traveled the world documenting people living in destroyed, displaced, and marginalized communities. The sharpness of his perspective shattered a closely held denial that I released in the writing of "Boom!"

To Doug Peacock, Rick Bass, Alexandra Fuller, Brooke Williams, and Teresa Cohn, true soul mates, my love and devotion for the years of playful teaching through wildness and experimentation as we tried to define and share an "ecology of residency" with a generation of students in Centennial Valley. And to Robert Newman, Steve Tatum, Mark Bergstrom, Louisa and Frank Carter, Mary Tull, Erin Halcomb, and Melody and John Taft, who made a true residency at Lakeside, Montana, possible.

Geralyn Dreyfous and Ellen Friedman are examples of how women take care of each other and dream large. Support from the Compton Foundation made all the difference. And I want to acknowledge Barbara Tanner and Deon Hilger as loving benefactors of the Art, Advocacy, and Landscape curriculum.

What I could never have imagined is the invigorating and warm community I have found at the Harvard Divinity School. I want to particularly acknowledge Dean David Hempton for his compassionate leadership and Janet Gyatso for her spiritual guidance and friendship. Stephanie Paulsell, in a class on Contemplative Prayer, sent me on a pilgrimage of faith that has me praying again; Charles Hallisey, in a transformative class on Shinran, the thirteenth-century Japanese Buddhist monk, uttered two sentences that broke me wide open after my brother's death by suicide: "This happened. Now something else can occur."

Charles Stang, director of the Center for the Study of World Religions, has a revolutionary religious imagination. With the grace of Corey O'Brien and

Matthew Whitacre, Ariella Ruth Goldberg, Jennifer Conforti, and Hal Edmonson, the staff of CSWR have created a sense of family. A special acknowledgment belongs to Dorothy "Dorie" Lee Goehring for helping me organize and discuss the early stages of the manuscript with true insight. To the residents of God's Motel, where we have been living in community for the past two years, thank you for your endless gestures of kindness, humor, and salvation.

Susan Swartz continues to teach me about belief through her art and life. My love to Susan and Jim Swartz for showing us what we can build together at HDS.

Sam Myers, director of the Planetary Health Alliance, has been my spirited mentor and colleague with the Constellation Project. Robin Kelsey, dean of the humanities, is bringing forth an elegance of thought through the lens of environmental humanities. Deep bows to both with their partners Kelsey Wirth and Sara St. Antoine. Dan Schrag, director of the Harvard Center for the Environment, has been a steady influence. I am grateful for his supportive friendship, alongside Jorie Graham, Sharon Harper, and Sheila Dennis.

The Coda is adapted from the talk "The Liturgy of Home," given at the Harvard Divinity School on April 12, 2018, as part of the Ingersoll Lecture series that dates back to 1893. It can be heard in its entirety here: www.youtube.com /watch?v=6Lr_YJHADFw. Deep gratitudes to Karin Grundler-Whitacre, Marguerite Farrell Jenkins, and Sue Beatty.

Many of these essays have appeared, in slightly different form, in the following publications: *Adventure Journal*, *Audubon Magazine*, *Canyon Country Advocate*, *Condé Nast Traveler*, *High Country News*, *The National Parks Magazine*, *Orion*, and *Yale 360*. Others have appeared in anthologies: *The Artists Field Guide to Yellowstone* (Trinity University Press, 2019), edited by Katie Christiansen, and *Hearth: A Global Conversation on Community, Identity, and Place* (Milkweed Editions, 2018), edited by Annick Smith and Susan O'Connor.

I have had the privilege of working with brilliant editors: Chip Blake, Steve Casimiro, Katie Christiansen, Roger Cohn, Chris Conley, Kevin Doyle, Tim Fitzpatrick, Bill Hedden and Eleanor Bliss, Erik Hoffner, Paul Larimer, Rona Marech, Alisa Opar, Tim Peterson, and Jennifer Sahn. *The Oxford English Dictionary* helped clarify the terms "imago" and "refuse." Ann Braude clarified Mormon sisterhood. Key conversations were had with Colum McCann, Andy Friedland, Christina Seely, Carol Folt, Anne Kapuscinski, Lee and Ed Riddell, Jack Turner, and Charles Wilkinson.

Deep joy with my collaborators: Joanne Dornan, a shared love of grouse; Ben Roth and Felicia Resor, with the support of Maggie Kaplan in "The Council of Pronghorn"; Harvey Hix and the late Craig Arnold at the University of Wyoming; Colin Peacock and Dena Adler, for sharing their ceremony of love; Sarah Hedden, her gift of tea; Allyson Mathis and Andy Nettell of Back of Beyond Books, for their care in making the broadside "Erosion" after the 2016 election; Alisha Anderson, for her insights at Great Salt Lake; Mary O'Brien, her activism like lightning; Scott Slovic and his community of scholars in China; Kate Kelly, her belief in radical change; Mr. Brian Raabe, his care at Larkin Mortuary; Mercedes Orales, spirit. And my respect to Tim DeChristopher for his integrity and spiritual spine in all things just.

My special bow to Darol Wagstaff for the length of his friendship and the unconditional love he gave to our brother, Dan. And to Madi Quissek, for her love and life cut short on June 7, 2019.

Monette Clark, conscience; Steven Barclay, my right arm; Gail Hochman, loving diplomat.

This is Sarah Crichton's book. It has been a privilege to work with her as my editor for the last decade. Her humanity, greatness of spirit, and astute editorial eye have stretched me, inspired me, and allowed me to grow as a writer. Our pilgrimage to the desert brought this collection into view. I appreciate the care of Jenna Johnson and all those whose hands have blessed this book at Farrar, Straus and Giroux.

I am especially grateful to Ross Donihue, cartographer extraordinaire, of Good Maps, whose map "Eroding Public Lands" is not only a geographic map but a political one of heartbreak and hope.

Unspeakable gratitude to my father for his dignity, strength of character, and loving support; Jan Sloan, for her great heart; my brother Hank, for his gravity and radiant soul; Lynne Tempest, my sister, honesty, always; Louis Gakumba, Rosette Kibamba, Malka, and Sheja, family; Lyn Dalebout, vision. The Tempest clan, the Williams clan—bloodlines as bedrock. Linda Asher and Ann Backer are my spiritual mothers.

To Dan, for all that was unsaid, but felt. Wild horses carry his spirit.

These essays were written at night. To the great horned owls who stayed.

And day and night, my love to Brooke: Awe.